PHILOSOPHY OF ART

"This book will take its place as the very best introduction to the subject on the market . . . Carroll, because of his vast knowledge of the popular arts as well as traditional high arts, both old and new, is able to provide an enormous variety of examples that will speak to a wide audience."

Professor Peter Kivy, *Rutgers University*

"This is analytic philosophy at its best: thorough, rigorous, even-handed, eminently readable throughout . . . Carroll's book generates an enthusiasm for the subject and liveliness of debate which will guarantee that its student readership will profit from it and be engaged by it."

Professor Peter Lamarque, *University of Hull*

Philosophy of Art is a textbook for undergraduate students interested in the topic of philosophical aesthetics. It aims to introduce the techniques of analytic philosophy in addition to a selection of the major topics in this field of inquiry. These include the representational theory of art, formalism, neo-formalism, aesthetic theories of art, neo-Wittgensteinianism, the Institutional Theory of Art, as well as historical approaches to the nature of art. Throughout the book, abstract philosophical theories are illustrated by examples of both traditional and contemporary art including frequent reference to the avant-garde. In this way the reader's understanding of art theory as well as the appreciation of art is enriched.

Noël Carroll is the Monroe C. Beardsley Professor of the Philosophy of Art at the University of Wisconsin-Madison. He is currently also President of the American Society for Aesthetics and has been a documentary screenwriter and a journalist. His other books include *The Philosophy of Horror* (Routledge, 1990) and *A Philosophy of Mass Art* (1998).

Routledge Contemporary Introductions to Philosophy

Series Editor:

Paul K. Moser
Loyola University of Chicago

This innovative, well-structured series is for students who have already done an introductory course in philosophy. Each book introduces a core general subject in contemporary philosophy and offers students an accessible but substantial transition from introductory to higher-level college work in that subject. The series is accessible to nonspecialists and each book clearly motivates and expounds the problems and positions introduced. An orientating chapter briefly introduces its topic and reminds readers of any crucial material they need to have retained from a typical introductory course. Considerable attention is given to explaining the central philosophical problems of a subject and the main competing solutions and arguments for those solutions. The primary aim is to educate students in the main problems, positions and arguments of contemporary philosophy rather than to convince students of a single position. The initial eight central books in the series are written by experienced authors and teachers, and treat topics essential to a well-rounded philosophy curriculum.

Epistemology
Robert Audi

Ethics
Harry Gensler

Metaphysics
Michael J. Loux

Philosophy of Art
Noël Carroll

Philosophy of Language
William G. Lycan

Philosophy of Mind
John Heil

Philosophy of Religion
Keith E. Yandell

Philosophy of Science
Alexander Rosenberg

PHILOSOPHY OF ART
A contemporary introduction

Noël Carroll

London and New York

First published in 1999
by Routledge
11 New Fetter Lane, London EC4P 4EE

Simultaneously published in the USA and Canada
by Routledge
29 West 35th Street, New York, NY 10001

Routledge is an imprint of the Taylor & Francis Group

Typeset in Aldus Roman by RefineCatch Limited, Bungay, Suffolk
Printed and bound in Great Britain by
St Edmundsbury Press, Bury St Edmunds, Suffolk

British Library Cataloguing in Publication Data
A catalogue record for this book is available from the British Library

Library of Congress Cataloging in Publication Data
A catalog record for this book has been requested

ISBN 0–415–15963–6 (hbk)
ISBN 0–415–15964–4 (pbk)

To Peter Kivy,
the Leader of the Band.

Contents

Acknowledgments

The author wishes to thank Philip Alperson, Jim Anderson, Sally Banes, David Bordwell, Hugh Carroll III, Jinhee Choi, Dong-Ryul Choo, Peter Kivy, Peter Lamarque, Steven Nadler, Prashant Parikh and Elliott Sober for their generous suggestions for improving this book. They, of course, are not responsible for the errors herein. I don't know who is.

Introduction

What is philosophy?

The analytic philosophy of art

Analysing concepts

Some peculiarities of philosophical research

The structure of this book

The aims of this book

Introduction

What is philosophy?

The word "philosophy" has many different meanings. Sometimes people tell you about their philosophy of life. They usually mean something like their deepest and most abiding beliefs. This is certainly an acceptable usage of the word in ordinary language but it is a broader conception of philosophy than that which will preoccupy us in this book. Herein, "philosophy" will generally refer to a certain academic discipline.

Of course, like many academic disciplines, philosophy can be approached in a number of different ways. That is, there are many different schools of philosophy, such as existentialism, phenomenology, marxism, deconstructionism, and so on. Though related in various respects, the different schools of academic philosophy often have different aims and emphases. The type of philosophy that we will be exploring in this book is often called *analytic philosophy*. In fact, the title of this book could be accurately expanded as the *Analytic Philosophy of Art: A Contemporary Introduction*. This book is an introduction to some of the major techniques and central problems of the analytic philosophy of art.

But what is analytic philosophy? It is a school of philosophy primarily practiced in the English-speaking world. Thus, it is sometimes called "Anglo-American" philosophy, though that is a somewhat misleading label because it is not by any means the only form of academic philosophy in the English-speaking world. However, it is a very prominent school, some might say the dominant school, of English-speaking philosophy, and it has exerted considerable influence throughout the twentieth century. But this is only to suggest the "where" and the "when" of analytic philosophy. The "what" remains to be explained.

This school of thought is called *analytic* philosophy. So a natural first question is: "What exactly does this school of philosophy analyse?" Simplifying drastically, we might say that what analytic philosophy analyses are concepts. That is why it is sometimes also called conceptual analysis. Though by this point in history, many philosophers would argue that this is not all that analytic philosophy does, for purposes of introducing the topic, it is fair to say that this is what many analytic philosophers have attempted to do in the past and what many, at least part of the time, continue to do today. They analyse concepts.

Concepts, of course, are fundamental to human life. Concepts organize our practices. The concept of a person, for example, is central to myriad practices, including politics, morality, the law, and so on. The concept of a number is fundamental to mathematics, while the concept of knowledge is indispensable throughout the widest gamut of human activities. Without such concepts, the activities in question would not exist. For example, without the concept of a person, there would be no morality as we know it for it is persons, not mere things, to which morality pertains.

A rough and ready way to characterize analytic philosophy is to say that it is concerned with the analysis of concepts that are key to human practices and activities, including not only those of enquiry, like science, but, as well, of pragmatic endeavors, such as governance. Analytic philosophers, in this regard, may trace their heritage back to Socrates, who walked the streets of ancient Athens asking "What is knowledge?" and "What is justice?" in ways that undermined commonplace and often complacent answers to these questions, thus paving the way, the analytic philosopher might say (in a slightly self-congratulatory tone of voice), for more rigorous analyses.

Those of you who've spent some time thumbing through college bulletins have probably noticed that the philosophy section is full of titles that take the form "the philosophy of _____. The blank is often filled in by the name of some other field – as in the philosophy of science, or of logic, or of art, law, history and so forth. Philosophy generally seems to be the philosophy of something. But what sort of something?

That something is a practice, like law or religion. Very often it is a practice involved with acquiring knowledge – like physics, psychology, history, and the like. But it may also be a practical activity, such as ethics. Philosophy begins when the people involved in the relevant practices become self-conscious – when they begin to wonder about just what it is that they are doing or just what they are really talking about.

That is, each one of these practices organizes its field of operation in terms of certain concepts, which are applied according to certain criteria. In addition, each of these practices employs certain recurrent modes of reasoning – certain ways of connecting concepts – which modes are appropriate to the point of achieving the goals of the practice in question. These concepts and modes of reasoning are what make the practice possible – they are what, so to speak, constitutes the practice. And it is such concepts and modes of reasoning that analytic philosophy analyses.

To be more concrete, consider the case of the law. It is a practice. It possesses a large number of key concepts – concepts without which there would be no practice of law. One such concept, quite obviously, is the very notion of law itself. What is a law? Under what conditions – according to what criteria – do we classify an injunction as a law? This is the kind of question that practitioners of the field ask when they become self-conscious about their practice. It is the point at which the philosophy of law takes off.

In asking "What is a law?" different options need to be explored. Is a law just what some duly appointed assembly decides is a law in accordance with certain established procedures? Or is a law – a genuine law – such that it must follow from or at least be consistent with deep principles – perhaps deep constitutional principles or deep moral principles, involving human rights? What arguments can be brought forward on behalf of these different options?

Such questions, needless to say, are not idle. They may come to the fore when, for example, someone maintains that a draft law is illegal. Of course, to allege that a draft law – or, for that matter, any law – is illegal – i.e., is against the law – brings us to the very brink of paradox. In order to resolve such paradoxes and puzzles, as arise frequently in our practices, we need to take a close look at our concepts. And that is the vocation of analytic philosophy.

In addressing questions such as "What is a law?" analytic philosophers, among other things, attempt to identify the criteria that we use to categorize things one way rather than another. Sometimes this is dismissed as merely playing with words. However, when one considers how very much can ride on questions of categorization, it seems that analytic philosophers are generally less naïve than those who disparage them as "mere logic choppers."

Throughout much of the twentieth century, analytic philosophy has increasingly become a "second order" form of enquiry. It is the philosophy of this or that – the philosophy of physics, or of economics, or of art. Analytic philosophers take as their domain significant forms of human practice, but unlike the social scientist, the analytic philosopher does not look for recurring patterns of social behavior within said practices. Instead, the analytic philosopher tries to clarify the concepts that make activities within the relevant domains possible. Analytic philosophers, in other words, do not attempt to ascertain answers to empirical questions like "How many people obey the law?" but rather address questions like "What does it take for something to count as a law?" or, to state the matter in more linguistic trappings: "What does it mean to call something a 'law'?"

Undoubtedly, learning how many people obey the law is crucial for designing social policy. But discovering what a law is, or attempting to do so, is an important project too, since if we ignore this question, we will be left wondering whether our practice is intelligible – whether it hangs together, and has any rhyme or reason. By interrogating the deep concepts that organize our practices – that make our practices possible – the analytic philosopher attempts to reveal what sense those practices have. This is not the only form of philosophy imaginable, but it is a significant form. Indeed, philosophers of other schools must also be analytic philosophers at least some of the time. For example, the marxist philosopher must ask "What is exploitation?"

Perhaps the notion that what analytic philosophers do is to analyse or clarify concepts strikes you initially as somewhat obscure. In what follows, it is to be hoped that that feeling of obscurity will be relieved. However, even at this juncture, the idea of clarifying concepts should not be utterly alien to you, since for the last few pages, we have been analysing a concept – namely, the concept of analytic philosophy. To the extent that you have followed the discussion so far, you have taken your first steps as an analytic philosopher. If you wish to know more about it, things are going very well.

The analytic philosophy of art

Analytic philosophy analyses the concepts that are fundamental to our practices. Art is a recurring form of human practice. Some have argued that all human societies show evidence of artistic activities. The purpose of the analytic philosophy of art is to explore the concepts that make creating and thinking about art possible. Some of these concepts include: the very concept of art itself, as well as the concepts of representation, expression, artistic form, and aesthetics. These concepts will be discussed at some length in this book.

But there are also further concepts that the philosopher might look at, such as interpretation, forgery, creativity, and artistic value, among others. A philosopher of art might concentrate on specific artforms – asking "What is literature (dance, music, film, drama, and so forth)?" Or, she might explore the concepts of certain artistic genres, such as fiction, comedy, tragedy, poetry, and the like. All these and more are the concepts that the analytic philosophy of art takes as its subject matter.

As with the philosophy of law, so with the philosophy of art, coming to understand these concepts is an important contribution to the life of the practices in which they figure, often constitutively. We have suggested how central the concept of the law is to the practice of jurisprudence. Similarly, the concept of art is fundamental to our artistic practices.

Without some sense of how to classify certain objects and performances as artworks, the Museum of Modern Art wouldn't know what to collect, the National Endowment for the Arts wouldn't know to whom to give money, nor would the United States government know which institutions deserve tax relief for the preservation of our artistic past. Nor even, without some command of the concept of art, would economists know how to evaluate empirical claims like "Art is a significant component of the financial well-being of New York City."

But far more important than the preceding "official" uses of the concept of art is the role the concept plays in our personal, ongoing commerce with artworks, since how we respond to an object – interpretively, appreciatively, emotively, and evaluatively – depends decisively upon whether or not we categorize it as an artwork. Suppose we come across a living, breathing couple seated at opposite sides of a wooden table, staring intently at each other. Ordinarily we might pay no attention to them at all, or avert our glance out of a sense of politeness. But if we categorize the situation as an artwork – as the performance piece *Night Crossing* by Marina Abramovic and Ulay – our response will be altogether different.

We will shamelessly scrutinize the scene carefully, attempt to interpret it, perhaps in terms of what it says about human life and relationships. We will try to situate it in the history of art, comparing it to other artworks in various genres. We will contemplate what it expresses and what feelings it arouses in us, and we may evaluate it – possibly commending it for drawing our attention to neglected realms of experience, or for moving us, or for making its point with a startling economy of means. Or maybe we will criticize it for being boring or hackneyed. But in any event, it is clear that once we categorize the situation as an artwork, our response to it will differ radically from the way in which we regard comparable seated couples in "real" life.

Or consider surgical procedures. In the everyday course of life, we do not think of them as alternatives to a night at the opera. But when such procedures are incorporated in a performance piece such as the work *Image/New Image(s) or the Re-incarnation of Saint-Orlan* and we categorize Orlan's plastic surgery as a work of art, we see it in a different light. We note the interesting color arrangement of the surgeons' uniforms and we ask about the meaning of Orlan's self-elected decision to go under the knife – what does it say about society, about women, about personal identity, about art history and the ideals of female beauty found there? That is, we react to the event completely differently from how we would, had we happened upon an ordinary gall-bladder operation. The attempt to interpret the meaning of your typical gall-bladder operation is out of place, but the attempt to interpret an artwork is usually appropriate. Yet interpretation here hinges on whether or not we classify the item in question as an artwork – on whether we correctly apply the concept of art to it.

Thus, clarifying our concept of art is not merely a matter of dry, academic book-keeping. It lies at the living heart of our artistic practices, since categorizing candidates as artworks puts us in a position to mobilize a set of art responses that are the very stuff of our activities as viewers, listeners and readers. In order to play the game, we need a handle on the concept of art. And it is the task of the analytic philosophy of art to make sure that that handle is a sturdy one by reflecting upon the concept of art and articulating its elements in as precise a manner as possible.

As already indicated, the concept of art is not the only one that preoccupies analytic philosophers of art, though for the reasons just stated, it is a central one. Representation, expression, artistic form, aesthetic experience and aesthetic properties are also of great interest. Consequently, much of the remainder of this book will be spent analysing these six concepts. Other concepts might have been chosen for analysis; however, for a text of this length, these should supply the inquiring student with a serviceable introduction to the field.

Analysing concepts

The phrase "analysing concepts" has been bandied about extensively in this introduction. But what does it involve? How do you go about analysing concepts? Since so much time will be spent in what follows analysing concepts, some opening comments may be helpful here.

Like most issues in philosophy, there is substantial debate about what concepts are and how to analyse them. However, there is one very standard approach (though as we shall see in Chapter 5, it has not enlisted universal assent). We can call this standard approach the *method of necessary and sufficient conditions*. It proceeds by breaking concepts down into their necessary and sufficient conditions for application. Although this method is controversial, we shall presume its practicability for most of this text, if only because it is a powerful tool for organizing and guiding research, even if ultimately it rests on certain questionable assumptions.

The standard approach takes concepts to be categories. Applying a certain concept to an object is a matter of classifying it as a member of the relevant category. Calling an object an artwork involves determining that it meets the criteria or conditions required for membership in the category. Analysing a concept is a matter of breaking it down into its component parts, where the component parts are its conditions for application.

Think of the concept bachelor. What is a bachelor? A bachelor is an unmarried man. We can break down or analyse the concept of bachelor into two component parts – manhood and unmarriedness. In order to be counted as a member of the category bachelor – in order to apply correctly the concept of bachelor to a candidate – the candidate must meet two conditions: he must be a man and he must be unmarried. Individually, each of these conditions is necessary for anything to count as a bachelor, and together (conjointly) they are sufficient (just enough) to categorize a candidate as a bachelor. Analysing the concept of bachelor – which might also be called "defining 'bachelor'" – is a matter of articulating the necessary and sufficient conditions for applying the concept bachelor to, for instance, the boy next door.

This method of analysing concepts should seem fairly commonsensical. When you want to know what something, like a bachelor, is, you want to know (1) the feature or features of the kind in question that every proper member of the category possesses; and (2) you want to know what feature or features differentiate members of the relevant kind or category from members of other kinds. For example, if you want to know what a bachelor is – how to apply the concept bachelor – then you want to know what all bachelors have in common *and* also what sets bachelors apart from other kinds of things, such as husbands and spinsters.

That is, you want to know what feature or features are *necessarily* possessed by all the proper members of the category, such that absence of the feature in question precludes membership in the category (were the boy next door married, he would not be a bachelor). *And* you want to know what feature or features are *sufficient* to differentiate members of the relevant category from members of other categories (were the boy next door an unmarried male, he could not be a husband or a spinster). Unmarriedness and maleness are each individually necessary conditions for bachelorhood; together, these criteria represent a sufficient condition for bachelorhood.

There is a very useful way of setting out these ideas. Since we will employ it throughout the text, it will be beneficial to introduce it here. "x is a necessary condition for y" means that something can be a y *only if* it is an x. Someone can be a princess only if she is a woman. Being a woman is not a sufficient condition for being a princess. But it is necessary; it is a necessary requirement for being a princess that one be a woman. Someone may be a woman and not a princess, but one cannot be a princess and not a woman. Womanhood is a necessary condition for princesshood, or, to state it formulaically: y is a princess only if y is a woman. Here the truth of "y is a woman" is a necessary condition – an unvarying requirement – for the truth of "y is a princess."

We cannot, however, say that *if* y is a woman, then she is a princess. Most women are not princesses. Womanhood is not a sufficient condition for princesshood; it is not enough to establish princesshood. Something else needs to be added. A likely candidate is that y be of royal lineage, where that is to be determined by the laws of the lands in question. Then we could say that *if* y is a woman and of the right royal lineage, then y is a princess. That is, the antecedent clause of the proposition – "y is a woman and of the right royal lineage" – guarantees the truth of the consequent clause of the proposition "y is a princess."

In the preceding example, womanhood and the right royal lineage are each individually necessary conditions for princesshood and conjointly they comprise a sufficient condition for princesshood. To summarize this information formulaically, we can say: y is a princess *if and only if* (1) y is a woman and (2) y is of the right royal lineage.

The locution "if and only if" signals that this analysis is proposing necessary conditions (the "only if" conditions) and sufficient conditions (the "if" conditions) for princesshood. Similarly, y is a bachelor if and only if (1) y is a male and (2) y is unmarried. Here conditions (1) and (2) are each on their own necessary conditions for bachelorhood and together they are jointly sufficient for bachelorhood.

This kind of analysis is often called a real or an essential definition. That it is a definition of the relevant concept should be evident. It is an essential definition because it attempts to get at the essential features of the concept – its necessary and sufficient conditions of application. It is said to be a real definition of the concept because unlike so many dictionary definitions it does not simply track how people commonly use the concept, but allegedly discovers the real conditions of application of the concept.

You will encounter many definitions of this sort in this book – set out in terms of the schema "x if and only if y." Some of these will include analyses of pictorial representation and artistic form. There will also be a large number of proposed analyses of the concept of an artwork, articulated in terms of necessary and sufficient conditions. Sometimes the text will refer to these as theories of art, sometimes as essential or real definitions. The variations in terminology should not throw you. In each case, we are talking about attempted analyses of the concept of art.

This brief review of the method of necessary and sufficient conditions or, less cumbersomely, the essential definition approach to analysing concepts, is intended to give you some idea of what is meant by the phrase "analysing concepts." After all, we've been using and will use that notion a lot, and you have a right to some concrete sense of what that abstraction might involve. However, it was also noted that this approach to the way in which we go about applying concepts is controversial and that alternative views will be explored in the last chapter of this book.

Yet until the last chapter, we will be employing this approach to analysing concepts pretty much without worrying about its adequacy.

This might strike you as strange and even irresponsible, if the approach is really disputed. But let me make two remarks on behalf of this procedure.

One objection to the essential definition approach is that many of our concepts are applied without resort to necessary and sufficient conditions. Arguably, many of our concepts do not have necessary and/or suffficient conditions of application. There is no reason to presume that the concepts that we explore by means of this method will turn out to be analysable in terms of necessary and/or sufficient conditions. That is a fair observation. However, since we won't know whether a given concept is congenial to this mode of analysis until we've tried it, we have no grounds for dismissing this approach from the get-go.

Second, even if the method of definition does not turn out to be the best way of understanding how we go about applying concepts, the method still has immense *heuristic* value. By "heuristic value," we mean that the method of definition, even when it fails, can assist us in making discoveries. The method alerts us systematically to the richness and complexity of the phenomenon that confronts us.

For example, when a philosopher of art, like Aristotle, proposes that representation is a necessary condition of art, we consider that conjecture by asking whether indeed everything we categorize as art is representational. If we think of color field painting, we will reject this conjecture as *too exclusive*. But we will learn something by refuting this conjecture. We will not only learn that the representational theory of art is false, but that the realm of art encompasses more different kinds of things than imagined in Aristotle's philosophy and that of his descendants, and this will sensitize us to the need to acknowledge nonrepresentational art in subsequent theorizing.

Similarly, if we hear that self-expression is a sufficient condition of art, that prompts us to ask whether or not that criterion really picks out only artworks. Of course, it does not, because there is a great deal of self-expressive behavior in everyday life – like the tantrums of a hungry infant – that are not artworks, not even performance art. So, we reject the self-expression analysis of art because it is *too inclusive*. But in this instance we not only learn that the self-expression theory is false, but that subsequent theorizing must be alert to the distinction between self-expression that is art versus that which is not. The method of definition, then, is conducive to an awareness of "joints" in the data that any future attempts at dissection must respect.

Attempted analyses of concepts in terms of necessary and sufficient conditions, even where they fail, abet discovery. They systematically flush out data and distinctions that enrich our understanding of art. They awaken us to the breadth and diversity of the world of art, while also charting its boundaries. In this way, the philosopher's preoccupation with analysing concepts can also contribute to our appreciation of art in all its luxurious and wondrous manifestations.

Some peculiarities of philosophical research

If this is your first course in analytic philosophy, some of its techniques, patterns of reasoning, and modes of argument are apt to seem strange to you. This is likely to be especially true if your background is in the empirical sciences. Given the subject of the analytic philosophy of art – human practices – you might presume that it is some kind of social science. But philosophy is not a social science, and thinking of it in those terms will only be frustrating to you. So in order to avert unecessary misunderstandings, something needs to be said at the outset about the peculiar status of philosophy in contrast to empirical research.

Philosophy is not social science. This is not to say that it is better or worse than social science. It is just different. Nor is it to claim that social scientists are never philosophical. But when they are in their philosophical mode, that is different from their empirical mode.

Consider the empirical claim: there is more art in Paris than there is in Spokane. The sociologist assesses this claim by counting up the artworks in Paris and the artworks in Spokane. This is an empirical matter, a matter of observation and statistics. But all this empirical research rests on an assumption – namely that the sociologist knows how to apply the concept of art. How else will she count the artworks? But determining the correct application of our classificatory categories – analysing the concept of art – is not an empirical question.

One doesn't settle it by taking polls, running experiments, or making observations. One settles the issue conceptually, by reflecting on the idea of art. This is the job of the analytic philosopher, or of the social scientist in a philosophical mood. It involves clarifying the classificatory categories that we will use in organizing our empirical observations, but this is different from gathering data and requires different techniques. It may require contemplating proposed necessary and sufficient conditions for art status. This is not accomplished by going out into the field, but by reflecting upon how we apply the concept of art, testing it intellectually against what we believe to be established applications of the concept, and even using thought-experiments (such as imagined examples) to see whether proposed reconstructions of the category of art mesh with our considered intuitions. Of course, intuitions are anathema to social scientists, but they are mother's milk to analytic philosophers.

You might say that this does not mark a difference between philosophy and social science, since the social scientist has access to the relevant intuitions through polling. But we cannot discover the concept of art by polling. Why not? Because many people have false beliefs about what is art. In the earlier decades of the twentieth century, the vast majority of people thought that in order for paintings to count as artworks, they had to be representations. But this was wrong. A social scientist relying on a poll like this would miscount all the artworks in Paris in 1930; he would overlook too many paintings by Mondrian, Malevich, Kandinsky and others.

The philosopher is not interested in establishing what most people believe is art, though this is a worthwhile thing to know, and we should be grateful for any information that the social scientist can provide on this subject. Instead, the philosopher wants to know how to apply the concept of art correctly or justifiably. But constructing standards of correctness is something that most social scientists consider outside their bailiwick.

Because the analytic philosopher of art is concerned with a different direction of research from the empirical social scientist, her methods are different. For reflecting upon the nature and structure of our concepts, like the concept of art, logic, definition, thought experiments and counterexamples (including imagined ones), and deductive argument are her primary tools – rather than laboratory experiments, polls, ethnographies, empirical observations, and the like. Of course, this is not to deny that social scientists may also avail themselves of the strategies that are so fundamental to analytic philosophers, but only to note that these strategies are at the very soul of analytic philosophy, whereas their use is generally less central and frequently optional for the social scientist.

Another way to suggest the difference between the philosopher and the social scientist is to say that the philosopher is preoccupied with what *must* be the case, whereas the social scientist is more concerned with what probably is the case most of the time. The philosopher tries to identify a necessary condition of art – a feature of a work that it must *necessarily* possess in order to count as an artwork. A social scientist is happy to discover what most people in a given society are *likely* to consider art. That is why the social scientist prefers questionnaires. The philosopher instead opts for logic, deductive argumentation, essential definitions, counterexamples and such in order to determine what must be the case, irrespective of what most people are probably disposed to call art.

Because analytic philosophy is so different from empirical research, many entering students distrust it or are puzzled by it. Its methods seem wholly speculative – totally an affair of the armchair. And armchair speculation is not what is encouraged in the empirical sciences; in fact, it is generally discouraged. This is why students sometimes find analytic philosophy so exasperating. It defies their expectations and it goes against their empirical training. If we really want to learn what comprises our concept of art, they ask, why not hand out questionnaires, run some tests, or launch a survey?

But, as we have seen, not all such questions can be resolved empirically; some require conceptual analysis. Nor is it correct to suppose that conceptual speculation and empirical research are locked in some zero-sum competition – that all is empirical research, with no other options.

Conceptual analysis may, in fact, complement empirical research sometimes – for example, it may supply the social scientist with the concept of art that she needs to find the artworks in Spokane. As well, in further cases, some of our questions may require primarily conceptual analysis, whereas in still other cases, empirical research is indispensable. The nature of our questions will determine the best method of research. "What is pornography?" invites conceptual analysis; "How much pornography is there in Glasgow?" calls for empirical research. Both avenues of inquiry have their purposes, which, in turn, shape their distinctive techniques, procedures, and modes of reasoning and argument.

It is because of this that the student unfamiliar with and perhaps even suspicious of the methods of analytic philosophy is advised to exercise a little patience. As she thinks her way through the various analyses in this book and comes to appreciate the nature and diabolical complexity of the problems we examine, she is likely to see the point and the efficacy of the techniques of analytic philosophy. If nothing else, analytic philosophy provides one with a set of powerful intellectual resources, applicable not only to the philosophy of art, but elsewhere as well.

Perhaps the disgruntled student will finally turn the resources of analytic philosophy against the analytic philosophy of art, venting her frustration in a gesture of revenge that shows the whole enterprise rests on a conceptual error. But then she will have become a philosopher, indeed, an analytic philosopher.

The structure of this book

This book is divided into five chapters. The first four chapters of the book have a parallel structure. Part I of each of these chapters reviews various theories of art – analyses or essential definitions of art, set out in terms of necessary and sufficient conditions. These theories include, respectively: representational theories of art, expression theories, formalist theories, and the aesthetic definition of art. The shortcomings of each of these theories are then, in turn, elaborated at some length.

However, in each of these chapters it is also noted that even if the concepts people have used to define all and only art – such as representation, expression, form, aesthetic experience and aesthetic properties – fail to supply necessary and sufficient conditions for all and only art, these concepts – representation, expression, form and aesthetics – are still applicable to many works of art, and, therefore, still warrant philosophical analysis in their own right (regardless of their adequacy as defining features of all and only art). Thus, in Part II of each of the first four chapters, analyses of representation, expression, form and the notion of aesthetics are explored.

Like the concept of art, these concepts are of central importance to the conduct of our artistic practices and our interaction with artworks. If the first part of each of the first four chapters is primarily critical – raising objections to a series of some of the best-known theories of art – then the second part of each of these chapters is constructive, suggesting analyses of some of the most important categories that we use when talking and thinking about art.

The dominant, unifying theme of this book is the attempt to analyse the concept of art. A discussion of successive attempts to provide an analysis of art initiates the first four chapters. These attempts are taken to be aimed at providing *classificatory* theories of art rather than *commendatory* theories of art – theories that say what art *is* rather than what art *should* be. The problem with commendatory theories of art is that they, in effect, only count as artworks those that are good – that is, works that accord with certain canons of what art should be. This, of course, is problematic, because there is such a thing as bad art – we talk about it all the time – and, consequently, any theory of how we classify objects and performances as artworks needs to encompass the bad and the ugly, as well as the good stuff. Unfortunately, a number of the theories canvassed herein are inadvertently commendatory theories rather than classificatory in nature.

Though it is a recurring problem, this is not the only problem with the theories rehearsed in the first four chapters. Each theory also raises other vexsome issues as well. By the fifth chapter of the book, we will have encountered so many failed definitions of art that it will be time to ask whether there might be some deep philosophical problem with attempting to analyse the concept of art in terms of sets of necessary and/or sufficient conditions.

Chapter 5 differs in its structure from the earlier four chapters insofar as it is devoted *solely* to the question of how we go about identifying or classifying candidates as artworks. Part I of Chapter 5 begins with the proposal that it is impossible to define art; that artworks are identified by family resemblances, rather than by essential definitions. This idea is called Neo-Wittgensteinianism. It is a very tantalizing suggestion, but ultimately it proves to be impracticable.

Part II of Chapter 5 returns us to the project of attempting to analyse the concept of art by means of essential definitions. Specifically, we look at two of the most discussed recent definitions of art: the Institutional Theory of Art and the Historical Definition of Art. Both of these theories of art have many virtues, but they have not proven invulnerable to a series of substantial objections.

Thus, we find ourselves once again without a definition of art. This provides a reason to return to the suggestion, first broached by the Neo-Wittgensteinians, that perhaps the method we employ for identifying art-works is not an essential definition, but something else. After all, we do manage to identify artworks with an amazingly high degree of agreement. How do we do it? What governs our classification of candidates as artworks?

In Part III of Chapter 5, historical narration is advanced as the primary way in which we sort artworks from other things. This is neither a matter of definitions nor of what the Neo-Wittgensteinians call family resemblances. In fact, this solution to the unavoidable philosophical question of the way in which we identify artworks is a pet idea of the present author. On the one hand, it may appear cheeky to you that I should conclude this book with my own brainchild; on the other hand, it is one of the perks of spending all this time writing the book. And, in any case, I do believe that the historical narration gives us a reliable method for distinguishing the art from the nonart.

The aims of this book

This book has several aims. The first is informational. A great many of the theories reviewed in this book are what might be called canonical. They are theories that anyone who cares for art should know about. They have, in some cases, influenced art making and art appreciation for centuries and, in other cases, their influence has extended at least for decades. Understanding these theories and the various criticisms of these views is essential for anyone who aspires to become a full-fledged citizen of the artworld.

At the same time, maybe needless to say, familiarity with these theories and the criticisms they have attracted is part of the indispensable operating knowledge that one needs in order to follow and join in contemporary discussions in the philosophy of art. Like any conversation, especially ones of any level of sophistication, the dialogue of the philosophy of art requires that one share certain background knowledge with the other participants in the exchange. This book is designed in such a way that the selected package of information it contains should be enough to get you started. It is far from a comprehensive review of every topic worthy of the attention of a philosopher of art. But it should provide you with sufficient entree into the field.

In addition to supplying information, the book also attempts to be an introduction to the techniques of analytic philosophy. Reading this book, it is hoped, will help you understand how to go about analysing concepts, how to investigate proposed definitions critically, how to think about exceptions to theories, how to argue on behalf of positions you believe in, and so on. Ultimately, though a great deal of the technique displayed in this book is critical, the aim of the book is to enable you to construct your own approaches to and theories of the concepts of art, representation, expression, artistic form, aesthetics, and many others. There is still a great deal of room for improvement in the philosophy of art, and inevitably it is up to your generation to move the discussion to the next stage of philosophical development.

There is one final note that needs to be made about the philosophical technique exhibited in this book. A great deal of this technique is critical in nature. Many of the skills that this book exercises involve ways of showing that theories and viewpoints are mistaken. This emphasis on criticism can lead to certain misgivings. It may seem to you at times to resemble nothing so much as lawyers haggling over next to nothing or forensic pedantry. And this may leave the depressing impression that the philosophy of art is little more than destructive, an invitation to hollow cynicism.

However, it is important to keep in mind that it is through criticism that knowledge and understanding are advanced. Refuting a theory not only tells you that it is wrong or inadequate (end of story). It also gives you a clue about what remains to be done. Taking note of what one theory has overlooked or neglected makes you aware of what should not be overlooked or neglected the next time around. Some of the shortfalls of the representational theory of art, as you will see, prepare the way intellectually for formalism and expression theories of art. In this manner, criticism can add positively and energetically to the incremental acquisition of knowledge.

As well, criticizing a theory or an analysis of a concept not only informs you about its weaknesses; it may also alert you to its strengths, which you may go on to incorporate, perhaps with refinements, into your own analyses. The method of historical narration defended at the end of Chapter 5, for instance, certainly profits from, while also critically modifying, the Neo-Wittgensteinian insight that identifying art may not be a matter of essential definition. Philosophical criticism, that is, is not only destructive; it can be constructive and productive as well.

It is very profitable to consider philosophies comparatively – to weigh the strengths and weaknesses of rival ideas against each other. Even mistaken viewpoints can supply part of the puzzle, while putting competing positions next to each other can winnow out the chaff from the wheat, thereby segregating the elements of more promising syntheses. Philosophical theories often evolve dialectically. Each step forward involves the rejection of parts of previous philosophies and the assimilation of other parts. In either case, criticism is the engine that drives philosophical evolution and should not be misconstrued as mean-spiritedness. It is an integral part of all analytic philosophy, including the analytic philosophy of art.

Welcome to the dialectic.

CHAPTER 1
Art and representation

Art and representation

Part I
Art as representation

Art, imitation and representation

The earliest known theories of art in Western philosophy were proposed by Plato and his student Aristotle. The particular artform that most concerned them was drama. In his *Republic*, Plato presented a design for an ideal state. In the course of outlining his utopia, he argued that poets – particularly dramatists – should be outlawed. In order to justify the exclusion of dramatic poets from the ideal state, Plato had to give reasons. And the reasons Plato found had to do with what he regarded as the nature of drama. According to Plato, the essence of drama was imitation – the simulation of appearances. That is, actors in plays imitate the actions of whomever they represent. In *Medea*, the actors, for example, imitate having arguments. Plato thought that this was problematic primarily because he believed that appearances appeal to the emotions and that stirring up the emotions is socially dangerous. An emotional citizenry is an unstable citizenry, ready to be swayed by demagogues rather than by good sense.

Arguments like Plato's against poetry are still heard today when it comes to discussions of the mass media. Often we are told that TV with its seductive imagery – its seductive appearances – makes for an unthinking electorate. Carefully designed, visually arresting, political advertisements appeal to the emotions of the voters rather than to their minds. If Plato were alive today, he would probably want to censor political advertisements for the same reason that he wanted to ban dramatic poetry.

Aristotle, however, believed that Plato's case was overstated. Though he agreed that drama provokes an emotional response from audiences, he did not think that this is all that drama does. Tragedy evokes pity and fear in spectators, but, he said, it does this for the purpose of *catharsis* – that is, for the purpose of purging the emotions. The meaning of "catharsis" is disputed among scholars. Some say that it means "clarifying" the emotions; others that it means "purifying" them; and still others that it means "evacuating" them. But, in any case, it is clear that Aristotle thought drama stimulated emotional responses for a beneficial purpose, even if we are uncertain about the precise nature of the purpose he had in mind.

Furthermore, Aristotle also thought that Plato was mistaken in presuming that drama did not address the mind of the audience. He maintained that people can learn from imitations, including dramatic imitations, and that the acquisition of knowledge from imitations is a major source of the pleasure that spectators derive from playgoing. Specifically, Aristotle thought that from dramatic poetry, viewers and readers could learn about human affairs – about how human events are likely to turn out once certain forces are put in motion (for example, once a powerful and resourceful woman like Medea is thrown over for her younger rival). Thus, Aristotle argues implicitly that there is enough good in drama for us to desist from implementing Plato's recommendation. Dramatic poets can remain in the righteous city.

Though Plato and Aristotle disagree in their diagnosis of the effects of dramatic poetry, they nevertheless agree on its nature. Both take poetry to be involved essentially in the imitation of action. Dramatic poetry represents human affairs by simulating human events on stage. Plato and Aristotle also talk about painting in their discussions of poetry, and, again, both agree that painting is essentially a matter of imitation – of verisimilitude. Plato describes painting as analogous to pointing a mirror toward things – an idea Shakespeare extends to drama when Hamlet instructs the players to hold a mirror up to nature.

What painters try to do, on the Platonic–Aristotelian view, is to reproduce the appearances of things – to copy them – not only people, but objects and events. Their view of painting parallels the view of their culture. Popular Greek stories of the painter Zeuxis, for instance, applaud him because he was able to draw pictures of grapes of such surpassing likeness that birds tried to eat them.

Since Plato and Aristotle primarily thought of dance and music as accompaniments to dramatic (or religious) spectacles, or poetic recitals, they thought of these artforms as subservient to the purposes of representation. They did not regard them so much as separate artforms, but as supplements or adjuncts of drama. They were parts of drama, and, as such, they were supposed to serve the imitative purposes of drama. Thus, along with drama and painting, Plato and Aristotle thought of music and dance as primarily imitative or representational arts.

When the Greeks used their word for "art," they had a broader conception in mind than we do today. For them, an art was any practice that required skill. Medicine and soldiering were arts on this conception. Thus, Plato and Aristotle would not have defined the arts, in their sense, as solely involved in imitation. However, it is clear that when they talk of what we call the *arts* – things like poetry, drama, painting, sculpture, dance and music – Plato and Aristotle thought that these shared a common feature: they were all involved in imitation.

Undoubtedly they did not think that these activities were the only ones that involved imitation; Aristotle talks about the way in which children imitate their elders. But imitation, for Plato and Aristotle, was at least a *necessary condition* for the kinds of practices we call art. That is, being an imitation – of a person, place, object, action or event – is a general feature that anything categorized as an artwork (in our sense) must possess. This is the theory of art that we find presupposed in the writings of Plato and Aristotle. We may state it thus:

x is an artwork only if it is an imitation.

In this formulation, the phrase "only if" signals that imitation is a necessary condition for art status. If a candidate for art status lacks the property of being an imitation of something, then it is not an artwork. For Plato and Aristotle, to be an artwork requires that the piece in question be an imitation of something. Nothing is an artwork, unless it is an imitation.

Today, after almost a century of abstract painting, this theory seems obviously false. Certain well-known paintings by Mark Rothko and Yves Klein do not imitate anything – they are pure fields of color – and yet they are considered major works of twentieth-century art. Thus, the theory that art is imitation appears to us to fail as a general theory of art, since it fails to be fully comprehensive. Too much of what we know to be art does not meet the alleged necessary requirement that anything that is art be imitative.

Art history has shown us that the theory of art associated with Plato and Aristotle is too exclusive; it confronts too many exceptions; it fails to count as art everything that we regard as belonging to the category of art. Walk through almost any art museum today, and you should be able to find some counterexamples to this theory.

Yet, in deference to Plato and Aristotle, we should also add that their theory was not as obviously false to them as it is to us, since the primary examples of art in their day were imitative. When they went to the theater, or when they went to the unveiling of a new sculpture, what they saw were imitations of heroes and gods and persons and actions – pieces of stones that looked like men, dancers that mimed human action, and plays that re-enacted important mythological events – like the destruction of the

House of Atreus. Thus, given the data that history had dealt them, the theory of art that Plato and Aristotle presupposed was fairly well motivated by what was available to them. It is only through the benefit of hindsight that we can see how far off they were.

So, in their own time, the imitative (mimetic) theory of art advanced by Plato and Aristotle had some initial plausibility. It coincided with the dominant examples of Greek art and it also informed readers about what to look for and to appreciate in the art of their contemporaries, namely its verisimilitude. That is, the theory of Plato and Aristotle had a pretty good fit with the data; it did a reasonable job of at least picking out what was important – or, perhaps, most important – in Greek artistic practices.

Due to the initial success of this theory, it was repeated in the Western tradition for centuries. The theory became especially important in the eighteenth century, since it was at that time that theorists began to codify our modern system of the fine arts.

What is meant by a "system of the fine arts?" Here, what we have in mind is a way of grouping certain practices – like painting and poetry – into a category distinct from other practices – like astronomy and chemistry. Prior to the eighteenth century, practices were grouped in a number of different ways. Music and mathematics, for example, might be placed in the same category. However, in the eighteenth century, a certain way of grouping various practices became canonical. Painting, poetry, dance, music, drama and sculpture came to be regarded as the fine arts – the arts with a capital A. These are the practices, with the later addition of a few others, like film, that nowadays we expect to be listed in the section of college bulletins devoted to the arts programs; and these are the kinds of things we expect to find represented at art centers. We do not expect to find scale models of space stations there.

Today this way of grouping the arts seems natural to us. But it was not always so. It is not until the eighteenth century that this way of classifying the relevant activities became more or less fixed. A particularly important text in bringing this about was *The Fine Arts Reduced to a Single Principle*, which was written by the Frenchman Charles Batteux in 1747. Notice that the title of this book indicates that the practices in the group called the fine arts are not assembled helter-skelter; they are not thrown together under the same title arbitrarily. Rather, it is said that there is a *single principle* to which all the pertinent activities can be reduced. And what is that principle? Imitation.

Batteux wrote, "We will define painting, sculpture and dance as the imitation of beautiful nature conveyed through colors, through relief and through attitudes. And music and poetry are the imitation of beautiful nature conveyed through sounds, or through measured discourse." For Batteux, membership in the system of the fine arts required that a practice meet a certain necessary condition, namely that it be imitative. In this, Batteux articulated a presupposition widely upheld in the eighteenth century – that art, as we call it, is to be defined essentially in terms of the Platonic–Aristotelian notion of imitation.

At first, it may seem strange to you that this characterization could ever have taken hold. You may wonder, for example, how music could have been regarded as an imitative art. Here, theorists argued not only that music could imitate beautiful sounds in nature – like birdsongs and thunder – but, more importantly, that it could imitate the human voice, for example, in spirited conversation.

Similarly, though much dance, such as social dance, does not appear imitative, eighteenth-century theorists, essentially reformers, advocated that theatrical dancing – dance as art – become imitative, following Aristotle's philosophy of drama, in order to join the modern system of the arts; the result was the *ballet d'action*, which dominated the dance stage of the nineteenth century. Moreover, the commitment to imitation also encouraged serious painters (painters dedicated to making art with a capital A) to continue their pursuit of greater and greater feats of realism (the attempt to approximate the perceptual appearance of things as closely as possible).

Thus, for several reasons, the authority of the imitation theory of art persisted well into the nineteenth century. A proponent of the theory could still claim that the imitation theory of art did a good job of describing existing art properly so called, since the vast majority of the most prominent examples of painting, drama, opera, dance, sculpture and so on were imitative (if only, in some cases, because practitioners aspired to meet the criterion necessary for cherished membership of the system of the fine arts). And, as well, there were also theories – such as the view that music imitates the human voice – that enabled apparent counterexamples to be explained away. Indeed, the influence of the imitation theory of art can still be found in the twentieth century: until only a generation ago, one could hear people saying of an abstract painting that it isn't art because it doesn't look like anything. And even today, some people will say that a certain film is not art because it lacks a story – that is, because it is not an imitation of action.

Of course, views like this are presently regarded as philistine – the opinion of people uninformed about art and, unfortunately, unashamed by displaying their ignorance. But that ignorance does not come from nowhere. It is a residue of the imitation theory of art, which theory, until the nineteenth century had, as we have indicated, some empirical credibility. Several things, however, have happened since then to undermine the theory decisively.

By the late nineteenth century and early twentieth century, visual art clearly begins to deviate from the aim of imitating nature. Visual art departs from the aim of copying how things look; photography could do that. German expressionist painters left off trying to capture exactly the look of things and, instead, distorted them for expressive effects. Cubists, action painters, and minimalists diverged from nature even further until finally making paintings whose referents, if any, were completely unrecognizable became a dominant tradition. Consider, for example, the work of Josef Albers, whose vocabulary comprises squares of color.

These examples of modern art refuted the imitation theory of art as a general philosophical conjecture, since they show that something can be a work of art that is not an imitation. Moreover, these examples also lead us to take another look at the tradition of visual art. The imitation theory claims that all art is imitative. Art in the twentieth century shows that that theory is false. But these counterexamples also encourage us to take a second look at art history and to ask whether the imitation theory was ever accurate. Contemplating the examples of twentieth-century art, I think we are inclined to realize that the imitation theory never got it quite right. Minimalist art, for instance, reminds us that there was always visual art of pure visual design, from carpets and pottery to illuminated texts and Islamic wall patterns. The history of pure visual decoration is as longstanding as the history of figuration.

Similarly, once alerted to the oversights of the imitation theory with respect to visual art, we need to reconsider the case of music. Is music really imitative? In times gone by, when music served primarily the function of accompanying words – in opera and religious chant, for example – one might have been tempted to assimilate music to the imitative arts. But with the triumph of symphonic music – pure orchestral music – in the early nineteenth century, the generalization that all music is representational was no longer tenable, if it ever was, since there was nonvocal music – marches and dance accompaniments – prior to the Romantic symphony. Likewise, modern drama has not only deviated from the imitation of action – in Futurist plays like Giacomo Balla's *To Understand Weeping* – giving rise to the dreamlike spectacles of Robert Wilson, but it also alerts us to the history of nonimitative performance, including many rituals and processions. And postmodern dance, with its emphasis on the perception of movement for its own sake, reminds us that much dance, including ballet *divertissements*, does not imitate, but rather explores the possibilities of human performance.

Furthermore, once we begin to poke holes in the imitation theory of art, we realize that it never really adequately characterized literature. Since Plato and Aristotle thought of literature in terms of dramatic poetry, it is easy to see why they thought it was imitative – it involved actors imitating the speech of characters. Even lyric poetry spoken aloud can be characterized this way. But once we start to think of literature in terms of novels and short stories, the idea that it is imitative, where imitation involves copying or simulating appearances, becomes strained. For novels are made up of words, and words don't look like their referents. The words that describe Holden in *The Catcher in the Rye* do not perceptually simulate anyone.

In order to deal with this problem, and others, the friend of the Platonic–Aristotelian theory may leave off talking in terms of imitation in favor of representation. By representation, here, is meant something that is intended to stand for something else and that is recognized by audiences as such. A portrait, for example, is intended to stand for whomever it is a portrait of, and viewers recognize it as such. This, of course, is an example of imitation, and imitation is a subcategory of representation. However, the notion of representation is broader, since something can also stand for something else without looking like it. For example, the *fleur-de-lys* can stand for the royal house of Bourbon without resembling it.

Moreover, by speaking of representation rather than imitation, conceived literally, the Platonic–Aristotelian theorist can deal with the problem of literature, since the description of the Battle of Borodino in *War and Peace* represents it without literally copying it. Likewise, many twentieth-century abstractions in visual art, like the paintings of Mondrian, represent something – such as ultimate reality – without rendering its literal appearance.

Reconstruing the imitation theory of art as the representational theory of art yields a position of greater generality, since the concept of representation is broader than the concept of imitation. But even with this additional breadth, the representational theory of art remains unsalvageable, since much art is not representational.

Stated formulaically, x represents y (where y ranges over a domain comprised of objects, persons, events and actions) if and only if (1) a sender intends x (e.g., a picture) to stand for y (e.g., a haystack) and (2) the audience realizes that x is intended to stand for y.

But there are many works of art that are not representations in this sense. Consider architecture: many of the finest buildings in history are not intended to stand for something. The cathedral of St. Peter in Rome does not stand for a house of God; it *is* a house of God. Similarly the Capitol Building in Washington, D.C. does not stand for the legislature; it houses the legislature. The representational theory of art may provide the means for incorporating much literature under the rubric of art, but it still leaves much architecture of the sort we are apt to regard as art outside the category. Thus, the representational theory of art, like the imitation theory of art, is too exclusive to serve as a general theory of art.

Of course, the problem with the representational theory of art is not simply that it excludes too much architecture from the category of art. It also excludes important and obvious examples of art from every other artistic genre as well. Some orchestral music may be representational, but most is not. Some abstract paintings are essentially formal exercises representing nothing, and there are even songs and poems like this. And there are also abstract films, videos, photographs, dances and even theater pieces (performance art) that stand for nothing, but are presented as occasions for concentrated perceptual experiences. These examples are primarily modern in origin. But the representational theory of art is not only refuted by modern examples. For as we have already indicated, decorative art throughout the ages provides an ample field of counterexamples – works based in the pleasing play of forms, representing nothing.

The neo-representational theory of art

Neither the imitation theory of art nor the broader representational theory of art appears successful. Neither gives us a general theory of art; neither designates a necessary property of all artworks. However, there is a recent variation on the representational theory of art which seems, at least at first blush, less susceptible to counterexamples than its predecessors. We can call this variation the neo-representational theory of art, though, it must be admitted, that this is a bit of a misnomer, since the theory does not claim that in order to be an artwork a candidate must represent something in the sense stipulated above. The neo-representational theory makes a weaker claim, namely that in order to count as a work of art, the candidate must be about something (i.e., it must have a subject, about which it makes some comment). Moreover, that about which the artwork expresses something may be the artwork itself or art in general.

Stated briefly, the theory maintains that:

x is an artwork only if it is about something.

This theory can be expanded by being more explicit about what is involved in being "about something."

x is an artwork only if x has a subject about which it makes some comment (about which it says something, or expresses some observation).

This notion might also be stated by alleging that in order to count as art, a candidate must have some semantic content. Indeed, it is in virtue of the requirement that all artworks possess semantic content that we call this theory neo-representationalism, since the concept of semantics and that of representation are intimately connected.

According to the neo-representational theory of art, anything that is a work of art necessarily possesses the property of aboutness – it has semantic content; it has a subject about which it expresses something. *King Lear*, for example, has a subject, governance, about which it says something: a house divided shall not stand. Likewise, Picasso's *Guernica* is about something, aerial bombardment, about which it expresses horror.

Perhaps the easiest way to see what is attractive about neo-representationalism is to note how it handles some difficult cases of modern art. One genre of modern art is the readymade or the found object. Marcel Duchamp is a name often associated with this genre. Two of his more notorious works are *Fountain* and *In Advance of a Broken Arm*. The former is an ordinary urinal; the latter is a snow shovel. These are called readymades or found objects because they came readymade off the factory assembly line; Duchamp did not make them – he, so to speak, found them.

Though today there may still be some people who deny that these readymades are artworks, practicing artists, critics and art historians treat these works as central moments in twentieth-century art. Thus, there is at least a *prima facie* case for regarding them as artworks. But, assuming that they are artworks, a puzzle arises. If *Fountain* and *In Advance of a Broken Arm* are artworks, why aren't things that look just like them – ordinary urinals and snow shovels from the same factories – artworks too?

Duchamp's readymades are perceptually indiscernible from their ordinary, real-world counterparts. Yet we classify Duchamp's artworks and their ordinary, perceptually indiscernible, real-world counterparts in terms of radically different categories, and this has important consequences. We do not stand before ordinary urinals contemplating their meaning, nor do we store the snow shovels in our garage with velvet ropes around them to insure that visitors maintain a proper distance from them. Why not? Why do we treat things that look exactly the same so differently?

Because Duchamp's readymades are artworks, whereas ordinary urinals and snow shovels are not. But what property or properties do Duchamp's readymades possess that their indiscernible counterparts lack? Here, the neo-representationalist advances the tantalizing hypothesis that Duchamp's readymades possess aboutness, whereas their ordinary, perceptually indiscernible, real-world counterparts do not.

This argument is what is called an hypothesis to the best explanation – that is, neo-representationalism offers the best explanation of why we make the awesome categorical distinction between Duchamp's readymades and ordinary real things (the former counting as art; the latter not); and inasmuch as neo-representationalism is the best explanation, we have good inductive grounds for accepting it. By being the best explanation, neo-representationalism recommends itself to us.

But what does it mean to say that the readymades possess aboutness? That they have a subject about which they say something. For example, art historians often maintain that *Fountain* and *In Advance of a Broken Arm* are about art – about the nature of art – about which they insinuate that artworks need not be literally created or sculpted by the labor of the artist (the artist need not literally be an artificer). This view contrasts with more sanctimonious views of art which regard the artwork as virtually a relic or spiritual imprint of the genius-artist. Or, it might be said, Duchamp makes the theoretical point that the essence of art is not manual labor or craft. In addition, *Fountain* might be "read" as a parody of scuplture – after all, like the monumental fountains that grace great cities, it is a fashioned stone artifact replete with running water.

In short, Duchamp's readymades warrant interpretations. It makes sense to ask what they are about. The sorts of interpretations rehearsed in the preceding paragraph answer that question. On the other hand, it does not make sense to ask what ordinary urinals and snow shovels are about. Ordinary urinals and snow shovels are not about anything; they have no semantic content; they are mute – meaningless. If you stand in your driveway after a blizzard, looking at your snow shovel and asking after its meaning, people will suppose you are either trying to avoid clearing off the snow or that you are a candidate for institutionalization. And if you stand in the men's restroom contemplating what the urinals express, you'll probably get arrested.

Our behavior, then, confronting readymades versus their indiscernible real-world counterparts is radically different. With readymades we presume that it is correct and appropriate to interpret them – we presume that they are about something and that an appropriate response to them is to determine what they have to "say" or what they imply concerning whatever they are about. This is not the appropriate response to ordinary urinals and shovels. Why not? Because the latter are not artworks and, therefore, are not about anything.

The neo-representational theory of art does a good job of explaining the difference between readymades and their perceptually indiscernible, real-world counterparts. Thus, it solves an important contemporary problem. But it is also proposed as a general theory of art – aboutness is not simply a necessary property of readymades, but of all art. So the question is: how generalizable is aboutness? Is it a property of all artworks?

Neo-representationalism maintains that aboutness or semantic content is a necessary condition of all artworks. Clearly, semantic content is not a feature of only artworks. Many other sorts of things – from sermons to advertisements to physics articles – have a subject about which they say something. So aboutness is not the unique mark of only artworks. But is it, nevertheless, a property that anything that is an artwork must possess (even if other things possess it as well)?

One way to argue for this conclusion is to begin with the premise that all artworks require interpretations. When one reads art criticism or art history books, one is struck by the fact that they are full of interpretations. It is natural to presume that all artworks are open to interpretation, since that is what people who are experts about art always seem to do with artworks – they interpret them. But if anything calls for an interpretation, then surely it must be about something – it must say something, have a meaning or possess semantic content.

This much seems built into the concept or the definition of an interpretation – that is, it is a necessary condition of interpretation that the object of interpretation have a subject about which it makes some comment. An interpretation is just the specification of that content. Anything that truly warrants an interpretation must be about something – otherwise it would not require an interpretation. Why else would it require an interpretation, unless it were about something? Thus, if artworks require interpretations, then they must be about something. This follows from what it is to be an interpretation.

Stated formally, this argument maintains that:

1 All artworks require interpretations.
2 If anything requires an interpretation, then it must be about something.
3 Therefore, all artworks are about something.

This is a strong argument in favor of neo-representationalism. Moreover, it should be clear that neo-representationalism is superior to the representational theory of art, since it is a broader theory. The central defining property of art that it proposes – being about something – is more comprehensive than the one advanced by the representational theory – standing for something else. For if x stands for y, x is about something, but there are more ways for x to be about something than standing for it. The film *Diary of a Country Priest* is about divine grace, but it doesn't stand for or represent divine grace. Thus, insofar as aboutness is broader than strict representation, neo-representationalism may not be as fatally narrow as the other theories we have examined so far.

The argument for neo-representationalism is logically valid, but that does not mean that its conclusion is true. The conclusion of a logically valid argument is only guaranteed to be true if the premises of the argument are true. So the question before us is whether the preceding premises are true. The second premise rests on or follows from the concept or definition of interpretation. It seems credible. So is the first premise of the argument – that all artworks require interpretations – acceptable?

One reason to dispute it originates in the practice of contemporary artists. Many contemporary artists aspire to create works of art that are designed to defy interpretation or to be utterly meaningless. Sometimes artists claim to do this in order to "deconstruct" the distinction between artworks and real things. This might be one way to view certain ready-mades – as examples of the supposed fact that ultimately there is no genuine difference between artworks and real things.

However, ironically, the neo-representationalist can argue that attempts along these lines really confirm the thesis of neo-representationalism. Why? Because artworks that are advanced to exemplify the thesis that artworks are ultimately real things are, in fact, not at all like real things, since such artworks have semantic content. They are about something – namely the nature of artworks – about which they have something to say: that artworks are actually real things. An artist cannot make an artwork whose point is that artworks are real things by simply making a real thing, since by saying something (by making a point) the piece is already more than a mute, meaningless real thing – because it has aboutness and warrants an interpretation.

Real things don't exemplify the property of real-thingness, though they possess it; something designed to exemplify real-thingness in order to make a theoretical point obviously has semantic content, semantic content of the sort that art critics will explicate by pointing to the artist's commitment to showing that artworks are ultimately real things. Even if the theoretical point that the artwork is intended to communicate is false, nevertheless in attempting to communicate a theoretical point, the work in question is necessarily about something. Thus, neo-representationalism is not challenged by avant-garde artworks that are "against interpretation," since by attempting to resist interpretation for the sake of disclosing the true nature of art, they, instead, mandate interpretation. Consequently, and paradoxically enough, modern artworks predicated on refuting neo-representationalism actually count in its favor.

Unlike the imitation theory of art and the representational theory of art, neo-representationalism does a nice job of handling cases of modern art. Much modern art is about the nature of art; thus it will satisfy the requirement of aboutness. Of course, not all modern art concerns the nature of art. Some modern art is concerned with metaphysical, political, spiritual or psychological matters. But neo-representationalism will have no problem with these works either, since they are all about something, even in cases where the artworks are abstract or nonfigurative.

Moreover, neo-representationalism looks like it can deal with a number of the other counterexamples that beset the representational theory of art. Much music and architecture that does not stand for anything nevertheless possesses expressive properties. The Pentagon, for example, expresses strength and substance, while some pure orchestral music strikes us as joyous. Might we not say that what these examples are about – what they mean, what comprises their semantic content – is their expressive content: strength, on the one hand, and joyousness, on the other?

And lastly, with respect to decorative art, the neo-representationalist will point out that many of the seemingly abstract decorations on artworks from remote cultures are not at all truly meaningless, but, when understood in their correct historical context, they will be seen to have religious or ritual significance. Thus even art that is allegedly merely decorative generally has aboutness.

Neo-representationalism, then, is a powerful theory. It has the resources to cover a lot of the ground that is inhospitable to the imitation and representation theories of art. It is far less exclusive than either of those views and this bodes well on its behalf. It is a more encompassing theory than the other theories in this family of representational theories, but is it encompassing enough? There are several reasons to think that it is not.

First, it is not certain that the way in which the neo-representationalist deals with some of our earlier counterexamples is really convincing. Confronted by certain cases of pure orchestral music and non-representational architecture, the neo-representationalist notes that they may possess expressive properties and that this is what such works are about. But this seems questionable. Suppose a piece of pure orchestral music is sad. Is this really what it is about? Does it truly have a subject, sadness, about which it expresses something? Does the possession of a property amount to being about the property?

It seems strained to say so. It possesses the property, but what does it say about it? If a painting possesses the property redness, mere possession of the property hardly counts as being about redness. Though you may possess red hair, you are not "about" having red hair. Being about a property surely requires more than mere possession of the property. So, the neo-representationalist's solution for dealing with the hard cases of much pure orchestral music and nonrepresentational architecture is not actually successful.

Another way of getting at this objection is to note that when we say that a piece of music is sad, we are not really interpreting it in any robust sense of the word. Reporting that the music is sad is more a matter of describing a perceptible property of the work. In pertinent respects, it is akin to saying that the work has a fast tempo. Once again, that a work possesses a fast tempo is not enough to say it is about "having a fast tempo"; that would require some further level of articulation from the work that calls attention to, makes reference to, and/or implies some comment or point about its having a fast tempo. Because mere possession of a fast tempo does not involve these things, no interpretation is called for in a case like this to identify the music's subject about which it expresses something. We need not interpret the music in either the case of its possession of a fast tempo or its sadness, since there is nothing that the music is about in the neo-representationalist's sense. But if certain pieces of pure orchestral music and nonrepresentational architecture, even though they possess expressive properties, are not about these properties and require no interpretation, then they become, in effect, counterexamples to neo-representationalism.

If the neo-representationalist response to the preceding types of hard cases was too hasty, it may be that the neo-representationalist's method of dealing with decorative art is also problematic. The neo-representationalist makes the good point that often what appears to us as mere decoration occurs in cultural contexts where it has symbolic, perhaps religious or ritual, significance and, therefore, aboutness. But the question is whether all cases of decorative art can be handled in this manner. Isn't there some decorative art that is simply a matter of stimulating pleasure by its design or its appearance? This is often what we mean when we describe something as beautiful – that we find a pattern arresting and pleasing.

Surely some artworks are simply beautiful in this sense. They are, so to say, "beneath interpretation." They do not require interpretation. They work their magic, or, at least, they are intended to do so, solely in virtue of the perceptual impact they make on us. They are not about beauty; they are beautiful. They express nothing about beauty in general, nor about the particular beauty that they possess. Perhaps some decorative art does more than this; perhaps some of it has latent religious significance. But, equally, much decorative art – including aural as well as visual art – addresses us only on the perceptual level – by being only beautiful or intriguing – and it is valued for that very reason. This sort of art is not really about anything. It is stimulating in a pleasing way, while not being about stimulation. But if we grant that there is such art, as I think we must, then there is art that is not about anything.

Cases like this – of pure decoration – are not isolated exceptions. There is a great deal of art of this sort. Moreover, there is a great deal of architecture and music that, though it may possess expressive properties – and for that matter beauty – is not about anything. Thus, there is a great deal of art that the neo-representational theory fails to accommodate. Neo-representationalism is more comprehensive than the imitation theory and the representational theory of art, but it is still nowhere near comprehensive enough. Thus, it would appear that none of the views in this family of theories is satisfactory as a general philosophical theory of all art.

Part II
What is representation?

Pictorial representation

So far we have seen that representation-type theories of art are inadequate. Neither the imitation theory, the representational theory nor the neo-representational theory succeed in discovering a general property that all works, in order to count as artworks, must possess. For some art is nonrepresentational – some art imitates nothing, stands for nothing, and is about nothing. And yet, even though much art is not representational, much other art is. Consequently, despite the fact that much art is not representational – thereby falsifying representational theories of art – since much other art is representational, we still need a theory of representation, a theory that explicates that which the concept of representation comprises.

Visual art is the art that most people are disposed to have in mind first when we speak of representation and/or imitation. So it is a useful place to start our discussions of representation.

Clearly, much visual art is representational. Representation is so important to the history of visual art that there have been moments in bygone eras when visual art was thought of primarily in terms of pictures. And even today much visual art is representational. Typically, the vast majority of photographs, movies, videos and TV programs that surround us are representations, indeed, representations that many might say proceed by way of imitation. Consequently, we may initiate our discussion of the concept of representation in art by focussing on visual or pictorial representation which we intend to encompass such things as: frescoes of the Sun god from Afghanistan, Wunggadinda's snake image from Manning Creek in Western Australia, *A Lone Fisherman on a River in Autumn* by Wu Zhen, Rubens' *Minerva Protects Pax from Mars*, Courbet's *The Stonebreakers* and *Burial at Ornans*, Cindy Sherman's photograph *Untitled #228*, every shot in Ola Balogun's film *Agani Ogun* and every episode of *Ally McBeal*.

Traditional approaches to pictorial representation

Two traditional theories of pictorial representation are the resemblance theory and the illusion theory. The resemblance theory of representation states that x represents y just in case x resembles y. A picture of George Washington represents George Washington just because the picture looks like or is similar to George Washington visually. On the other hand, the illusion theory of pictorial representation maintains that x represents y just in case x causes the illusion of y in spectators. That is, a film of a battle scene represents the battle scene just because viewers of the film have the impression that the battle is unfolding in front of them. According to the illusion theory, a picture, whether moving or still, is a representation of y when it deceives viewers into believing that they are in the presence of y.

Obviously, the resemblance theory and the illusion theories of representation can be combined into one theory: x represents y just in case x causes the illusion of y in viewers by way of resembling y. However, you can hold one of these theories without holding the other. Thus, we will examine these theories one at a time, since if each of the theories is false by itself, it is unlikely that they will be true when added together. Two wrongs don't make a right.

As we have already seen, Plato thought painting to be strictly analogous to holding a mirror toward an object. A pictorial image, for him, was the analog of a mirror-image. Since a mirror-image is similar in a great many of its visual properties to whatever it is an image of, Plato held what we are calling a resemblance theory of representation. This is probably the view that most people would offer if you asked them in what a pictorial representation consists. Stated formulaically, the resemblance theory of representation maintains that:

> x represents y if and only if x resembles y appreciably.

Note that this theory claims two things. First that resemblance is a necessary condition for representation – that x represents y *only if* x resembles y. But it also claims something else, namely that *if* x resembles y, then x represents y. That is, the formula employs the locution "*if* and only if." The first occurrence of "if" here signals that resemblance is a *sufficient* condition for representation – that if something involves resemblance, then that is sufficient for counting it as a representation. The "only if" portion of the formula states that resemblance is a *necessary* condition for representation. Thus, the theory as a whole claims that resemblance is both a necessary and a sufficient condition for representation, or, somewhat less jargonistically, x represents y if and only if x resembles y appreciably (where "appreciably" means something like "in a significant number of respects"). Given the structure of this theory, we can proceed by first asking whether indeed resemblance is a sufficient condition for representation, and then go on to ask whether it is a necessary condition.

Is resemblance a sufficient condition for representation – if x resembles y, does it follow that x represents y? This seems false; it appears overly inclusive. Imagine two automobiles – both Jeep Cherokees. They roll off the assembly line one after the other, they are the same color, and they share all the same features. These two Jeep Cherokees will resemble each other maximally, but neither represents the other. The same story can be told of identical twins. Though they look like each other in every respect, neither represents the other. Thus, similarity, even very exact similarity, between two items is not enough – not sufficient – to say that one of the items represents the other item.

That resemblance cannot be a sufficient condition for representation can also be shown by contemplating the logical structure of resemblance versus the logical structure of representation. Resemblance is a reflexive relation. That means that if x is related to x (if x is related to itself in a certain way), then x is related to x (itself) in the same way (xRx if and only if xRx). Resemblance is like mathematical equality in this respect, since "If 1 = 1, then 1 = 1." But representation is not reflexive: I resemble myself in every respect, but I do not represent myself. Given the reflexivity of the resemblance relation, if I resemble myself, as I do, then I should represent myself, but this does not follow. Consequently, resemblance is not a sufficient condition for representation.

Another feature of the logic of resemblance is that resemblance is a symmetrical relation. That is, if x is related to y, then y is related to x in the same way (xRy if and only if yRx). If I am Pat's brother, then Pat is my brother. If I resemble my sister, then my sister resembles me. But representation is not a symmetrical relation. If a picture of Napoleon resembles Napoleon, it follows that Napoleon resembles his picture, but it does not follow that Napoleon represents his picture. For though resemblance is a symmetrical relation, representation is not. Thus, resemblance cannot serve as a model for representation, since resemblance and representation have different logical structures, the one being symmetrical and the other not. Resemblance cannot be a sufficient condition for representation, because there will be many cases of resemblance – such as the fact that Napoleon resembles his portrait – that will not warrant attributions of representation. It is not the case that if Napoleon resembles his portrait, then Napoleon represents his portrait.

One might try to get around this objection via amending the

resemblance theory by stipulating that x must be a visual design. Then the theory states that if x, *a visual design*, resembles y, then x represents y. Thus, even if Napoleon resembles his portrait, we will not say that he represents it because Napoleon is not a visual design. But this calls attention to a problem with the resemblance theory that we have not mentioned yet. What most visual representations resemble most are other visual representations. A *picture* of Richard Nixon looks more like a *picture* of Bill Clinton than it looks like Richard Nixon. So on the present version of the resemblance theory, we would be forced to say that a visual design of Richard Nixon represents a picture of Bill Clinton, since it resembles Clinton's picture more than it does Nixon. And this would be an unfortunate result.

To remedy it, one might try to refine the resemblance theory further, stipulating that if x is a visual design and y is *not* a visual design then x represents y. This will block counterexamples such as the case where we will have to say that the picture of Nixon represents the picture of Bill Clinton.

But this revised theory will have further unacceptable consequences, because some pictures *do* represent other pictures. Photographs of Raphael's *School of Athens* in art history textbooks do represent it just as postcards from scenes of the movie *Batman* represent them. Thus, rewriting the theory this way results in a bad theory – a theory that excludes certain obvious cases of representation. If our previous objections showed that the resemblance theory was too inclusive, this last objection shows that it is also too exclusive.

Resemblance, then, does not appear to be a sufficient condition for representation. But is it a necessary condition? Is it the case that if something is a representation, then it must resemble (appreciably) whatever it is a representation of? Are all instances where x represents y also instances where x resembles y? There is at least one argument that suggests that this is not the case.

In order to understand this argument, we need to think a bit more deeply about what we mean by a representation. When we say that one object represents another object, we mean, at the very least, that the first object is a symbol for the second object. To say a photograph of Madonna represents Madonna, we mean at the very least that the photograph is a symbol of Madonna. But what is a symbol? The pragmatist philosopher C. S. Peirce defined a symbol as a sign "whose special significance or fitness to represent just what it does represent lies in nothing but the very fact of there being a habit, disposition or other effective rule that it will be so interpreted."

To be a symbol for something else – to denote something else – is to stand for it, to refer to it, insofar as there is a rule that the symbol will be so interpreted. To represent something else is to be a symbol for it which, in turn, entails that at the very least – i.e., necessarily – that a representation stand for whatever it represents. But to stand for something does not require resemblance.

Consider a military map. A thumbtack can stand for an armored division, but it does not resemble an armored division. A thumbtack can denote an armored division without resembling it appreciably. A pepper shaker could serve equally well to represent the armored division. In a context like this one, what stands for the armored division is arbitrary. Appreciable resemblance is not necessary. But if the symbol relation (denotation) is the core of representation, and if denotation can obtain without resemblance, then resemblance is not a necessary condition for representation. And previous arguments have already shown that resemblance is not a sufficient condition for representation. Denotation is enough to establish representation; it alone is a necessary and a sufficient condition for representation.

Or, to state the argument more prosaically:

1 x represents y if and only if x denotes y.
2 If x denotes y, then x may not resemble y.
3 x represents y.
4 Therefore, x denotes y.
5 Therefore, x may not resemble y.
6 Therefore, x represents y and x may not resemble y.
7 Now, suppose that resemblance is a necessary condition for representation.
8 If resemblance is a necessary condition for representation, then it is not (possibly) the case that x represents y and that x may not resemble y.
9 Therefore, it is not the case that x represents y and x may not resemble y.
10 Therefore, resemblance is not a necessary condition for representation.

This argument takes the form of a *reductio ad absurdum* – a reduction to absurdity (where "absurdity" means a "contradiction.") This sort of argument proceeds by *supposing* what one intends to disprove (as in premise #7 above) in order to show that it leads to an absurdity (a contradiction – note that in the preceding argument steps #6 and #9 contradict each other). Since a contradiction is an unacceptable result, it must be eliminated. That is, we must eliminate the most probable source of the contradiction. Since we had no contradiction before we made the supposition (in premise #7), that step appears to be the likeliest source of our contradiction.

So we surmise that it must be false (step #10 above). Thus, resemblance is not a necessary condition for representation.

We can call this the "core argument" against resemblance because it maintains that since what is fundamental to representation is denotation and since denotation does not require resemblance, resemblance is not a necessary condition for representation – there can be representation without resemblance. This argument looks compelling, though we shall have to return to it shortly in order to see whether it is genuinely successful. Nevertheless, for the time being, let us grant for the sake of exposition that it advances a *prima facie* case against the resemblance theory of representation.

As already mentioned, another traditional theory of representation is the illusion theory. According to the illusion theory:

x represents y if and only if x causes the illusion of y in spectators.

The archetypal story of the country bumpkin who rushes onstage during a melodrama to save the heroine from the villain encapsulates the illusion theory. Likewise, with respect to pictures, the illusion theory says that genuine pictures of Joan of Arc deceive viewers into believing that the Maid of Orleans is before them, just as the Greeks claimed that Zeuxis's pictures of grapes were so effective that birds tried to eat them.

But the illusion theory has even more problems than does the resemblance theory. First of all, it is wildly at odds with our normal experience of pictorial representations. Under standard conditions, who is ever really fooled by them? Who ever tries to reach into a still life to slake one's thirst with the wine pictured therein? Nor does anyone ever try to get out of the way of the charge of the Light Brigade when viewing paintings or movies of that event. That is, in normal circumstances, our behavior indicates that we are not fooled into believing that what is pictured is really before us.

Perhaps in extraordinary conditions, someone might be deceived into believing that what is pictured is really in front of them in the "flesh," but typically this is not what happens. Typically we know that we are looking at a picture, not its referent. And if we know that this is the case, then we do not believe we are looking at the subject of the picture "in the flesh"; we are not deceived. Thus the illusion theory grievously misdescribes our experience of pictorial representations and cannot be an adequate theory of it.

Nor does the illusion theory make much sense out of our practice of looking at pictures. When viewing pictures, we often appreciate the verisimilitude of the picture. But if we thought the picture was its referent, it would make no sense to appreciate its verisimilitude. It is nonsense to appreciate how much my car looks like itself. But if the illusion theory were true, that is what I would be doing if I said I appreciated the veri-similitude of a picture of my car.

Additionally, in order to view pictures properly, we must learn to "see through" their surface distortions. We must see through the shine off the varnish, or, if it is a film, we must see through the scratches on the emulsion. But in order to see through these features, we must know that we are looking at pictures and not their referents "in nature." However, if we know these are pictures, then, given our standard understanding of what it is to know something, we do not believe that they are their referents. Thus, again, there is no deception – no illusory belief – involved. So the illusion theory of pictorial representation is false for the standard case, which, of course, is the case that we expect a theory of pictorial representation to explicate. Therefore, we need another approach to the problem of pictorial representation.

The conventionalist theory of pictorial representation

The case for the conventionalist approach begins with the unimpeachable observation that there are different pictorial systems. For example, the ancient Egyptians employed different conventions of representation than the Italian painters of the High Renaissance. In the Egyptian system of representation, the nose of a figure is shown in profile while, simultaneously, the eye is represented frontally. This is why it is sometimes referred to as "the frontal eye" style. In a typical Renaissance painting, the eye and the nose are presented from a uniform angle of perception – from the same perspective: if the nose is in profile, so is the eye. Moreover, there are many other styles of representation cross-culturally and transhistorically. Of this, there can be no doubt; it is a fact.

Furthermore, it is often claimed that people from different cultures, steeped in their own systems of representation, allegedly have difficulty comprehending representations in alternative styles. It has been reported that tribal peoples from Africa had trouble identifying what Western photographs were photographs of. In order to comprehend the pictures of other cultures, the conventionalist argues, the spectator must learn the conventions of the relevant pictorial system just as in order to understand foreign languages, one must learn them. Like languages, the conventionalist argues, pictures consist of codes which must be learnt if pictures are to be understood by percipients.

Obviously, pictures often involve certain conventions or codes. In order to understand that the halo around the head of a woman in a painting signifies that she is a saint, one must know what those illuminated circles stand for. The conventionalist contends that all pictorial phenomena are like this. All pictures involve "reading" the relevant conventions or codes. Moreover, since these conventions vary from period to period and from culture to culture, to understand pictures from elsewhere requires learning the pertinent conventions.

The conventionalist approach is also notably consistent with the most important premise of the "core argument" against the resemblance theory. According to that argument, the central feature of representation is denotation. And what denotes what is arbitrary. A representation is a symbol and what fixes the reference of a symbol is some kind of rule or code. Thus, representation is conventional. Just as what words stand for what things is a matter of consensus, what configurations denote what objects is also a function of a social contract. I am calling this approach conventionalist, but it might also be called "semiotic": it holds that representations are signs whose referents are systematically established by conventions that correlate visual configurations with objects. Pictorial representation is a kind of language.

The resemblance theory and the illusion theory are naturalistic theories of pictorial representation in the sense that they presuppose that there is some universal psychological process that explains pictorial representation: either the percipient naturally detects certain similarities and surmises representation on the basis of this, or, on the other hand, the representation somehow causes normal spectators to believe that the referent of the representation is before them. But for the conventionalist, pictorial representation is an affair of acculturation. A picture represents by way of conventions which may vary over time and place. Comprehending what a picture is a picture of involves reading, or deciphering, or decoding it in virtue of some established system of conventions or codes. According to the conventionalist theory of pictorial representation:

> x pictorially represents y only if x denotes y in accordance with some established system of established conventions.

The relevant system here may or may not hang on resemblances, nor is there any claim that spectators will be deceived by pictures. Thus, the conventionalist theory is not susceptible to the kinds of objections raised against the traditional theories of representation. Moreover, unlike those theories, the conventionalist theory is more suited to explaining the apparent evidence of the cross-cultural incomprehension of alternative pictorial practices. Thus, in terms of its explanatory power and its resistance to standard objections, the conventionalist theory appears superior to its traditional rivals.

However, one objection to the conventionalist theory might be that it fails to explain why we experience certain pictures as more realistic than other pictures. The photographs in *Time* magazine seem more "realistic" to us than Egyptian wall drawings in the "frontal eye" style. Proponents of the resemblance theory would explain this phenomenon by saying that the pictures that resemble objects in nature more closely are the ones we experience as more realistic. But however we explain the phenomenon, it does seem that pictures in certain systems seem more "lifelike" than others. Moreover, this does not appear to square with the conventionalist theory, since on the conventionalist theory, all pictorial representations are arbitrary *and*, if they are all arbitrary, none should appear more realistic than others.

Nevertheless, the conventionalist has an explanation prepared for objections like this. The conventionalist maintains that the representations that *we* call realistic are merely the ones with which we are the most familiar. Once we become habituated to a given style of representation, it seems natural to us. Think of our relation to our own language. It seems natural to us; it seems strange that other people should call dogs by a different name from ours. But then other languages seem natural to the people raised to speak them.

The conventionalist wants to tell the same story about pictorial representation – for any group of people, the conventional system of representation with which they are most familiar will be called "realistic." Habituated in the "frontal eye" system, the Egyptians thought it realistic, whereas we find the Renaissance perspective more realistic because that is the system we know. But if one of us were to trade places with an ancient Egyptian, then we would both reverse our assessments.

Moreover, with respect to our own culture, the notion of realism has shifted over time. Giotto's work was once regarded as realistic, but now it seems much less so when compared to the work of David. The reason, the conventionalist maintains, is that the conventions of realism in the West have changed. Perhaps, various works of Cubism strike us as unrealistic now. But if Cubism were to persist and become the most dominant and familiar form of pictorial representation, then, the conventionalist predicts, it would come to strike us as realist, since the impression of realism is nothing more than habituation within a given symbol system. When Picasso made a portrait of Gertrude Stein, she noted that it did not look like her. Picasso told her not to worry because it would – that is, once his style became familiar, it would pass for realism.

Similarly, if pictures of people were always distorted in the German expressionist manner, then gradually expressionism would come to look like realism to us. In this respect, conventionalism is a very radical, counterintuitive doctrine. It is hard to imagine that we could ever come to regard Cubist or expressionist portraiture as realistic. But conventionalism is committed to this view, which is one reason why we may feel tempted to revert to some sort of naturalistic theory of pictorial representation.

A neo-naturalist theory of
pictorial representation

Part of the case for conventionalism rests on its explanatory power. It can explain the alleged cross-cultural incomprehension of alternative styles of representation. But there are also a great deal of phenomena that conventionalism cannot explain, and this counts against conventionalism.

First, there is evidence, based on cross-cultural research, that pictorial representations travel far more smoothly from society to society than the conventionalist suggests. After Japan became open to the West, Japanese artists were able to understand and then imitate Western perspective by perusing the illustrations in Dutch medical textbooks. That is, they understood a representational system alternative to their own without special tutelage. Similarly, Western cinematography is now employed cross-culturally; people in remote villages in India understand Hollywood motion picture images without taking film courses.

We can also confirm the ease with which pictorial styles cross cultural boundaries by considering our own case. We can recognize the kinds of things that Assyrian bas-reliefs represent (e.g., winged creatures) without knowing anything about Assyrian culture. Indeed, we can recognize what prehistoric cave paintings represent (e.g., bisons), and no one really knows anything about Neolithic pictorial conventions. Or, to consider more recent cases, Westerners can comprehend Japanese pictures in the "floating-eye" style without being tutored in Japanese representational codes.

In addition, there is evidence from developmental psychology that bodes ill for conventionalism. Children raised without seeing any pictures for the first year and half of their lives are able to recognize what pictures are pictures of on their very first exposure to them. That is, where children are able to recognize the relevant objects "in nature" (such as cats and cars), they will be able to recognize typical pictures of those objects without any special training in the pictorial styles of their culture.

But if comprehending what a picture is a picture of were simply a matter of applying conventions, then that would require that percipients be trained in the pertinent pictorial codes and conventions. However, in the preceding cases, there is no training. Therefore, contrary to conventional-ism, it does not seem that pictorial comprehension can be simply a matter of applying codes and conventions.

One would suppose that acquiring a set of pictorial codes, of the sort the conventionalist envisions, would be extremely analogous to acquiring a language. In both cases, what is involved is an arbitrary code. But as the preceding examples indicate, quite often mastery of pictures – seeing what they represent – is not like language acquisition at all. Learning a language takes a long time. But we are able to understand pictures – able to identify the kinds of things they stand for – without protracted training. We recog-nize Assyrian, Egyptian, Neolithic and Japanese pictures with no special education in these alleged codes, and the Japanese and the Indians recog-nize Western-style pictures without training, as do children in our own culture. It is unimaginable that linguistic comprehension could proceed in this manner. Thus, pictorial comprehension is not really very much like linguistic comprehension, which is our best model for understanding what is involved in coming to learn arbitrary conventions of the relevant sort.

Consider this disanalogy. On the evidence cited, it appears that after seeing one or two pictures in an alien representational style, people of different cultures are able to identify the picture of any kind of object with which they are already familiar. Similar powers are not in evidence with respect to words and languages. After viewing one or two Japanese pictures in the floating-eye style, a Westerner can negotiate almost any picture in that style. But if I learn one or two Japanese words, I am nowhere near being able to understand almost every Japanese sentence. This suggests that pictures are not arbitrary symbols in a system of con-ventions and that comprehending them is not a matter of reading, deciphering, decoding or of the application of merely conventional pat-terns of inference. There is, with respect to recognizing the generic kinds of things that pictures represent, no pictorial dictionary of the sort that we need to acquire in order to master the vocabulary of a language. But if pictorial comprehension is so different from linguistic comprehension, can it really be but an affair of conventions?

Against the evidence and argument just marshaled, the conventionalist is apt to reply: there is also evidence of cross-cultural incomprehension with regard to pictorial pick-up. However, here it must be stressed that the evidence is not really so clear-cut. There is some question about the qual-ity of the photographs that tribal peoples failed to recognize, and, in some cases, the reasons behind their failures can often be explained by noting that they did not understand what they were being asked to do. Ques-tioned about what a given picture was, some Africans identified it with an indigenous fabric, because that is what the paper on which the picture was printed reminded them. However, once they understood the task they were being invited to perform, they had little difficulty saying what the picture was of.

Moreover, even if there ever was some initial hesitancy in comprehending the relevant pictures, in contrast to linguistic acquisition, it took virtually no time for native informants to master Western picturing. This claim is, of course, also borne out by the way in which Western pictorially-styled photography, film and TV has been disseminated to every corner of the globe without special training. Peoples of different cultures appear able to pick up, almost immediately, that which is being represented, without being tutored, or with only minimal instruction, in dramatic contrast to what it would take for them to master a foreign language.

So, the anthropological evidence for conventionalism is at best mixed and surely controversial, while, additionally, there is a great deal of evidence – such as the smooth dissemination of pictorial comprehension across cultures and generations – which is difficult to assimilate into the conventionalist model. These considerations argue strongly against conventionalism. But furthermore, the evidence we have been looking at suggests a theory of pictorial representation that is rival to conventionalism.

We have noted that people across cultures and children within our own culture are able to evince the capacity to recognize what pictures are pictures of without special training. That is, where they are familiar with the kinds of objects represented in pictures, they are able to recognize the generic kinds to which the referents of the pictures belong simply by looking, rather than by means of subtending processes of reading or decoding. The capacity to recognize what pictures picture appears to evolve in tandem with the capacity to recognize objects – once we are able to identify something, such as a horse, "in nature," we have the capacity to recognize a picture of a horse, drawn from a typical viewpoint. Pictorial comprehension is not primarily a matter of learning and employing an arbitrary code or set of conventions. Rather, it seems to involve a natural capacity, already evident in young children. But if this is plausible, then perhaps what pictures are are objects designed to trigger this natural capacity.

Pictorial comprehension involves a natural capacity to recognize what a picture is a picture of simply by looking – i.e., without mobilizing processes of reading, decoding or inferring – in cases where the percipient is already familiar with the kind of object pictured. If we suppose that pictorial representations are designed with the function of eliciting pictorial comprehension, then we can hypothesize that:

A visual design x pictorially represents y (an object, person, place, action, event or another visual design) only if (1) x has the intended capacity to cause a normal percipient to recognize y in x simply by looking (wherever the percipient is already familiar with the class of things to which y belongs), and (2) only if percipients recognize y in x because they realize (1).

This may sound like a reversion to the traditional illusion theory of art, but it is not. According to the illusion theory, viewers are deceived into believing that the referents of the picture are before them. But this theory does not claim that any deception is involved; it stresses *recognition*, not deception, and it claims that viewers perceptually recognize y in x, not that they are perceptually deceived into taking x for y. On the present view, spectators recognize y in x at the same time that they realize that x is a picture (and not what the picture stands for). Thus, the preceding theory is not liable to the earlier objections to the illusion theory, nor is it a version of the traditional illusion theory. Instead, we may call it a *neo-naturalist theory of pictorial representation* in honor of its reliance upon the idea that pictures trigger certain *natural* capacities.

To return to the conventionalist argument, it proceeds by way of a process of elimination (what is called a disjunctive syllogism). It claims that:

1 Pictorial representation is a matter of resemblance, or illusion, or convention.
2 It cannot be a matter of resemblance or illusion (given the earlier arguments).
3 Therefore, it is a matter of convention.

This is a valid form of argument. However, it will only yield a logically compelling conclusion if the first premise truly enumerates all the relevant, competing alternatives. That is, the conventionalist must eliminate all the rival theories. And at this point in the debate, we can see that the conventionalist has failed to list all the pertinent alternatives. The conventionalist has failed to consider neo-naturalism as an alternative, rival account. Thus, we need to determine that conventionalism is superior to neo-naturalism before we can think about endorsing the conclusion of the conventionalist argument

Indeed, we should hesitate before assenting to the conventionalist argument because we have already seen a number of ways in which neo-naturalism is a superior hypothesis. Moreover, there are further considerations in favor of neo-naturalism.

Recall the conventionalist account of pictorial realism: we think some pictorial styles are more realistic than others, but this is only because we have been habituated in the allegedly more realistic style. I have already said that this is a counterintuitive doctrine. But that is not an argument. Here is an argument.

Within our own culture, we have been able to comprehend the emergence of new styles of realism. For example, the addition of shadows as depth cues in pictures was recognized as a breakthrough in pictorial realism. But how could such things be hailed as breakthroughs if realism is just a matter of convention and habituation? There is too little time for such innovative conventions to be learned and even less time for us to become habituated to them. In fact, if conventionalism were true, it would be hard to understand how such breakthroughs could be possible, since we will always be more habituated to the existing style than to the breakthrough style. Thus, conventionalism cannot explain the unexceptionable fact of the evolution and reception of progressively more realistic styles of pictorial representation.

On the other hand, neo-naturalism can. Successive breakthroughs in realism can be said to discover more and more effective ways of triggering our natural recognitional capacities.

Conventionalism also claims that *any* pictorial style will be thought of as realistic, once it becomes familiar. This seems unlikely; few would call Picasso's portraits realistic, though they have been around for three and a half generations. But neo-naturalism can explain this too. Some representational styles provide fewer or less reliable recognitional cues than others, and Picasso's portraits in these respects are less realistic than the images of people we see on the evening news.

Clearly, then, neo-naturalism is an alternative to conventionalism – a rival theory that the conventionalist has yet to eliminate. Arguably, it proposes an even better explanation of certain phenomena than conventionalism does. But perhaps the conventionalist can use what we previously called the "core argument" against the resemblance theory in order to defeat neo-naturalism.

Neo-naturalism says that x is a representation of y only if x triggers the recognition of y in x in percipients. But is recognition a necessary condition of representation? According to the "core argument," denotation is fundamental to representation, and clearly x may represent y – x may denote y – without our being able to recognize y in x. Remember our example of the thumbtack or a pepper shaker standing for an armored division. Consequently, can't we run the core argument against the resemblance theory with equal force against neo-naturalism, replacing the notion of resemblance in the earlier argument with the notion of recognition in a new argument?

That is:

1 x represents y if and only if x denotes y.

2   If x denotes y, then x may not trigger the recognition of y in x.
3   x represents y.
4   Therefore, x denotes y.
5   Therefore, x may not trigger the recognition of y in x.
6   Therefore, x represents y and x may not trigger the recognition of y in x.
7   Now, suppose that recognition is a necessary condition for representation.
8   If recognition is a necessary condition for representation, then it is not (possibly) the case that x represents y and that x may not trigger the recognition of y in x.
9   Therefore, it is not the case that x represents y and x may not trigger the recognition of y in x.
10 Therefore, recognition is not a necessary condition for representation.

Earlier we did not probe this argument against the resemblance theory, though we noted that it might not be as compelling as it appears. Now we need to consider whether it presents a decisive objection to either the resemblance theory or to neo-naturalism with respect to pictorial representation. One reason to think that it does not concerns the first premise of the "core argument."

The core argument as stated is logically valid, but a logically valid argument can turn out to be false, if any of its premises are false. Moreover, the first premise of the core argument – as it is directed against either the resemblance theory or neo-representationalism – may be false.

The first premise states that "x represents y if and only x denotes y." That is, denotation affords necessary and sufficient conditions for representation. But from our perspective, this premise is ambiguous. If we are talking about representation *simpliciter*, the premise is true. A thumbtack can represent an armored division when we stipulate that it stands for one. But if we mean by "representation" a "*pictorial* representation," then the premise is false. That denotation alone marks representation *simpliciter* does not entail that it defines every particular subcategory of representation. It does not define pictorial representation entirely, for example.

Though a thumbtack can represent an armored division, a thumbtack is not a pictorial representation of one. Obviously, a thumbtack is not a picture of an armored division. Consequently, inasmuch as the core argument is supposed to pertain to pictorial representations, but implicitly rides on the notion of representation *simpliciter* as its central premise, the core argument appears to commit the fallacy of equivocation.

A fallacy of equivocation occurs when a concept in an argument is used with different senses. For example, if I say "All bachelors are male. Hilary Clinton is a bachelor (of arts). Therefore, Hilary Clinton is a male," the argument is unacceptable because the concept of bachelor is not being used univocally – that is, with the same meaning throughout the argument. In the first premise, it pertains to gender, whereas in the second premise it pertains to scholastic status. To deduce that Hilary Clinton is male because she is a bachelor (in the academic sense) is a fallacious inference.

The first premise of the argument is true when read in the gender sense, but false when read in the academic sense, while the second premise is true when read in the academic sense but false when read in the gender sense. For the conclusion of the argument to follow from the premises, the concept of bachelor would have to be applied in the same sense in both premises so that both premises are true under the same reading. Instead, in our example, the argument shifts fallaciously – or equivocates – between different meanings of the word "bachelor," and thereby commits the informal logical fallacy of equivocation.

Moreover, we can also see an equivocation in play in the conventionalist's core argument. The first premise of the argument is true, if we read it as a definition of representation *simpliciter*. But it is false if we are talking about pictorial representation, since a skid mark can stand for the Pacific Ocean without being a picture of it. So, if we read the core argument as concerned with pictorial representation, the argument fails, when its first premise is disambiguated – when we grasp that "representation" in the first premise really has to mean "pictorial representation" in order to get the job done.

Moreover, the equivocation in the first premise infects the rest of the argument. Specifically, the apparent contradiction between steps #6 and #9 disappears once we remove the pertinent ambiguity, since "x represents y *simpliciter* and may not trigger the recognition of y in x" is not inconsistent with "it is not the case that x *pictorially* represents y and x may not trigger the recognition of y in x."

Or, to state the major problem with the core argument succinctly, it fails because it conflates the issue of defining pictorial representation with the definition of representation *simpliciter*; it mistakes proving that representation *simpliciter* does not require recognition (or resemblance) with proving that pictorial representation might not require recognition (or resemblance). That one can represent something without mobilizing the recognitional capacities of the percipient does not show that one very particular kind of representation, namely pictorial representation, does not require recognition.

So, neo-naturalism is not fazed by the strongest conventionalist argument against this type of theory, and neo-naturalism appears to possess more explanatory power than conventionalism. Yet the neo-naturalist can still learn something from conventionalism. For even if recognition is a necessary condition for pictorial representation, it is not a sufficient condition, since, though we may recognize faces in clouds, clouds are not representations of the faces we see in them. Why not? Let us exploit the conventionalist proposal that denotation is also a necessary condition of representation and incorporate that suggestion into the statement of neo-naturalism.

This results in a more complex statement of the neo-naturalist theory of pictorial representation, namely:

> A visual design x pictorially represents y (an object, person, place, action, event or another visual design) if and only if (1) x has the intended capacity to cause a normal percipient to recognize y in x simply by looking; (2) the relevant percipients recognize y in x simply by looking; (3) x is intended to denote y; and (4) the relevant percipients realize that x is intended to denote y.

This is quite a mouthful, but it appears to give us a stronger account of the most basic type of pictorial representation than does conventionalism. It exploits the conventionalist's emphasis on denotation, but it doesn't mistake representation *simpliciter* for that very special type of representation we call "picturing."

However, at least one question may still remain for the careful reader. Though neo-naturalism appears superior to conventionalism, how does it compare to the resemblance theory of pictorial representation? Here let two comments suffice. First, neo-naturalism and the resemblance theory *may* be combinable, since it may turn out that the psychological mechanism that is a cue for percipients to recognize the referents of pictures is resemblance. Of course, resemblance may not be the mechanism; something else may be. But this leads to a second comment. Whatever the mechanism is that secures pictorial recognition is a job for psychologists to discover. It is enough for philosophy to say that recognition (however it is to be explained scientifically) is essential to pictorial representation. That is, philosophy attempts to say what pictorial representation is, not how it works psychologically.

Representation across the arts

Thus far we have been concentrating on defining the nature of pictorial representation in the visual arts. But there are more kinds of representation than pictorial representation when it comes to the arts. So it will be useful to conclude this chapter with a brief discussion of representation across the arts.

Speaking broadly, we may say that by "represent" we mean that x represents y (where y ranges over a domain comprised of objects, persons, events, and actions) if and only if (1) a sender intends x (e.g., a picture) to stand for y (e.g., a person), and (2) an audience recognizes that x is intended to stand for y. This is a general characterization of representation; it applies to many varied kinds of representation.

Representation can obtain in the arts in a number of different ways. It is useful to consider four types of representation in order to characterize the ways in which representational practices differ with respect to different artforms. These four types of representation sit on a continuum in terms of the different, though sometimes overlapping ways that audiences can come to comprehend or understand that x stands for y.

These four points on the continuum include:

1. Unconditional representation. This is the sort of representation that obtains by triggering the audience's innate recognitional capacities – capacities that enable viewers to recognize that the referent of the *Mona Lisa* is a woman simply by looking at the picture. In cases of unconditional representation, we can recognize that x stands for y on the basis of the same recognitional powers that enable us to recognize y's "in nature." If we can recognize women in the real world simply by looking, then we can recognize that the *Mona Lisa* pictures a woman by means of the same perceptual processes we use to recognize women. As was argued in the previous section, pictorial representation falls into this category.

But standard dramatic representation does as well, since when an actress represents eating by imitating eating – by lifting a fork to her mouth and simulating chewing – the audience recognizes her actions as a portrayal of eating without recourse to any specialized codes. Often the psychological mechanism subtending such examples of direct recognition has been discussed in terms of similarity, though, as indicated above, the idea of natural recognitional powers is also available. Whether similarity or natural recognitional powers afford a superior explanation of the phenomenon in question or whether the two ideas should be combined is an issue which we may ultimately leave to the psychologists to resolve. The relevant point here is only that much representation in the arts – for example, in mass market movies, TV, theater, painting and sculpture – proceeds by triggering innate recognitional capacities and, in that sense, is immediate (i.e., not mediated by the manipulation of an arbitrary or conventional code). In rare cases, even music can achieve this type of representation by, for instance, simulating birdsongs.

2. Lexical representation. If some representation is unmediated by arbitrarily established codes, other forms of representation are coded, or lexicographic, or semiotic. In these cases, in order to realize that x stands for y, a spectator must know the relevant codes. In dance, certain gestures and movements are correlated to definite meanings in a dictionary-like fashion. In the Romantic Ballet, for example, when a character draws a circle around her head, that means "I am pretty." One cannot realize this simply by looking; one must also know the relevant lexicon. Similarly, Indian mudras function in the same way.

The conventionalist maintains that all representation is of this sort, and, though we have produced reasons for rejecting this extreme view, it is certainly true that much representation in art falls into this category. Of course, the boundary between unconditional and lexical representation often yields mixed cases, since what we sometimes recognize in an unmediated way is a socially (rather than an artistically) coded signal (e.g., we unconditionally recognize the fire truck in part because it is red, but its being red is the result of an antecedent social code).

3. Conditional specific representation. Sometimes we recognize what is being represented only on condition that we already know what is being represented. One is unlikely to realize that poison is being put in the king's ear in the play within the play in *Hamlet*, unless one already knows that this is what the play within the play is supposed to represent. Once we know that this is what is intended to be represented by the playlet, we easily pick up what the otherwise obscure gestures stand for. But most of us, in all probability, would be at sea without such antecedent knowledge.

This is not a case of unconditional representation, since we wouldn't have a clue as to what is going on without being told (by Shakespeare). Being told, here, is, in other words, a condition for understanding the representation. However, once told (i.e., once the condition is met), we can use our native recognitional powers to decipher the otherwise elusive gestures.

Nor is this a case of lexical representation, since there is no pre-established code for ear poisonings in drama. The actor proceeds by imitation, not by strictly coded signaling. Lexicographical or semiotic representation is, of course, conditional, insofar as it depends upon the existence of a code, but not all conditional specific representation need be lexical, since in many cases it can operate by engaging natural recognitional capacities, once those have been alerted or cued in terms of what to expect (i.e., what to be looking for).

Deciphering a case of conditional specific representation can involve a complex interplay of cognitive abilities requiring natural recognitional capacities working in concert with fragments of lexicographic knowledge (as well as other factors). However, this category still marks an important difference, since in order to mobilize the relevant cognitive capacities, we need the clue that something is being represented. Indeed, representations in this category require that we know that something specific – for example, an ear poisoning – is being represented. In this, it contrasts with the next category.

4. Conditional generic representation. Here the spectator is able to detect or to recognize that x stands for y on condition that she knows that *something* is being represented. For example, unless you know that I am trying to represent *something*, you might not take my rolling arm movements to stand for waves. But if you know that I intend to represent something, even if you do not know antecedently what I want to represent, you would be likely to see my arm movements as waves rather quickly; it would be one of your first hypotheses. Likwise, if we know that a piece of music is a tone poem, then we are likely to interpret certain "rushing" or "flowing" phrases as water.

Simply knowing that an artistic signal is meant to be representational, even if we are not told exactly what it represents, leads us to mobilize our natural recognitional capacities, our linguistic associations, and knowledge of strict semiotic codes, along with other factors, in order to determine appropriately what the representation is a representation of, without being told its specific, intended meaning.

The contrast between conditional specific representation and conditional generic representation can be illuminated instructively by contemplating a game of charades. Indeed, you might try to get the hang of the distinction by playing charades. Imagine two teams – A and B. Team A gives a player on Team B a saying which she must elicit from the other members of her team by means of gestural promptings. Suppose, as well, that she tries to do this by acting out the whole saying. Since the members of Team A know the saying – since they know what her gestures are intended to represent – they relate to her performance as an instance of conditional specific representation. They try to fit her gestures to what they know it represents. They are able to follow and to appreciate her gesticulations because they know exactly what she is trying to signal.

Her fellow team members, however, know only that she intends to signal something. They do not know exactly what it is. They try to infer what it is, using a variety of cognitive skills that they put into gear simply because they know that she is playing charades. If they were not playing charades, they might not think that she was trying to signal anything at all. But knowing that she is playing charades, knowing that she intends to represent something, they try to determine what. And they are quite often successful at this.

For Team B, their teammate's gestures are regarded as conditional generic representations at the same time that for observers from Team A, they are conditional specific representations. That is, members of Team B disambiguate her gesturing on condition that they presume that something is represented, though they know not what beforehand. For members of Team B, the charade is a matter of conditional generic representation and, alerted to this, they use this understanding as a framework for interpreting the array, exploiting all kinds of clues to infer what is being represented. Team A, on the other hand, knows what is being represented ahead of time. For them, following the charade is a matter of matching gestures with the saying they are designed to recall. They know the solution to the problem that the player from Team B is trying to crack, and they use that knowledge to appreciate player B's ingenuity.

Clearly, the players on Team A and the players on Team B are engaged in different cognitive tasks, which we can characterize as responding to conditional specific representations, on the one hand, and responding to conditional generic representations, on the other. Moreover, this is not simply a matter of charades, since artworks can employ either sort of representation as well. Honegger's *Pacific 231* and Berlioz's *Symphonie Fantastique* are examples of conditional specific representation, while the thunder in Beethoven's *Pastoral* is more of the nature of conditional generic representation (one wouldn't hear it as thunder unless one knew that the piece was illustrative).

Though these four points on the continuum of representation are not exhaustive and though they can be combined and melded in particular cases in very complex ways, they nevertheless are helpful in characterizing the typical ways in which different artforms – or groups of artforms – employ representation. All the arts – including painting, sculpture, theater, dance, literature, photography, film, video, and even music – can employ all these categories of representation. It is not the case that any one of these categories correlates with all and only one artform. However, though each of the relevant artforms can employ every one of these categories, particular artforms – or groups of artforms – tend to emphasize or to rely upon certain of these categories more than others. Thus, we can enlist these four categories to begin to describe the typical, though not the unique, representational practices of the different artforms.

For example, it is true that dance representation can fall into all of the four categories, and it is also true that representation in other artforms can instantiate each of these categories as well. And yet it does seem that dance relies on some of these categories more than the other arts do – or at least more than the neighboring arts of dramatic enactment (such as realist theater, movies, and TV).

That is, contrasting dance with theater, film and TV, dance seems to rely more on categories 3 and 4 than do theater, film and TV. This is not to say that dance does not employ categories 1 and 2; perhaps dance even employs these categories as much or more than it does categories 3 and 4. Nevertheless, theatrical dance as we know it does employ forms of conditional representation more than the dominant forms of theater, film and TV do in Western culture. Indeed, these artforms rely more exclusively on category 1 than on the other categories of representation on our list. Call this difference in choice of representational strategies a *proportionate difference* in the representational means between dance and its dramatic neighbors.

This is not to deny that theater, film and TV as typically practiced may use category 2. And in certain avant-garde cases – such as Brakhage's film *Anticipation of the Night* – they may even deploy forms of conditional representation. Nevertheless, in the main (the mainstream), theater, film and TV use categories 3 and 4 to a lesser extent than they use category 1, whereas, while dance uses category 1, it also relies very heavily on using category 2 and, especially, on categories 3 and 4 for purposes of representation. This should be clear from the degree to which even mainstream dance representations depend on accompanying descriptive texts – such as program notes – for intelligibility, whereas mainstream theater, film and TV are generally accessible without such enabling texts.

Thus, there is a proportionate difference between the choice of representational means between dance, on the one hand, and theater, film and TV, on the other. Dance relies more on conditional representation (of both sorts) than they do. But what of music? Though there is much less representation in music than in dance, when there is representation in music, doesn't it rely heavily on conditional representation too (think of the *1812 Overture*)? Is there no difference between music and dance with respect to the representational means toward which they gravitate?

Certainly, there is: dance uses unconditional representation more than music does. So where dance differs from theater, film and TV by its emphasis on forms of conditional representation, it differs from music in its far more frequent use of unconditional representation. Of course, it is also in virtue of their primary reliance on unconditional representation that the dominant practices of theater, film and TV distinguish themselves from music.

Moreover, dance differs from the remaining temporal art – literature – insofar as literature operates almost exclusively via lexicographic representation (words and grammar), depending on that category of representation vastly more than dance does, or, for that matter, than do theater, film, TV, and music.

Though representational painting, drawing, and sculpture depend primarily on unconditional representation – as theater, film and TV do – they also depend on conditional representation, deploying titles, captions, and backstories (e.g., knowledge of the myths, historical events, religious parables and so on that the images depict) in order to be fully intelligible. In this, these artforms, as well as much photography (given its dependence on captions) are perhaps closer to dance than they are to realistic theater, film and TV. But one suspects that they still do not rely upon conditional representation to the extent that dance does. In this regard, these artforms appear to fall somewhere between dance, on the one hand, and film, theater and TV, on the other hand, in terms of their proportionate emphasis on unconditional versus conditional representation. And, of course, the representational practices of these artforms are also differentiated along another dimension – that of stillness versus movement – from the standard representational practices of theater, dance, film and TV.

Painting, drawing, sculpture and photography can be distinguished from music, of course, due to their heavy reliance on unconditional representation, whereas, in turn, they use lexical representation far less than literature does. This is not to neglect the fact that there are pictorial codes, but only to note that however important they are for these artforms, they are still less fundamental here than they are with respect to literature.

Using the preceding four categories of representation, then, along with the notion of a proportionate difference between existing artforms (or, at least, groups of artforms), we can say something about the representational tendencies toward which artforms gravitate. However, what we can say about these artforms pertains to what is characteristic, not unique, about their use of representation. We are not speaking about what is unique about representation in each of these artforms, since, as we've seen, each artform employs the same types of representation that the other artforms do. Where they differ, when they differ, is in virtue of the differential, proportionate emphasis they place on the different types of representation available to them.

Chapter summary

The relation of representation to art is an enduring one. In the earliest philosophies of art in the West, representation was taken to be an essential feature of art. This view persisted for centuries and was instrumental in the formation of what we think of as the modern system of the arts. However, the development of nonrepresentational art in the nineteenth and twentieth century rendered the representational theory of art obsolete, while also alerting theorists to the fact that it had never really been fully comprehensive.

However, even if the representational theory of art is false as a general theory of art, it is still the case that a large amount of the art with which we are familiar is representational. Though not all art is representational, much is. Thus, a theory of representation is still an urgent task for the philosophy of art.

This is perhaps most obvious with respect to pictorial art – which includes not only painting, but film, photography, video and TV. As a result, a large portion of this chapter has been spent discussing pictorial representation, which, we have suggested, is best analysed by what was called a neo-naturalist theory of pictorial representation.

Still, pictorial representation is not the whole story of the relation of art to representation, since there are more kinds of representation than pictorial representation. Consequently, we spent the concluding section of this chapter examining the variation in representational practices across the arts. We noted that each of the various arts does not possess a unique form of representation. Each artform can exploit the same package of representational strategies that the other arts can. Where the arts differ, when they differ, with regard to their representational practices, it is a matter of a proportionate difference in the way in which each of the arts – or groups of arts – relies, in varying degrees, upon alternate strategies of representation.

Annotated reading

Students interested in readings pertaining to the classical representational theories of art should consult Books 2, 3 and 10 of Plato's *Republic* and Aristotle's *Poetics*. These works are available in many editions. Students are advised to shop around for the versions that they find most readable and that most suit their pocketbook. The best background article on the system of the fine arts is Paul Oskar Kristeller, "The Modern System of the Arts," reprinted in *Essays on the History of Aesthetics*, edited by Peter Kivy (Rochester, NY: University of Rochester Press, 1992).

One version of the neo-representational theory of art can be found in Arthur Danto, *The Transfiguration of the Commonplace* (Cambridge, MA: Harvard University Press, 1981). The term "neo-representationalism" derives from Peter Kivy, who also criticizes the view. See his *Philosophies of Arts: An Essay in Differences* (Cambridge: Cambridge University Press, 1997), Chapter 2.

For an introduction to the topic of pictorial representation, see Monroe Beardsley, *Aesthetics: Problems in the Philosophy of Criticism* (Indianapolis, Indiana: Hackett Publishing Company, 1981), Chapter 6. The first chapter of Nelson Goodman's *Languages of Art* (Indianapolis: Hackett Publishing Company, 1976) makes a powerful case for the conventionalist theory of pictorial representation. Flint Schier's *Deeper Into Pictures: An Essay on Pictorial Representation* (Cambridge: Cambridge University Press, 1986) defends a robust form of neo-naturalism, though students should be forewarned that this is a very difficult book technically. A good place to start to read about representation across the arts is Peter Kivy's *Sound and Semblance* (Princeton, NJ: Princeton University Press, 1984), especially the second chapter.

Finally, in this chapter we have only discussed pictorial representation from the perspective of cases where the pictures in question are pictures of existing things. We have not broached the more complicated question of pictorial representations of fictions. This topic, however, is dealt with in the suggested readings by Beardsley, Goodman and Schier. It, along with many other relevant issues, is examined at length in Kendall Walton's *Mimesis as Make-Believe: On the Foundations of the Representational Arts* (Cambridge, MA: Harvard University Press, 1990). Like the book by Schier, Walton's book is also a very formidable read.

CHAPTER 2
Art and expression

Art and expression

Part I
Art as expression

The expression theory of art

For centuries, representation was taken to be the central, defining feature of art. Where representation was understood in terms of imitation, the role of the artist could be analogized to holding a mirror up to nature. Speaking very broadly, the emphasis in imitation theories of art was on the outward aspects of things – the look of objects and the actions of humans. In a loose sense of the word, art was characterized in terms of primary concern with the *objective* features of the "external" world – with nature and observable behavior.

But, in the West, as the eighteenth century dissolved into the nineteenth, ambitious artists – both in theory and practice – began to turn inward; they became less preoccupied with capturing the appearance of nature and the manners of society than with exploring their own subjective experiences. Where artists still described landscapes, the landscapes were charged with a significance beyond their physical properties. The artists in question also attempted to register their reactions – the way they felt – about the landscapes. Whereas under imitation theories of art, artists are said to attend foremost to mirroring the objective world, by the early nineteenth century, artists were becoming more attentive to the subjective or "inner" world of experience.

An important example of this seismic shift in artistic ambition was the Romantic movement. In 1798, in the Preface to his *Lyrical Ballads*, Wordsworth maintains that poetry "is the spontaneous overflow of powerful feelings." That is, the role of the poet is not essentially to mirror the action of other people, but to explore his or her own feelings. Romanticism places premier value on the self and its own individual experiences. Where the poet contemplates some outward scene, the scene is not presented for its own sake, but as a stimulus for the poet to examine his or her own emotional responses to it.

The world is presented from an emotionally saturated point of view, where the emotional perspectives of the individual poet are more important than simply describing whatever gave rise to it (such as a skylark or a Grecian urn). For the Romantic poet, the artist was not devoted to the slavish imitation or representation of the external, objective world, but to the presentation of an inner, subjective world – the presentation of the emotions and feelings of the artist. And in music, as well, the work of composers like Beethoven, Brahms, Tchaikovsky, and others came to be regarded as the projection of powerful feelings.

Romanticism profoundly influenced the course of subsequent art. We still live in the shadows of Romanticism. Perhaps the most recurrent image of the artist in popular culture today remains the emotionally urgent author (composer, painter, etc.) trying to get in touch with his or her feelings. Many twentieth-century art movements, from German Expressionism to Modern Dance, can be seen as direct descendants of Romanticism. Moreover, as these developments deviated more and more from the strict canons of imitation – by employing distortion and abstraction for expressive purposes – they made ever more evident the inadequacies of imitation and representational theories of art.

For not only were these experiments themselves often counterexamples to the reigning theories of art; they also encouraged people to take a second look at the historical record, where interested parties saw that Romanticism and its vicissitudes were not something altogether new under the sun, but that the expression of emotions was something with which art had been engaged perennially. Were not Shakespeare's sonnets expressive? Thus, art both new (Romanticism and the rise of absolute music) and old called for a new kind of comprehensive theory, one more inclusive than and more sensitive to emotional expression than representational theories of art. And it is in this context that expression theories of art come to the fore.

Representational theories of art treat the work of the artist as akin to that of the scientist. Both, so to speak, are involved in describing the external world. But by the nineteenth century, any comparison between the scientist and the artist was bound to make the artist look like a poor relation in terms of making discoveries about the world or holding a mirror up to nature. Here, science clearly had the edge.

So, there was a social pressure for art to come up with some vocation that both distinguished itself from science and, at the same time, made art equal in stature to science. The notion that art specialized in the expression of the emotions was particularly attractive in this light. It rendered unto science its own – the exploration of the objective world – while saving something comparably important for art to do – to explore the inner world of feeling. If science held the mirror up to nature; art turned a mirror at the self and its experiences.

By the beginning of the twentieth century, the philosophy of art was prepared for a sea change. From a purely intellectual point of view, representational theories of art were due to be retired; they failed to characterize art – both recent and past – comprehensively. Moreover, in situating art in the same league as science, they made art seem prime for obsolescence. Consequently, theory, practice, and social exigencies all conspired to dispose the artworld favorably toward expression philosophies of art.

Throughout the twentieth century many different versions of the expression theory of art have been propounded. Until mid-century, such theories were probably the most common approach on offer. At root, all expression theories maintain that something is art only if it expresses emotions. "Expression" comes from a Latin word which means "pressing outward" – as one squeezes the juice out of a grape. What expression theories claim is that art is essentially involved in bringing feelings to the surface, bringing them outward where they can be perceived by artists and audiences alike.

Though expression theories of art differ in many ways, one kind of theory, popularized by Leo Tolstoy, thinks of expression as a form of communication. When I express myself to you, I communicate to you. Of course, not all communication is art. So how does one differentiate between an artistic communication and other sorts? According to this kind of theory, what marks art is that it is primarily concerned with the expression or the communication of emotion. With art, an inner emotional state is externalized; it is brought out into the open and transmitted to viewers, readers and listeners.

But how are we to understand this notion of the transmission of an emotion? Basic to the idea of a transmission is the concept of a transfer. To transmit something is to transfer it. But what does an artwork transfer? According to the expression theorist, what is transferred is an emotion. An artist looks at a landscape and feels gloomy. Then she draws the landscape in such a way that the viewer experiences the same sense of gloominess. "The artist expresses her gloominess" here means that she has a feeling of gloominess which she conveys to or instills in her audience by drawing in a certain manner.

This conception of expression involves several things. First, the artist must have some feeling or emotion. Perhaps it is directed at a landscape or an event, like a military victory. But whatever the emotion is directed at, the expression theory of art requires that the artist experience some emotional state. The artist expresses this state – brings it outside himself, so to speak – by trying to find some configuration of lines, shapes, colors, sounds, actions, and/or words that are appropriate to or that "match" that feeling. Then, these configurations stimulate the same kind of emotional state in the audience.

In the film *Amistad*, Steven Spielberg expresses his outrage at the institution of slavery. That is, he makes something that enables the film audience to feel the same kind of outrage toward slavery that he feels. Notice that on this sort of expression theory it is necessary that the artist feel something and that the audience be brought to feel the self-same (kind) of emotion. That is, for this version of the expression theory, there must be an artist, an audience, and an emotion that they share. So, x is art only if an artist transmits the self-same feeling state that the artist experienced to an audience.

Here, we have three necessary conditions for art – an artist, an audience and a shared feeling state. But clearly this is not enough to define art. Suppose I am very dejected; I've just lost my job. I am weeping, my shoulders are hunched together, and I talk in a slow, distracted manner. You see me and, in a manner of speaking, catch some of my sadness. Suppose you start to think about losing your own job – since you are next in line to go at our common workplace – and you feel sad too. Clearly, I am experiencing sadness and my behavior has you feeling bad as well – possibly sad about your own prospects in the same way I despair about my own. But I have not created an artwork, have I?

No, and at least one reason for saying this is that by weeping I don't intend to make an artwork, or even to make you feel my pain. I'm so unhappy that I don't care what you feel. I am upset, but it is not my intention to transfer that feeling to others. When an artist expresses her feelings, she does it intentionally. That is her aim. She wants to get her feelings out in the open where everyone, including herself, can contemplate them. Something is an artwork only if it is an *intended* transmission to an audience of the self-same emotion that the artist experienced.

But what of greetings cards? – condolence cards, for example? Suppose that you are in the business of writing them? Are you an artist? Such cards express emotions. But they are very generic emotions. That's why they can be manufactured and sold on a large scale. They are rather impersonal. Even if the people who compose them feel sad and even if the recipients feel sad too, we hesitate to call them works of art almost all of the time. Why?

Perhaps because the emotions they communicate are too general. The Romantics placed a high value on the articulation of individual experience. But the emotional experience conveyed by a greetings card is not individualized. It pertains, for example, to any dead relative, friend, or even mere acquaintance. But we expect artists to say things that are original and specific, not canned. So let us add to our list of necessary conditions that a work of art is an intended transmission to an audience of the self-same, *individualized* emotion that the artist experienced.

This is still not yet an adequate definition of art for an obvious reason. Suppose that a painter receives an eviction notice while you are visiting his studio. He takes a can of red paint and splatters it on the wall, cursing profusely while he hurls it. He's angry, and his anger is pretty specific – he's defacing the wall, which is a well-chosen tactic for hurting his landlord, and the expletives he's shouting about the landlord's weight, sexual proclivities, ethnic background and so on are all tailored to the landlord, and not just anyone. Imagine that we are infected with the painter's ire toward his landlord. Is this episode one of the painter's artworks?

This seems unlikely. The expression theorist of art typically tries to explain this conclusion by saying that there is a distinction between the artistic expression of an emotion and the mere ventilation of an emotion. Art is not a matter of ranting, even if our ranting inflames others in the same way that we feel enraged. We often vent our emotions to loved ones who come to share our feelings. But this is not art. Why not?

An artist examines her emotions; it is not simply that she is possessed by them. For the artist, her emotional state is like the sitter who poses for a portrait. She struggles to find its texture and its contour. As she reflects upon her emotional state, her activity is controlled. She explores it deliberately and attempts to find just the right word, or color, or sound to express it. She tries alternatives. If she is a poet, first she opts for one word, but then replaces it with another which better captures how she feels. Making a work of art is not a matter of exploding, venting or ranting; it is a process of clarification.

Typically, an artist begins a work – a poem, a song, or a painting – with an insistent, but nevertheless vague feeling. She tries to bring this feeling into sharp relief. She works on it, bringing it into clearer focus. Partly, she does this by externalizing it – by experimenting with different ways of expressing it. A dancer will combine several phrases, a painter several brushstrokes, a composer several chords, and then stand back from them, inquiring whether they are right – where "right" means "do they feel right?" or "do they get the emotion exactly right?" This process clarifies the emotion for the artist at the same time that the emotion inspires and informs the artist's choices.

The artist is working through the emotion by striving to articulate it in her medium. The artist is doing what we all do when we ask ourselves what we really feel about something. The first few sentences that we utter may be vague and fragmentary. But we keep revising them, striving to be more accurate and precise. Similarly, a painter is working at the same game, only he is using lines, shapes and colors, rather than words. What color is my emotion? Is it jagged or smooth? He tries one line, but then shortens it. The painting is under the guidance of the emotion, but as the picture acquires more detail and definition, so does the emotion. Painting just is a way of getting at the specific emotion, a way of clarifying what it is – a way of clarifying what the artist is feeling.

This is a controlled activity, not an outburst. The artist studies her emotion in the way a biologist studies a cell. She pokes it in different ways, using phrases or movements the way a biologist uses a reagent. She examines it from different angles and with different techniques, getting closer and closer to what is unique about it. By the time she is done, if she has been successful, she will have captured her feeling precisely and enabled viewers, listeners, or readers to do likewise. She has tasted the flavor of her emotion in all its particular richness and distinctiveness, and she has made it possible for others to do the same.

For example, in his Sonnet LXXIII ("That time of year thou mayst in me behold"), Shakespeare clarifies that particular experience of intensification that we feel for loved ones when we realize that they will some day perish. In successive stanzas, Shakespeare introduces different metaphors of death, extinction and passing, thereby inducing a very particular mood in the reader, one that is all the more precise for the accumulation of connected tropes, which through their diverse colors sketch an emotional state that is complexly mixed, not simply despondent, but touched with a saving vitality as well.

Of course, the audience does not experience the numerically same emotion that the artist does; his emotion occurs within the boundaries of his body, while each of us experiences our emotion where we live. Yet, what is shared is the same clarified emotion-type. Moreover, we are interested in art, on this view, because it affords the opportunity to experience, if not always new emotions, at least emotions more elaborated, articulate and precise than we ordinarily do. Art enables audiences to discover and to reflect upon emotional possibilities. So, the notion of clarification needs to be added to the expression theorist's account of art. Let us say that something is art only if it is an intended transmission to an audience of the self-same, individualized feeling that the artist has experienced and *clarified*.

Needless to say, an artist might clarify her feelings by just focussing on them mentally. That is, it is at least conceivable that one could get clear on one's emotional state simply by thinking about it. The emotion, then, would be clarified but not externalized. Yet could an artwork exist entirely, so to speak, inside someone's head? This would appear to violate our ordinary understanding of art which regards an artwork as a public affair. It would also seem inconsistent with the notion of expression which fundamentally rests on the idea of something "inside" being brought "outside." Thus, in order to block cases of completely mental artworks, the expression theorist should add that the process of the clarification and transmission of emotions be secured by means of lines, shapes, colors, sounds, actions and/or words. This guarantees that an artwork is, at least in principle, publicly accessible – that it is embodied in some publicly accessible medium.

Here, it is useful to note that rather than stating this requirement in terms of *artistic* media, it has been stated more broadly in terms of publicly accessible media – lines, colors, shapes, sounds, actions and/or words. This has been done in order to avoid circularity in the definition, since the expression theorist is trying to define *art*; thus if the expression theorist mentions "art" (*art*istic media) in the definition, he is assuming the very concept he is supposed to be explicating.

Likewise, the expression theorist does not say that the process of transmission and clarification must proceed by means of music, literature, drama and any other artform because this way of framing the matter presupposes that we have a way of picking out *art*forms prior to defining the notion of *art*. Thus, to evade circularity, expression theorists, like Tolstoy, have attempted to characterize art by enumerating the relevant media for making art without in the process invoking the concept of art either explicitly or implicitly.

Assembling the preceding considerations, then, we can state one very representative version of the expression theory of art formulaically as:

> x is a work of art if and only if x is (1) an intended (2) transmission to an audience (3) of the self-same (type-identical) (4) individualized (5) feeling state (emotion) (6) that the artist experienced (himself/herself) (7) and clarified (8) by means of lines, shapes, colors, sounds, actions and/or words.

We might call this version of the expression theory "the transmission theory" because it requires (in condition #2) that the clarified emotion be communicated to an audience. Another version of the expression theory could be obtained by dropping this requirement, allowing that something is an artwork as long as it involves the clarification of an emotion, irrespective of whether it is intended to be transmitted to an audience. We can call this the "solo expression theory of art," since it maintains that something is an artwork so long as its creator has clarified her emotional state (if only to herself) by means of lines, colors and so on. The transmission theory and the solo expression theory are the two most widely discussed expression theories of art.

Expression theories of art seem superior to representational theories of art. They seem more comprehensive. Not only are they better suited to accommodate the subjective stylistics of much advanced art since Romanticism. They pertain generally to art of the past. Romanticism called our attention to the artist's portion in the creation of an artwork – to the fact that an artwork embodies the artist's attitudes, feelings, emotions, and/or point of view toward his subject. Romanticism emphasized these features of the artwork forcefully. But once Romanticism called attention to the subjective dimension of its own creations, people were able to see past art as possessing these features as well.

Perhaps artists in the past had thought that they were merely mirroring reality. But in hindsight, after Romanticism, people could see retrospectively that their works came inscribed with points of view and evinced attitudes, feelings and emotions toward their subjects. Maybe the expression theorist of art might add, "How could it be otherwise?" Thus, the expression theory of art is not only an impressive theory of Romantic art and its legacy; it also does as good, if not a better, job of tracking pre-Romantic art. Its approach to music, for example, seems nowise as strained as imitation and representational theories of art. Speaking of even pure orchestral music as expressive of feeling seems correct, whereas speaking of it generally in terms of representation appears almost silly.

Just in terms of comprehensiveness, expression theories are superior to rival imitation and representational theories. But expression theories of art also suggest an important role for art, one which invests it with a mission comparable to science. If science explores the outer world of nature and human behavior, art, according to the expression theory, explores the subjective world of feeling. Science makes discoveries about physics and markets. Art makes discoveries about the emotions. The naturalist identifies new species; the artist identifies new emotional variations and their timbres. Thus, the expression theory of art not only explains what makes something art in a more comprehensive manner than previous rivals did; it also explains why art is important to us. These are two consequential recommendations in its favor.

Objections to the expression theory of art

The expression theory of art has exerted a great influence. Many people, including artists, still think that it is our best characterization of the nature of art. When artworks are criticized for being too impersonal or an artist is said to lack a voice of his own, the odds are that the complaint can be traced back to an implicit assumption that the expression theory of art is correct. But even if expression theories of art are influential, we must still ask whether or not they are convincing.

The transmission theory says that something is an artwork only if it is an intended transmission to an audience of an emotion. As we have already seen, an alternative theory, the solo expression theory, denies that instilling the relevant emotion in audiences is required. Thus, an obvious place to start our interrogation of expression theories of art is to ask whether or not intending to make a work for an audience is a necessary condition for art status.

The solo expression theorist argues that one can make art without having in mind the intention to communicate to an audience. One can make a work of art for oneself. Reputedly, Franz Kafka and Emily Dickinson did not want their work disseminated publicly. Can't I make an artwork – a picture, say – and put it in my closet under lock and key, thereby insuring that no one will ever see it? Is it any less an artwork for being locked away? And what if as soon as I made my picture, I burnt it? Surely it is an artwork, since if I had chosen to show it, everyone would say so. Doesn't it seem arbitrary to say that it is not an artwork just because I do not intend to exhibit it to anyone else?

After all, the picture unexhibited is the same as the picture exhibited. They are perceptually indiscernible. If I showed it to others, they would say "that's art." Why should the fact that I do not intend to show it to anyone else demote it to the status of nonart? That sounds rather capricious. This is how the solo expression theorist might argue against the transmission theorist. And if the solo expression theorist is right, this is an argument that anyone can bring against the transmission theory stated in the previous section.

The "no intended audience necessary" argument initially seems right. Surely a poet has made an artwork even if as soon as he writes it, he shreds it. And if he shreds it immediately, he certainly appears to intend that no one else shall see it – that it is not for the eyes of any audience. But, appearances not withstanding, the poet's activity in writing the poem may still – at least in one sense – indicate an intention to communicate to others.

In what sense? Well, the poet has written his poem in the words of and in accordance with the grammar of some natural language. This makes his poem publicly accessible. Were someone else to see his poem before he shredded it or pasted it back together afterwards, it would communicate. The poet has made his artwork in an idiom that by its nature is accessible to others – that is intended to communicate to others. By adopting a publicly accessible medium, the poet shows an intention to communicate, since he has chosen to make something that is communicable. He has made something designed for an audience. Even if he does not want an actual audience for his work, he has made something that, in principle, invites an audience. Both Kafka and Dickinson wrote works that audiences could have (and do) comprehend, even if their authors did not want them published.

Here the poet's actions, so to say, speak louder than his words. He says that he does not want an audience, but by employing a natural language he makes something designed for public consumption. Thus, at best, his intentions in this matter seem mixed or even conflicted. On the one hand, he acts to insure that no one will see his work. Nevertheless, he makes something that, in principle, is designed for audience reception. So in adopting language as his means, the poet does intend to make something that, at least in principle, is designed to communicate to an audience. The poet has acted such that his poem will not be read by others, but he has also acted intentionally – in choosing to write in a publicly accessible language – to make something that is, in principle, communicable – i.e., that is available to a potential audience.

And perhaps this may be enough to save the audience condition of the transmission theory which, in light of the preceding objection, we may amend thus: x is an artwork only if it is intended, at least in principle, to transmit something to an audience. This would take care of the cases of Kafka and Dickinson and of related cases where the author essays her work only for practice purposes. Furthermore, this seems to be an eminently sound addition to the theory anyway, since artists usually make works only intended *in principle* for audiences, without necessarily having any particular existing audiences in mind.

Some readers may be unpersuaded by this argument. It rests on the presumption that the artist in question is employing some publicly accessible medium – language, or perhaps certain established genres of music or painting. Thus, so the argument goes, in mobilizing some publicly accessible medium, the artist is implicitly addressing an audience – or, at least, a potential audience. But, you may object, what if the poet, in order to thwart even the possibility of an audience, writes in a way that is completely inaccessible publicly – in an idiolect (a private language) – utterly of his own invention and impenetrable, in principle, to anyone else? Might that be an artwork, one that shows that the audience condition is not universal?

Two things need to be said here. First, if someone makes something that is truly incomprehensible to everyone else, it is extremely unlikely that we would regard it as an artwork. Art does seem to require some, if only minimal, quotient of public accessibility. If something created by an artist were absolutely unintelligible to anyone else, why would we take it to be an artwork? Perhaps this is the truth behind the requirement of an intended audience.

Second, if the poem were written in a completely private language, one wonders whether it would be accessible even to the poet. How could he recall what it truly meant from one reading to the next, if his language were genuinely private? And if the poem is accessible to neither the poet nor anyone else, is his composition really even a poem?

Language is, in principle, a public affair, and it is doubtful that there could be a private language – of words, of images, sounds or shapes. But once the artist deploys a publicly accessible medium, he works with the intention to make something that is, at least in principle, transmissible to an audience, even if he goes on to destroy it.

Of course, even if the artist destroys his artwork, it might still be argued that it was not only in principle intended for a potential audience, but that it also had an actual audience, namely the artist himself. For an artist is not only a creator; he is also the first audience for his artwork. The poet typically stands back from his work in order to gauge its effect and, in doing so, he becomes its first audience. The role of the artist and that of the audience are intimately linked, and every artist is his own first audience.

Artistry requires that the artist play the role of audience member in order to proceed – in order to revise and correct her work. She is her own first critic and, to be self-critical, the artist needs to take up the position of a spectator. Thus, once we remind ourselves that the artist herself is also essentially a member of the audience, we must grant that the artwork is something intended for an audience.

If these arguments are correct, then the transmission theory should be preferred over the solo expression theory. Art must be intended, at least in principle, for some potential audience. However, it is not evident that the other conditions of the transmission theory can be defended as successfully.

In addition to requiring that artworks be intended for audiences, the transmission theory also requires that artists transmit the self-same feeling that they've undergone to audiences. The artist must be sincere. There are two necessary conditions here. First, the artist must have experienced a certain emotion, and, then, she must transmit just that emotion to audiences. Let us call these the "experience condition" and the "identity condition," respectively. Are either necessary conditions for being an artwork?

The identity condition does not seem very satisfactory. Surely artworks can arouse emotions in audiences which their creators do not feel. An actor playing Iago intends to inspire hatred for his character in the audience. But he need not be feeling hatred toward Iago in order to do so. Rather, he applies various acting techniques to rouse the audience's animosity. If the actor were as worked up as the audience about Iago's nastiness, he would probably forget his lines – or maybe kill himself! Actors and their audiences need not be in the same emotional states; indeed, often the actor would destroy his performance, if he were. Many (most?) actors are too busy calculating their emotional effect on the audience to emote genuinely themselves. So the identity condition does not apply universally.

Similarly, art in many genres relies upon certain formal strategies in order to move audiences in the ways they do. Suspense stories, for example, employ certain tried and true narrative techniques for the purpose of inciting anxiety in audiences. To put the audience on the edge of its seat, the author need only deploy these forms in the right way. He need not feel suspense as he rachets up the audience's apprehensiveness. Indeed, he might feel amusement as he tightens the screw – laughing to himself "Boy, this will make them squirm." Certainly, at least some suspense stories are art, but provoking suspense in audiences does not require that the authors in question feel the same thing that readers, viewers, or listeners do.

Indeed, it is said of Beethoven that he would make audiences weep over his improvisations, only to laugh at their folly and his own power. Clearly, in such a case, the artist and the audience are not feeling the same thing.

Much art is commissioned. Suspense films might be one example. But in the past, artists were often hired to celebrate all sorts of things, from royal weddings and saints' days to military victories. There is no reason to suppose that an artist must feel moved on behalf of the cause he celebrates in order to move others. An artist may be cynical. A Native American might direct a rousing cavalry film while simultaneously feeling contemptuous of his audience. And some advertisements may be art, though the people who compose them need not have the same enthusiasm for Alka-Seltzer or Burger King that they mean to provoke in consumers.

One might say that such people are not really artists, but hacks. Yet that is merely a bit of name-calling and not an argument. Surely a cynic can make a moving artwork. Moreover, if one says that someone who fails to transmit his genuine feelings is not an artist, that begs the question. It renders the identity claim true by definition rather than by confronting the real world of possibilities.

These problems with the identity condition also point up problems with the experience condition, since they indicate that an artist need not share the same feelings with the audience. They might have some other feeling – glee rather than suspense. But, in addition, it may not be the case that the artist has any feelings at all when creating the artwork.

Again, in many genres, arousing emotions may be a matter of putting established forms through their paces. If the artist knows how these forms work – if the actor knows what gestures inspire pity – she need not feel anything at all, let alone what the audience feels, in order to move them to tears. Thus, in order to be a work of art, the artist need experience no emotions at all, let alone exactly the emotions felt by the audience.

Here, it might be objected that, even if in order to inspire pity, the artist need not experience it while composing her artwork, it must be the case that at some time or other the artist must have experienced the relevant sort of pity. But does this really seem necessary?

Consider horror. Imagine a horror writer. Perhaps she has never been frightened by a horror story in her life, but she knows how to scare other people. Surely this is conceivable. And it is equally conceivable that when she does what she has to do to frighten readers, she does not laugh up her sleeve. To her, it's just a job of work. She may think that it is peculiar that other people are frightened by her stories. But she does it anyway. She has to pay the rent; she has to feed the family. Likewise, why suppose that psychopaths can't be effective actors; they are often reputed to be able to move people, but purportedly they feel nothing.

It will do no good to say that feelingless artists cannot make good art or even that they cannot make art at all. That remains to be seen on a case-by-case basis. Thus, we cannot necessarily rule out of bounds the possibility that there might be some works of art that fail to meet the experience condition. Of course, the proponent of the transmission argument may respond that, given human nature, it is impossible that an artwork be made without feeling, since humans are always in some emotional state or other; so, there is no such thing as a feelingless artist.

But this is problematic for several reasons. First, it does not seem true that we are always in some emotional state or other, and, thus, there is no reason to predict that an artist is always in some emotional state. Yet, even if it were the case that an artist is always in some emotional state, it would not help the transmission theorist much, since he claims not only that the artist must be in some emotional state, but that she be involved in clarifying that state. However, an artist may be in some emotional state while composing her work without being involved in trying to clarify that state. She may not be aware that she is in that state. Or, a singer may indeed be anxious about her taxes and peripherally aware of this as she belts out a happy tune, but she does not dwell on it, and, therefore, does not clarify it.

Not only does the clarity condition impede the preceding defense of the experience condition; it has problems of its own. According to the transmission theory, artists essentially clarify their emotions. They do not serve them up raw. But this does not seem to be the aim of all art. Some art, like Beat poetry and Punk Art, appears to covet pure, unrevised emotion – it aspires to let it all hang out. It is the stylistic purpose of some art, that is, to mine the emotions of the artist as close to the nerve as possible. Revision might even sometimes be thought of as a disqualifying betrayal – a matter of selling out – in such art. But then clarification cannot be a necessary condition of art, if there are certain creditable artistic styles where it should not obtain.

Nor are the only counterexamples here of recent vintage. Reportedly,

Coleridge's poem "Kubla Khan" came to him during a reverie. It arrived, so to speak, in one shot, with no clarification. He transcribed it almost mechanically as it came to him – as if in a trance, a trance that was interrupted (which is why we only have a fragment of the poem). Coleridge was not engaged in a process of clarifying his emotion as he wrote "Kubla Khan"; it came to him in a flash, and disappeared just as quickly. Thus, since if anything is an artwork, "Kubla Khan" is, art can occur without any process of clarification.

The transmission theorist assumes that the clarification of emotion is the aim of all art. But this is not true. Some art is designed to project vague emotions. Symbolist Art of the late nineteenth century is of this sort. It trades in vague, ambiguous and even amorphous moods. It is meant to suggest emotional states, rather than to clarify them. Neither the artist nor the audience aspires to emotional clarification. Symbolism is an art of intimation in which feelings are prized for their elusiveness. But since Symbolist works are artworks, clarification cannot be a necessary condition of all art.

The Surrealists also present problems for the transmission theory. One of their compositional techniques was called the "Exquisite Corpse." One person would write the first line of a poem, fold the paper over, and pass it to another person, who, without reading the preceding line, would write the next line of the poem. This procedure can generate poems of any length. But the process cannot be called one of clarification, since there is no emotional state that need be shared by all its authors. That is, there is no single emotional state that the poem aspires to clarify. Yet, this procedure has generated artworks. So, again there appear to be historical counterexamples to the clarification condition.

Indeed, the Exquisite Corpse is not only a problem for the clarification condition. It causes difficulties for other conditions of the transmission theory as well. Since there need be no single emotion that gives rise to the finished product and since the emotions the finished product evokes may diverge from those of the authors who contributed to it, Exquisite Corpse poetry challenges the identity condition of the transmission theory; while, additionally, since none of the authors of an Exquisite Corpse need be in any emotional state at all, this type of poetry also renders the experience condition underinclusive.

The Exquisite Corpse is an example of aleatoric art – art generated by chance procedures. Not only poetry, but painting, music and dance can be made in this way. Merce Cunningham and John Cage made artworks by casting the runes of the *I Ching*. In this, their aim was to short-circuit their own subjective processes of decision-making and replace them with a thoroughly random, objective procedure. Artists, including Cage and Cunningham, have also used probabilistic computer programs to this effect. They have done this in order to remove themselves in important ways from the compositional process.

Aleatoric works of this sort are regarded as art. But if these works are art, then it cannot be true that artworks must be intended to transmit the emotions of their makers to audiences, since, if anything, aleatoric techniques are designed to factor out the influence of the artist's emotional experience. Chance rules rather than the artist's subjective experience govern the final shape of the artwork. Aleatoric works of art are designed to thwart expression in the sense advanced by the transmission theory of art. Aleatoric techniques challenge the necessity of the identity, experience and clarification conditions of the transmission theory while also, at the same time, rejecting the notion that the artist intends to transmit anything pre-determined by her own experience. Her own experience has been taken out of the process; aleatoric strategies are adopted in order to make any intention to communicate her experience impossible to implement.

According to the transmission theory, the emotions communicated by artworks are individualized, not generic. From one day to the next, soap operas serve up the same sentiments – another disease strikes some endearing character, and we are sad in the same way today that we were yesterday. It's downright monotonous, virtually routine. But genuine art, it is alleged, explores individualized emotions. The complex feelings engendered for the mother in Toni Morrison's novel *Beloved* are likely to be unprecedented for most readers.

Undoubtedly, there are some works of art that explore uncommon, highly individualized emotional states. However, it overstates the case to presume that all art is like this. For centuries, artists painted the image of Christ as the Sacred Heart. Perhaps some managed to express their own highly individualized feelings toward Jesus. But many more probably struck pretty much the same reverential chord. The feelings of faith communicated by these artists, though probably sincere, nevertheless are often repetitive.

Indeed, the patrons who commissioned these works more or less expected these artists to transmit the kind of awe and reverence standardly appropriate to Christianity. Such works are numbered among the artistic treasures of the West, yet they are not, with respect to being individualized, less routine than soap operas. They may generally be of greater value than soap operas, but not because they trade in emotions that are less generic. Since such examples are clearly artworks, it cannot be the case that it is a necessary condition for art status that artworks traffic solely in the sort of individualized emotions that interest transmission theorists.

That artworks explore highly individualized emotions is a greatly admired feature of certain genres, such as modern drama. But it is not a feature of all art. The *Mahabharata* and the *Ramayana* paint with emotively broad brushstrokes. But they are classic artworks. The transmission theorist mistakes a good-making feature of some artforms (such as individualized emotions, and, for that matter, the clarification of emotion), as necessary conditions of all art. But this is to confuse what makes some art good of its kind with what makes any work art, or, in other words, it is to conflate issues of commendation with issues of classification.

A contemporary poem that communicates and clarifies an author's personal feelings may be good for that reason, but that does not entail that for anything to count as an artwork, it must meet these canons of excellence. For not only are there alternative, nonconverging canons of excellence for different artforms, but some works that are undeniably art are bad, perhaps because their emotions are not individualized where that is an expectation of the genre to which they belong. But bad art is still art; if failing to be individualized renders a poem bad, it does not at the same time disqualify it as art.

Another problem with the notion that artworks must communicate individualized emotions is that the very idea of an individualized emotion is very slippery and may even be incoherent. Most emotional states have something generic about them. In order to be afraid, I must think that the object of my state meets certain necessary conditions – that it be harmful, for example. All fear is similar, at least in this respect. So, what exactly does it mean to say that emotions must be individualized? Since most emotions are generic to some degree, where do you draw the line, in a way that is not arbitrary, between the ones that are individualized versus the ones that are not? Nor can one draw the line by saying that the individualized ones are absolutely unique. That would be incoherent, since most emotions belong to kinds – like fear – that have necessary conditions.

At this point, a defender of expression theories of art might say that all of our criticisms so far have really only been of details (like the requirements of individualized and clarified emotion) of the transmission theory and of the solo expression theory. However, challenging these details, it may be said, doesn't cut to the heart of the expression theory, since the bottom line of any expression (including the transmission theory and the solo expression theory) is that something is art only if it expresses emotion (whether or not it is an emotion sincerely felt by the artist). Until something is shown to be wrong with this presupposition, the expression theory of art remains a viable contender as a comprehensive theory of art.

But it is not plausible to maintain that the expression of emotion is a necessary condition of art. Some, perhaps most art, may be in the business of communicating and/or exploring emotions. But not all art is. Some art is about communicating and/or exploring ideas. A case in point is modern painting, of which a great deal in the twentieth century has been about the nature of painting.

The work of Frank Stella, for example, has been frequently preoccupied with calling our attention to the constitutive role that the edge of a painting plays in structuring composition. Many of Andy Warhol's neo-Dadaist experiments pose the philosophical question of what differentiates artworks from real things. M. C. Escher presents us with perceptual puzzles that encourage us to reflect on the peculiarities of our visual system, especially with respect to the way in which it is engaged by pictorial representations; you could say that his work is about pictorial representation. But it is not about emotions. It is cognitive, not emotive.

Similarly, many of the dances of postmodern choreographers in the 1960s, like Yvonne Rainer and Steve Paxton, were concerned with raising the question "What is dance?" They were not involved in either articulating the choreographer's emotions, or arousing emotions in the audience. These choreographers wanted to make the audience think, not feel. Specifically, they intended the audience to contemplate the question of what counts as a dance and why. These seem perfectly legitimate projects for artists to engage in and some of the work that has pursued this research is recognized as classic by art historians, critics, practitioners, and informed audiences. Thus, insofar as such "intellectual" work is art, the expression of emotion is not a necessary condition for art. Art need not be about feeling; it may take ideas, including the play of ideas, as its subject.

Here, the friend of the expression theory may resist this conclusion in one of two ways, either by denying that the preceding examples are art, or by arguing that, appearances notwithstanding, the work in question is concerned with the expression of emotion. The first line of counterattack seems ill-advised. It is hard to motivate in a non-question-begging way. The artworld appears to accept this work as art, and that provides at least a *prima facie* reason for thinking it so. On the other hand, if the expression theorist invokes her theory to support her conclusion that it is not art, then she has merely assumed what she is supposed to prove.

Alternatively, the expression theorist might argue that the work of Stella, Warhol, Escher, Rainer, Paxton, *et al.* is involved in expressing emotions, even if the artists are unaware of this, just because every human action expresses some emotion. Humans bring their emotions to everything they do, and they cannot help leaving traces of themselves behind.

There are two claims here: first, that we approach everything we do with some attitude, in some mood, with certain feelings, from some point of view, and so on; *and* we cannot avoid depositing the imprint of these states on whatever we create. Thus, these works express the feelings and personality of the artist, even if the artist intends otherwise. Therefore, the expression theory of art is not really inhospitable to such works.

But both of the presuppositions of this counterargument seem false. As I add up a long column of numbers, I need not have any garden-variety attitude, mood, feelings, or emotions. And if I have a point of view (the mathematical point of view?), it is not the sort of emotively charged point of view that is relevant to the expression theory of art. Moreover, if I can approach a column of figures without emotion, why suppose that it is impossible for me to calculate the disposition of architectual columns dispassionately?

However, and of greater significance, even if it is the case (which one doubts) that every human breath is accompanied by some emotional state, mood, attitude, and so on, then there is still no reason to believe that it will insinuate its way into the products of our endeavors. One can glean nothing of Newton's emotional state from the inverse square law nor of Einstein's feelings from the special theory of relativity. And there is no reason to think that things stand differently with artworks.

You might think that there is a difference here. Scientists attempt to remove their emotions, feelings, moods and so on from the outcomes of their research, and where they succeed, if they succeed, that is because they have special procedures and techniques that enable them to do so. But the same is not true of artists. Or, so the story goes.

But why presume this? Artists, too, have techniques for bracketing their emotions. Aleatoric strategies are one sort that we've already discussed, and there are others. Just as scientists know how to render their products austerely intellectual, so do many artists. Artists can organize their works in such a way that the only response a sympathetic spectator can make is to think about it. Perhaps finally the most effective way to convince an expression theorist of this is to confront her with a work of choreography like Yvonne Rainer's *Trio A* and to ask what emotion it could be *plausibly* taken to express? Count the expression theorist's silence in this matter as another piece of evidence against the claim that something is art only if it expresses emotion.

Nor does the case against the view that the expression of emotion is a necessary condition for art rest exclusively with a consideration of what we might call avant-garde "idea" art. Much traditional art does not express emotions. Much of it is designed merely to provoke pleasure in viewers or listeners. Call this the art of the beautiful, where beauty is the capacity to cause delight through the manipulation of appearances – both visual and aural.

Some music strikes us with its perfection, though we would be hard put to identify what emotion it expresses. We find the pattern on a handcrafted kelim ravishing, but associate it with no emotion in particular. Here the expression theorist, in order to save her viewpoint, may claim that these works express the emotion of pleasure. But this seems wrong. Pleasure is not an emotion, though it may accompany some emotions, and, in any case, these works do not *express* pleasure; they stimulate it. Much traditional art is merely beautiful, not expressive. Therefore, the expression of emotion is not a necessary condition for being an artwork.

The last necessary condition of the transmission theory is the requirement that artworks express emotions *by means of lines, colors, sounds, shapes, actions and/or words*. This condition says, in effect, that artworks must be in a physical medium. This condition seems to be a promising requirement, at least in spirit, though perhaps not in letter, since it is connected to the very plausible requirement that artworks be publicly accessible, at least in principle; which, in turn, would seem to mandate that they be physically detectable. However, there are at least two potential problems with this claim that are worth considering.

The first is fairly controversial. There is a kind of contemporary art, called Conceptual Art, some of which may represent counterexamples to the requirement. As its name suggests, Conceptual Art is important for its ideas. Often these ideas are about the nature of art. As well, Conceptual Artists are generally opposed to what they regard as the commodification of art. To resist commodification, they specialize in artworks that can't be sold – artworks that are ideas, rather than saleable objects.

In this spirit, an artist might declare that her artwork was comprised of all the ideas that she had about art before breakfast. Now, if this is art, it would refute both the letter and the spirit of the requirement that an artwork be embodied in lines, colors, sounds, shapes, actions, words and/or any other physical medium. But, of course, the question remains whether or not an example of Conceptual Art like this is art?

One reason to suspect that it is not is that it is not publicly accessible. But it may be. Often all that remains to be seen of Conceptual Art is its documentation. Perhaps the artist in the last paragraph exhibits the documentation of her (mental) performance piece – a neatly typed out list of descriptions of all the relevant thoughts she had in the stipulated time period. This might lead you to say: but then it is not a counterexample, since the list is in words. But the list is not the artwork – the thoughts were. Moreover, at the same time, the artwork is not inaccessible – we can contemplate it – through the artist's report of what she did (mentally). Thus, the work is accessible, though it is not, strictly speaking, in any physical medium – let's say her thoughts were not verbal, but are merely described rather than transcribed by her list. If such works are art, then it is not the case that artworks require incarnation in a physical medium.

Admittedly, this is an arguable case; many will not be swayed by it. However, there is another problem with the condition. If the condition is compelling, it is compelling in spirit, not in the letter, since the list – lines, colors, shapes, sounds, actions and/or words – must be incomplete. Even if artworks must be embodied in some medium that is publicly accessible, there is no way ahead of time to enumerate all the possible media that artists might employ. So, we have no way to finish the list.

Moreover, there may be ways of transmitting to an audience the self-same, individualized, clarified emotion that the artist experienced that we would not regard as constituting artworks. Imagine that artists make pills that do the job, or that they communicate by telepathy. I doubt that we would count these methods as artistic. But how will we justify excluding candidates like these from the list without courting circularity?

So adequately framing the last condition of the transmission theory is troublesome. We do not appear to have a way of completing the list, nor a way of disqualifying candidates from being added to it. We would like to say that something is an artwork only if it employs *artistic* means, but if we knew what comprised all and only artistic means, we would already have a definition of art at our disposal.

Thus far, we have only been considering the expression theories of art in terms of various purported necessary conditions. We have not asked whether when all the conditions are added together, they are conjointly sufficient. But one example should suffice to show that they are not.

Imagine that you have just broken up with your lover. You despise your ex-lover now. You sit down and write a letter to express your disdain. It's a long letter, written in publicly accessible language, and you use the space to clarify your emotions colorfully. It's individualized in the sense that you dwell graphically on the specific wrongs dealt to you. It's a very effective letter. You make your lover loathe himself/herself in the same way that you loathe him or her. And that's what you intended. But I doubt we would regard most such letters as art; nor if you told your lover off in this way while standing by the company microwave, I doubt we would view it as part of the history of drama. Yet these cases meet all the conditions of the transmission theory. Thus, the transmission theory does not supply jointly sufficient conditions for identifying art. Moreover, the examples need only be rewritten minimally to demonstrate the same failing with respect to solo expression theories.

Furthermore, cases like this are not exceptional. All sorts of everyday behaviors can be cited that are expressive in accordance with all the requirements of expression theories, but are not art. This is especially evident if we pare down the expression to the claim that something is art if and only if it expresses emotion, since so many things that are not art express emotion.

Scouting various expression theories of art, then, only the requirement that artworks be intended for audiences looks like it has a fighting chance to succeed as a necessary condition for art, and this condition need not have anything to do with the expression of emotion *per se*. Every other condition of the expression theories of art canvassed fails to be necessary.

Expression theories of art, like the transmission theory, therefore appear too exclusive. There is too much art that they do not accommodate. But at the same time, expression theories of art are too inclusive; the conditions are not jointly sufficient. Together they will count too much everyday expressive behavior as art when they shouldn't. Thus, expression theories of art are not nearly accurate enough. Though superior to representational theories of art, they fail to track all art satisfactorily in both its richness and its specificity.

Part II
Theories of expression

What is expression?

Some philosophers have attempted to define art in terms of expression, but, as we saw in the previous section, expression theories of art confront many problems. At present, such theories seem far from promising. However, even if not all art is expressive, much art is. We say that the music is joyful, the painting is sad, the dance is melancholic, the building is somber, the story is angry, and the poem is nostalgic. That is, the music expresses joy, the painting expresses sadness, and so on. So much of the language that we use to characterize a great deal of art rests on the notion of expression. Thus, even if expression theories of *all* art are unpersuasive, we still need to say something theoretical about expression and art, inasmuch as quite a lot of art is expressive. What exactly are we doing when we say that the music is joyful, or that a poem is expressive of anger?

The word "expression" can have broader and narrower uses in ordinary language. For example, sometimes it behaves like a synonym for "representation." We might say equally that "The White Paper expresses the British position" or that "The White Paper represents the British position." However, this sense of expression is broader than the one that concerns philosophers of art, since typically when they talk of expression, they intend it to contrast with representation. Thus, the sense of "expression" that concerns us is more narrow than the view of expression as representation.

Another broad meaning of "expression" in everyday speech is roughly "communication." Every utterance is an expression in this sense – "Shut the door" is an expression, as is "The rain in Spain falls mainly on the plain." But as we can see through our discussion of expression theories of art, this too is a broader sense of expression than philosophers of art have in mind. For them, what is expressed is not anything that can be communicated but only a subset thereof.

In ordinary language, it makes perfect sense to say that the poem expresses (communicates, represents) the Catholic idea of heaven. But when philosophers of art talk about what poems express, they are not thinking broadly about the communication of ideas. For them, what gets expressed are certain human qualities (also known as anthropomorphic properties) – notably, emotional tones, moods, emotively colored attitudes, and the like. That is, the concept of expression that concerns philosophers of art is the one in evidence in sentences like: "This artwork expresses joy"; or "This artwork is expressive of joyousness"; or "This artwork is an expression of joyousness."

When I say "this poem is angry" I could mean at least two things: that the poet reports that he is angry (perhaps a line of the poem states "we are angry") or that the poet expresses anger. To express anger involves more than merely reporting that one is angry. Reporting can be done in a dispassionate way. One could say "We are angry" in the same tone of voice that one could say "Everyone here is over five feet tall." In the relevant sense, when we express anger in life or in art, we manifest anger – we show it forth. There is a qualitative dimension to our utterance; the quality of our anger saturates our utterance. It is an angry utterance, not merely a statement that one is angry. Compare the statement "You numbskull!" with "I am angry with you." The first expresses anger; the second merely reports it.

To express anger, in this sense, is to get the feeling of anger across – to make it perceptible (to embody or objectify it). It is to project the quality of anger. Roughly speaking, then, to express anger is to manifest outwardly an emotive property – the emotive property of being angry. However, I say "roughly" here because, though emotive properties are a major object of artistic expression, there are some other kinds as well.

For example, an artwork may also manifest a range of other human qualities – such as courage. That is, we might say "The story is courageous" or "It expresses courage," or "It is expressive of courage," or "It is an expression of courage." Thus, what may be expressed are not only emotive qualities, but any human qualities, including emotional ones, and also character traits as well (such as courage, cowardice, honesty, meanness, stateliness, and so on).

The concept of expression that interests philosophers of art ranges over human qualities such as emotive qualities and qualities of character. For our purposes, expression is the manifestation, exhibition, objectification, embodiment, projection, or showing forth of human qualities, or, as they are also called, "anthropomorphic properties" (properties that standardly apply only to human persons).

This sense of expression contrasts with the notion of representation explored in the previous chapter. There the notion of representation applied to certain kinds of things, but not others; its domain, so to speak, comprised objects, persons, places, events and actions. These were the sorts of things that could be represented.

In contrast, the domain of expression comprises human qualities or anthropomorphic properties – i.e., the kinds of qualities and properties that can be applied generally only to human persons. These are the sorts of things that can be expressed by artworks. Saying that an artwork expresses x means that it manifests a property typically applied to humans – such as sadness, courageousness, and the like. In summary, then, to say that an artwork expresses x means that it manifests, exhibits, projects, embodies, or shows forth some x where x is a human quality (some anthropomorphic property) such as an emotive property or a quality of character.

Expression in this light is not the central defining property of art, since not all artworks need be expressive. But expression occurs quite often in art – it occurs wherever artworks manifest human qualities. Frequently we commend artworks (and/or parts of artworks) for their expressive powers. We say that the the movie was good because it captures the desolate feeling of the end of an affair perfectly. That is, it shows forth that quality of feeling with great lucidity.

Sometimes we condemn artworks for their expressive properties (the human qualities they manifest). Perhaps we say the second scene of a play exhibits inappropriate cruelty. It is a cruel scene, or it expresses cruelty excessively. But whether condemning or commending, or, for that matter, whether simply describing artworks (or parts thereof), the attribution of human qualities to artworks comprises a large part of our commerce with them.

But how do we go about attributing expressive properties to artworks? What conditions warrant saying, for example, that the piece of music (or a part of a piece of music) expresses certain human qualities? Suppose we hear a fanfare and it strikes us as regal, dignified and expressive of nobility. Or, perhaps a poem appears pessimistic and resigned. We make observations like this often. They lie at the heart of the way in which we describe and evaluate much art. But on what basis do we make such attributions?

One theory – which we may call the common view – maintains that:

An artist expresses (manifests, embodies, projects, objectifies) x (some human quality) if and only if (1) the artist has been moved by a feeling or an experience of x to compose his artwork (or a part thereof); (2) the artist has imbued his artwork (or some part of it) with x (some human quality); and (3) the artwork (or the relevant part) has the capacity to give the artist the feeling or experience of x when he or she reads, listens to and/or sees it again, and, consequently, to impart the same feeling or experience of x to other readers, listeners and/or viewers.

Thus, if we are speaking of the expression of indignation, then our ascription of it to a painting is warranted just in case the artist experienced indignation and her indignation moved her to make the artwork in the way she did; the painting has the quality of indignation; and the painting moves audiences, including the artist, to feel indignation when they see it.

The requirements that the artist compose her painting under the aegis of her experience of indignation and that the painting evoke or arouse indignation in subsequent audiences remind us of some of the conditions discussed with respect to the transmission theory of expression. These conditions are no less problematic here than they were previously.

According to the common view, it is a necessary condition that an artwork expresses x only if the artist experienced x and that that experience of x governed the composition of the artwork. We might call this the sincerity condition. So, if Beethoven's *A Major Symphony* truly expresses joy, on the common view, Beethoven must have felt joy while composing it in such a way that that experience shaped his composition of the work.

The sincerity condition certainly derives a great deal of its attractiveness from our everyday use of the notion of expression. In the course of daily events, we often observe expressive behavior in our acquaintances. Before a big date, we see that our friend is nervous. Her voice quavers. We say that her voice quavering expresses her nervousness. But, in ordinary speech, when we say that her voice quavering expresses nervousness, typically we think that it provides evidence that she is nervous. The perceptible property of nervousness in her voice, all things being equal, warrants our inference that she is nervous. If the voice quavering really expresses nervousness, then it is connected to her ongoing (occurrent) psychological state. It signals that she *is* nervous. The outward manifestation of nervousness is linked (some would say conceptually) to her inner state. This, at least, is probably the way we most frequently use the concept of expression in daily life.

The common view of expression in art extrapolates from this customary use of expression and applies it to artworks. In ordinary speech, genuine expression of an emotion indicates that whoever exhibits the emotion also has the pertinent emotion. The expression supports our suspicion that the agent in question possesses the relevant emotion (either contingently or necessarily typically) and that her possession of the emotion explains her expression. Thus, when it comes to art, the common view holds that for an artist to express a certain feeling requires that the artist have the feeling. If the artist lacks the requisite feeling, then he is not genuinely expressing it. This would seem to follow from the ordinary usage of the concept of expression.

But this argument assumes that the concept of expression is always applied in art in the way it is usually applied in life. And this is mistaken. When an actor makes a plaintive gesture, we do not suppose that the actor is mournful, even if we suppose her character is. Indeed, it is unlikely that the actor is gripped by grief, since if she were so gripped, she would probably forget her lines and her blocking. We do not presume that the expressive behavior of an actor onstage either necessarily or contingently counts as evidence of what she, the actress, is feeling. She may in fact be feeling nothing at all, but only reckoning her effect on the audience.

We do not require genuine sincerity from actors; after all, they're *actors*! Similarly, when a composer makes a despondent score, he may be feeling very happy that his notes fit together so nicely. Even if expressive behavior in everyday living usually (or necessarily typically) provides evidence of inner states, that is no reason to suppose that it functions likewise with respect to art.

For as we have already noted, much art is commissioned. A film director might be hired to make a film – say a *film noir* – that is supposed to project certain feelings. She knows how to do this – how to manipulate the lighting, the dialogue, and the pacing. She can do the job without feeling angst. We would not say the film is not expressive of anxiety, if we learnt that the director had been cheerful throughout the production. When we say a film is expressive of depression, we do not regard this as evidence that the film-makers were depressed.

Of course, it is not always the case even in ordinary speech that a sad expression warrants the inference of a sad mental state. Some people have sad faces all the time – that is, their faces have the characteristic look of sadness. They always look like they are about to burst into tears. But when we say that Margaret has a sad face – or that her face expresses sadness – we need not take this as providing evidence that Margaret is in the mental state of sadness. As they say, Margaret just has a "sour puss." Thus, though everyday discourse affords some support for the common view, it is not conclusive, since ordinary speech also countenances usage that does not suggest that expression requires the pertinent accompanying psychological state. And much art is like this. Thus, the way in which the proponent of the common view tries to deduce the sincerity condition from ordinary language is not as straightforward as it may have seemed at first.

Provisionally we might mark a distinction between two uses of expression. In one case, when we say that "x expresses sadness," we mean that x is an expression of sadness such that a genuine expression of sadness by a person either contingently or necessarily typically counts as evidence that the person is sad. Call this the expression sense. But another sense of "x expresses sadness" means only that x is expressive of sadness – that it gives the characteristic appearance of sadness – where *sadness* describes how something looks or sounds, but does not indicate that anyone is in the psychological state of sadness. Call this the expressive sense of "x expresses sadness." The expression sense is used far less frequently with reference to artworks than the expressive sense. Hence, it is false that we can only attribute an expressive quality, such as sadness, to an artwork if the artist has experienced sadness.

One way to see this is to recall that we often attribute expressive qualities to nature. We say the drooping, weeping willow tree is sad. Here we obviously mean that it is expressive of sadness; we cannot be implying that the tree is in a state of psychological sadness. Trees cannot be sad. Likewise, we might say that the picture of the weeping willow tree is sad. But a picture can't be in the psychological state of sadness either. So, as with the tree, we are saying that the picture is expressive of sadness, and not that the person who made the picture is sad.

In the case of the tree in nature, we can say that it has the expressive property of sadness, without saying that it suffers the mental state of sadness. Similarly, we can attribute sadness to the picture of such a tree in the same way. Since we are not compelled to claim that the tree must be in the mental state of sadness in order to say that it is expressive of sadness, by parity of reasoning, we can say that the picture is expressive of sadness, without attributing sadness to its creator. Therefore, it is an error to claim that an artwork necessarily expresses a certain human quality x only if the artist is moved by the feeling or experience of x.

The sincerity condition is one component of the common view; it appears to be false. It is not a necessary condition for expressing an anthropomorphic quality x that an artist be moved by the feeling or experience of x. But the common view also maintains that in order to express x the artwork must move audiences to feel or experience x. We can call this the arousal condition. An artwork expresses x only if it arouses x in the audience. But the arousal condition is no more compelling than the sincerity condition.

Undoubtedly much art does arouse emotions in audiences. But arousing emotions in audiences is not a necessary condition of artistic expressiveness. A piece of music can express hope, and I can apprehend that it expresses hope without becoming hopeful myself, just as I can see that George has a happy face without becoming happy every time I see George. If you say the weeping willow tree in the front yard is sad, I can see what you mean – I can detect the relevant expressive properties – without becoming sad myself.

If the arousal of the relevant emotion in the audience were a necessary condition for an artwork's expression of it, then wherever we find expressiveness in artworks, we would have to find ourselves literally moved to feel whatever the artwork expresses. But this is not true for all artworks that express human qualities. Here are three very common types of cases that show that the arousal condition is not necessary.

First, many of the works of art that do arouse feelings in audiences arouse audience emotions that are quite different than the ones expressed in the work. Parts of Dostoyevsky's *Crime and Punishment* express remorse, but readers do not feel remorse (that would be implausible – they haven't killed anyone); instead they feel pity. Thus, it is not the case that in order to express x (some emotion), the audience must be made to feel the same x. An artwork may express x, while arousing some altogether different feeling, y.

Second, sometimes artworks express human qualities other than emotive ones. A painting may express fortitude. But fortitude is not something that you can arouse in audiences. In cases like these, artworks can express x without making audiences feel x, since x here is not something that one can feel. And if we are moved to some feeling by an expression of fortitude, it is not fortitude, but something else, like admiration, in which case we are back to the objection in the preceding paragraph.

Third, some artworks are expressive of anthropomorphic properties like anger, but they lack the resources to arouse anger in audiences. Pure orchestral music is generally like this. To be aroused to anger, I must have some object toward which I direct my anger and that object must be subsumable under the appropriate kind of description – I am angry at Henry because he has wronged me or mine.

Literature can supply us with the requisite objects – like Simon LeGree – as well as the appropriate descriptions – the way he abuses his slaves. But pure orchestral music provides us with neither objects nor descriptions, and without them, it is hard to see how it can arouse us to anger. We cannot be angry without something to be angry about – without an object and the right reasons. And yet some music seems expressive of anger. We say we hear anger in the music. But we are not aroused to anger. With whom and for what reasons would we be angry? The music is mute on this score. Thus, some art is expressive of emotional states that it does not (and perhaps cannot) arouse in audiences. Moreover, this is not only the case with some music, but with certain abstract paintings as well.

Sometimes people speak as if the arousal condition alone provides necessary and sufficient conditions for attributing expressiveness to an artwork. It is obviously not a necessary condition, since many artworks are expressive of x without arousing the self-same feeling of x in audiences, or, for that matter, without arousing any feeling in the audience at all. We can detect expressive qualities without being infected by them.

And clearly arousal of emotion is not a sufficient condition for expression in art, since our emotions can be aroused by the mere dispassionate representation or description of certain kinds of events – like droughts, floods and massacres. Nor is the arousal condition, supplemented by the sincerity condition, much of an improvement, since, given the discussion so far, we can imagine artworks expressive of remorsefulness that neither reflect the artist's feelings nor arouse remorse in the audience; whereas still other artworks may arouse fear in the audience – fear which the artist shares – while not being expressive of fear (for example, a scientifically antiseptic photograph of an asteriod hurtling toward Earth).

So far we have been focussing attention on the sincerity and the arousal conditions of the common view. We have not said anything about the second condition in the theory – that an artwork expresses x (some human quality) only if the artist has imbued the artwork (or some part of it) with x. This condition does seem to be onto something. A scherzo is expressive of joy only if the artist has given it the quality of joyousness. In order to express joy, the quality of joyousness must be detectable in it. This does seem to be what warrants our attribution of joyousness to the scherzo.

However, the notion of the scherzo's being imbued with joyousness or its having the quality of joyousness is somewhat obscure and uninformative (is being imbued with the property of joyousness less in need of explication than the notion of being expressive of joyousness?) Therefore, let us see whether or not this condition can be made less mysterious. Perhaps that will yield a comprehensive theory of the grounds upon which we ascribe expressiveness to artworks.

Expression, exemplification and metaphor

When we say that an artwork expresses something, we have in mind some property or quality, namely some human quality, whether an emotive quality or a quality of character. For such an attribution to obtain, then, it seems fair to say that the artwork in question must be imbued with the quality. But what is it for an artwork to be imbued with a quality? That seems very opaque. Can we do anything to relieve that opacity?

When an artist makes an expressive artwork, she intends to show forth or to display some anthropomorphic quality. That is, there is some human quality that the artist wants to refer to in order to draw our attention to it. Perhaps the artist wishes to inform us about its existence or to put it forward so that we may contemplate it, reflect upon it, and familiarize ourselves with its distinctive appearances. In this respect, what the artist is doing is not so different from what a clerk in a hardware store does when he shows us a sample sheet of paint.

Suppose we want some blue paint. We go to the store and the salesman shows us a sheet of different shades of blue paint. There are little squares of various blue paints – a navy blue square, a prussian blue square, and so on – neatly arrayed on a piece of paper. If we ask, "What do you have in navy blue?" the clerk points to the appropriate square. This is intended to show me what the paint in the cans marked "navy blue" looks like. The little square is a sample of the color in the cans labeled "navy blue" that are presently for sale. It refers to the paint in the can; it symbolizes it. But it doesn't merely stand for the navy blue paint in the cans; the phrase "navy blue" can do that. Rather, the little square shows us some of the properties of the paint, at least with respect to color.

How does it do this? By being a sample of that color. It is an example of that color; it exemplifies that color. What is it about the color sample that enables it to exemplify the paint in the cans? It possesses the same property – navy blueness – that the paint in the cans do. It exemplifies the paint by being an example of the color of the paint – i.e., by possessing the same color property that the paint does.

Exemplification is a common form of symbolism. We encounter it at every turn in everyday life. At a restaurant, when the waitress brings out the dessert tray and shows us various slices of cake and pie, each of those desserts is functioning symbolically as an example of what we will get, if we order a certain piece of pastry. The piece of chocolate cake on the tray that the waitress shows us refers to the pieces of chocolate cake in the kitchen, and informs us about what we will receive, if we order a piece of chocolate cake. Similarly, the sneakers in the display window of a shoe store refer to the sneakers in the storeroom of the shop and inform us – by showing us an example – about the properties of the sneakers that are on sale. The display sneakers are able to do this by virtue of their possession of many of the same properties that the sneakers in the storeroom have.

Of course, it need not be the case that a sample possesses all the properties of that of which it is a sample. Standardly samples possess only some of the properties of the items they exemplify. In grocery stores, we are offered a small piece of sausage in order to exemplify the taste of the sausage. The piece of sausage in the package is larger in size than the sample. The sample exemplifies the taste properties, not the size properties of the sausage product. In order to exemplify the taste of the sausage, the sample must possess the same taste as its referent (the sausage in the package), but it need not have all the same properties of the packaged sausage. It need only possess the properties it is intended to exemplify.

Exemplification is a common form of symbolism, but it is not the same as representation. The domain of representation is persons, places, things, events and objects. The domain of exemplification is properties. In addition, possession of the relevant property is a necessary condition of exemplification; x cannot be an example of y, unless x possesses y-ness. A paint sample cannot exemplify navy blueness, unless is possesses the property of navy blueness. But x can represent y without sharing any of the properties of y; some of the music in the *1812 Overture* represents France without sharing any properties with France.

Of course, not every can of Coke exemplifies every other Coke can, even though each Coke can shares a massive number of properties with every other. Why not? Because ordinary Coke cans do not refer to other Coke cans. In order to function as a sample of other Coke cans, a Coke can must be selected and displayed in a communicative context where it functions as a symbol. So, in other words:

> x exemplifies y (some property) if and only if (1) x possesses y and (2) x refers to y.

But what do Coke cans, paint, sneakers, chocolate cake and so on have to do with art? Just as these objects function to exemplify certain properties of their kind, expressive artworks exemplify the properties that they express. We have said that artistic expression involves manifesting human qualities or anthropomorphic properties. The artist articulates the artwork in such a way that the relevant properties are exhibited for contemplation by the audience. That is, in expressing something the artist exemplifies it for the audience.

For example, the novelist tries to capture the qualities of a certain form of mourning – to articulate them so that the audience becomes aware of this kind of mourning in a way that informs us about certain properties of mourning we might experience or that we have already experienced or that we have observed others experiencing. By embodying certain properties of mourning the artwork refers to mourning – perhaps to the mourning a son feels upon the death of his father – and by articulating the qualities that attend that kind of mourning, audiences are alerted to the existence and contours of mourning, i.e., its characteristic properties.

Or, in other words, the artist, by way of the artwork, exemplifies mourning; the expressive artwork refers to mourning, and it shows forth the relevant properties of mourning by being sad (sad in a certain way). The artwork exemplifies mourning by referring to sadness by way of possessing the property of sadness. Just as the waitress exemplifies chocolate cake by means of a sample, so the artist exemplifies the sadness of loss by showing certain of its properties.

This does not require that the artwork make the audience sad. We can reflect upon the sadness exemplified by an artwork without becoming sad. The artwork can inform us about sadness – for example, about its rhythms, conditions, and so on – without arousing sadness in us. To exemplify sadness only requires referring to aspects of sadness by way of possessing them.

When we say that an artist imbues an artwork with a certain human quality, what we mean, more concretely, is that the artist fashions the expressive artwork in such a way that it exemplifies the relevant human quality. Suppose a composer wants to express a feeling of stateliness. She gives the music a slow, deliberate pace, rather than a fast, congested one. In this, she tries to capture the characteristic appearance of stateliness, its slow, deliberate cadence. She exemplifies stateliness by referring to it, by way of providing a sample of it. She offers an example of stateliness for listeners to contemplate, perhaps to compare its projection of stateliness or the lack thereof with events in their daily lives.

Saying that imbuing an artwork with an anthropomorphic quality involves exemplifying it makes some headway in explicating the notion of artistic expression. But the exemplification theorist will be the first to point out that this is not quite right. To see this, just recall our last example. We said that the composer exemplifies stateliness, in part, by providing a sample of it. And to be a sample, the music must possess the property of stateliness. But music, it may be argued, is not literally stately; people are stately. Similarly, if we say the music is sad in part because it possesses sadness, we cannot be speaking literally, since only persons are sad. Music is not a sentient being. How can it possess sadness? Sadness is a psychological state, and a piece of music has no psychology. Thus, the exemplification theory of expression as stated thus far cannot be right, since it is impossible for music to be a proper sample of sadness.

Here the exemplification theorist is likely to agree. More needs to be added to the view in order to deal with this apparent problem. What the exemplification theorist adds is that the music is only metaphorically sad, not literally sad. The music does not possess the property of sadness literally, but metaphorically. Expression on this augmented view, then, involves three elements: reference, possession and metaphor. Stated formulaically:

x expresses y if and only if (1) x refers to y, and (2) x possesses y (3) metaphorically.

Expression, then, is reference plus metaphorical possession, or, to say it even more compactly, expression is metaphorical exemplification.

Undoubtedly the notions of metaphorical possession and metaphorical exemplication are hard ones to understand. How does someone possess anything (my car, for example) metaphorically? One either possesses something or one doesn't. So, for our purposes, let us take this notion of metaphorical possession to mean that the artwork possesses some literal properties – pitches and tempos, for instance – that the audience is entitled to describe in terms of some appropriate metaphor.

This appears to do a better job with hard cases, like sad music. When we say the music is sad, we are ascribing the property of sadness to the music metaphorically, not literally. But, of course, when attributing a quality like sadness to the music, we cannot pick just any metaphor that we want. It must be a metaphor that fits the music – that is appropriate to the sounds and cadences of the music.

It would be absurd to attribute dourness to Beethoven's "Ode to Joy." Thus, if expressiveness in art is a matter of metaphorical exemplification, then in order justifiably to ascribe sadness to a piece of music certain conditions must be met: the music must refer to sadness, and it must possess sadness, at least in the sense that our metaphorical attribution of sadness is appropriate.

This, however, still leaves at least one question – what makes a metaphorical attribution appropriate? In order to answer this question, we need an account of metaphor. But there are many accounts of metaphor on offer, and we cannot explore all of them. So for purposes of exposition, let us look only at the account of metaphor most often associated with the exemplification theory.

We say that the scherzo in Mendelssohn's program music for *A Midsummer Night's Dream* is vibrant and spritely; that the architectonic structures of Poussin's landscapes are rational; that the film *Seven* is paranoiac. But, the exemplification theorist says, music can't be spritely, nor a picture rational, nor a film paranoiac. So these attributions must be metaphorical. But how do we go about assigning these metaphors appropriately?

A metaphor is at least the application of a name, or a category, or a descriptive term or phrase to something to which the label does not apply literally, but only imaginatively. "King Richard the Lion-Hearted" is a metaphor. King Richard did not literally have the heart of a lion; the sentence "King Richard was lion-hearted" is literally false. On the other hand, for the people of his times something about the phrase seemed right. The name seemed fitting. It did appear to pick out some important features of King Richard and articulate them pointedly. Why?

According to the exemplification theorist, metaphors involve the transfer of one set of labels from an indigenous field of application to an alien field. Lion-heartedness comes from the field of animal biology (where it is standardly applied) and gets transferred, so to speak, to the alien field of human character traits (where it is applied to the virtues of King Richard). But what is meant by "field" here?

Consider temperature terms: hot, cold, tepid. They form a descriptive scheme of interrelated categories. Their indigenous field of application – their "home" territory – is degrees of heat. When applied to degrees of heat, these terms are used literally. Boiling water is hot; ice water is cold; and tepid water is somewhere in between. But often we apply these terms to things other than degrees of heat. We apply them to things from alien fields. We say that singer's style is hot, that the commissar's is cold, and that the nice guy's is tepid. What we are doing here is transferring a scheme of labels (temperature terms) from its home ground of application to alien territory (a list of personalities), or, in other words, we are mapping temperature labels onto a scheme of human personality labels. The contrasts that are built into the indigenous temperature scheme are being mapped onto or projected onto the contrasts implicit in the alien personality scheme.

On this view of metaphor, metaphors are always systematic. Whenever we apply a metaphor, we are implicitly mobilizing an entire scheme of contrasting literal terms and projecting them onto an alien scheme. If we say that Tina Turner's singing style is hot, we are assuming that this contrasts with some tepid singing style (perhaps Al Gore's), even if we don't articulate, including to ourselves, the rest of the scheme-to-scheme mapping. We just say, that "Tina Turner's performance was hot," but this is really a fragment of a larger scheme-to-scheme mapping. Moreover, where a metaphor appears appropriate, that is a result of its fitting into the scheme-to-scheme mapping in the right way.

"Right way?" If I say that "Venus is to Jupiter as the the Indian Ocean is to _____ ," many of you will fill in the blank with "the Pacific Ocean." Why? Because if we are comparing planetary objects with oceans along the dimension of size, then the Pacific Ocean is the right answer, since it is the largest ocean on earth, just as Jupiter is the largest planet in our solar system. That is, the Pacific Ocean has the same relative position in the scheme of ocean-terms that Jupiter has in the scheme of planet-terms. If we uttered the metaphor "Jupiter is the Pacific Ocean of outer space," that attribution would be appropriate, since the "Pacific Ocean" bears the same contrastive relation to the other terms in its scheme of labels that Jupiter bears in its.

Metaphors, then, are always homologies. That is, they have the implicit form of "x is related to a as y is related to b" (x/a::y/b). And there is a logic to homologies. So a metaphor is appropriate when it accords with the logic of the larger homology of which it is a part. When I say that the movie *Seven* is paranoiac, that is appropriate because it fits a larger, though generally unstated homology, in which other movies (like *Meet Me in St.*

Louis or *Sleepless in Seattle*) correlate with other contrasting human qualities, like optimism. Or, *Seven* is paranoiac as *Meet Me in St. Louis* is optimistic.

Single metaphors, then, are parts of systems – underlying systems of contrasts. To say that Van Gogh's last paintings are delirious implicitly invokes a set of systematic contrasts where some other paintings are placid (say Monet's water lilies), and where still further paintings correlate with other emotional properties. Making a metaphor involves two different things: choosing one scheme of labels (deliriousness, placidity, and so on) and mapping that scheme of labels onto another scheme (Van Gogh's paintings, Monet's, and so on).

According to the exemplification theorist, the choice of the initial scheme of labels is flexible, some would even say arbitrary. I could choose a list of color terms – red and blue – and then map them onto a list of songs. Perhaps "Satisfaction" is red (metaphorically speaking) and "September Song" is blue. That is, we can opt to project any scheme of labels onto any other scheme of labels. Which scheme we project is almost arbitrary. However, once we decide on a scheme, the mapping we arrive at will not be arbitrary. If we choose to project the temperature schema onto the singing style schema, then it is not arbitrary that we call Tina Turner's style hot and Al Gore's tepid. If anyone said that Tina Turner's style were tepid, we would say that he made a mistake.

Though the choice of which scheme to project onto another is virtually wide open, the way we go about correlating items with each other in respective schemes does not seem to be. There is generally a surprisingly high degree of convergence in these matters. Given the nonsense syllables "ping" and "pong," most people will agree that violins go with ping and tubas go with pong. That is, there are certain criteria that make some mappings appropriate and others not, namely, that the structure of contrasts in the indigenous realm of labels should be isomorphic (or approximately isomorphic) with the structure of contrasts that inheres between the relevant items in the alien realm of labels.

This provides a neat way in which to determine whether the metaphorical attributions we make of human property terms to nonhuman artworks are appropriate. Thus, if a musical composition refers to a property (say, nobility) that can be attributed to it metaphorically in the appropriate way, then we are warranted in saying that the music is expressive of nobility. Consequently, the theory of expression as metaphorical exemplification has the great virtue of offering impressive clarity to a subject hitherto obscure.

Some problems with the theory of metaphorical exemplification

There is no doubt that the account of expression offered by the theory of metaphorical exemplification sketched above is attractive. It provides a very legible model of how we go about attributing expressive properties to artworks. And yet for all its admirable precision, it possesses certain nagging limitations. We may begin to explore these by asking whether the theory of metaphorical exemplification we've outlined supplies necessary or sufficient conditions for attributing expressive properties to artworks.

Is it the case that every expressive artwork metaphorically exemplifies its properties in accordance with the preceding account of metaphor? That account of metaphor requires that metaphorical terms be part of a larger matrix of contrasting schemes. This works very well when we are thinking of opposing columns consisting only of single labels, like:

hot	Romantic music
tepid	Muzak
cold	Electronic music

However, not all expressive attributions are so simple.

Suppose we say that a poem expresses some very complex emotional property, such as "late nineteenth-century, *fin-de-siècle*, bohemian, anarchistic despair and loathing." It is certainly very difficult to imagine reconstructing the indigenous scheme of contrasting labels that that complex property-label inhabits. Indeed, it is fair to presume there is none, unless we are shown otherwise. And yet many of the expressive properties that we attribute to artworks are at least this complex. For example, the movie *King Kong* is expressive of mid-century American brashness, naïveté, and sentimentality. Therefore, the theory of metaphorical exemplification that we are examining does not look like it possesses the resources to accommodate all the expressive properties we wish to attribute to artworks.

In the same vein, there appear to be many "one-off" metaphors – metaphors that do not seem to belong to a scheme of contrasts. For example, in the poem "The Highwayman," the moon is said to be a "ghostly galleon." But "ghostly galleon" does not belong to any neat list of descriptions that can be readily mapped onto an alien scheme of extra-terrestrial bodies that exhibit the same structure of contrasts. It is a one-off metaphor. But there also appear to be one-off metaphors with respect to expressive artworks.

I say that Tom Clancy's novel *Patriot Games* is very John Waynesque; this is intelligible without there being a scheme of actor-labels in which the name "John Wayne" contrasts with the names of other actors. Rather, the fact that we have certain associations with John Wayne in isolation from any scheme of labels is enough for us to see that the metaphorical attribution of John-Waynishness or a John-Waynesque mood to *Patriot Games* is apposite. Thus, the theory of metaphorical exemplification under discussion does not apply to every expressive metaphor with which we can describe artworks.

Nor is metaphorical exemplification a sufficient condition for attributing expressiveness to an artwork. Using the logical machinery of scheme transfer, we may say, metaphorically, that one painting appears (but is not literally) brittle, where this implicitly contrasts with some other painting or paintings that are strong. Thus, the theory warrants our saying that the painting expresses brittleness. But *brittleness* is not the sort of thing that gets expressed in artworks – it is not literally an emotive property or a human character quality. Thus, the theory that we are working with counts artworks that are not expressive as expressive. Here, the theorist may say that we really ought to reconsider what gets expressed in artworks by consulting his theory. But with equal justice, we may respond that the theory has failed to find its mark.

Also, remember that the theory of metaphorical exemplification maintains that the choice of the indigenous scheme is arbitrary. But this cannot be correct. If we map a scheme of farming devices onto an array of artworks, we can wind up with the conclusion that some poem expresses tractorness (rather than reaperness). But even if there is some poem that could be aptly described by this metaphor, it cannot *express* tractorness, since tractorness is not something that can be expressed. It is not the right kind of property – it is not an anthropomorphic property. Thus, the theory does not provide sufficient conditions for expressiveness, because it will count as expressive too many things that are not truly expressive.

It may be thought that this lacuna can be repaired by placing certain constraints on the kinds of schemes that can be mobilized for mapping expressive properties. Perhaps, the theorist of metaphorical exemplification will say that only schemes involving anthropomorphic properties are permissible. But there will be problems here too, since certain anthropomorphic properties are not the sorts of things that can be expressed. Imagine a scheme of human skin diseases being projected on an array of artworks with the result that some artwork, perhaps a horror film, correlates with impetiginousness. Surely, that is not an expressive quality that an artwork can have.

This is an outright counterexample for any exemplification theorist who maintains that the choice of a scheme for mapping is perfectly arbitrary. But it is also a problem for the exemplification theorist who wants to place constraints on which schemes are available for mapping, until she comes up with a way to set the constraints so that they will pick out all and only expressive properties. That is, the burden of proof here rests with the proponent of metaphorical exemplification.

So far these objections have primarily revealed limitations that can be traced back to the particular account of metaphor upon which the exemplification theorist usually relies. But perhaps that account can be reworked, or a better one can be found. Thus, it might be argued, these objections do not cut to the quick of a theory of metaphorical exemplification. Are there deeper objections?

The theory of metaphorical exemplification claims that *all* expressive properties are possessed by artworks metaphorically. That is, whenever we attribute expressive properties to artworks we do so metaphorically – whatever the correct account of metaphor is. This is the deepest commitment of the theory. The theory of metaphorical exemplification gives a general answer to our initiating question: "How do we attribute expressive properties to artworks?" The answer is: "Metaphorically." But is this true?

Is expression always metaphorical?

The friend of metaphorical exemplification argues that expression in artworks is *always* metaphorical, which we can understand as the claim that *every time* expressive properties, like sadness, are attributed to artworks, concepts like *sadness* are being used in an extended or metaphorical way. This must be the case, it is argued, since artworks are not the kinds of things that can be sad. Only sentient beings can be sad, i.e., only sentient beings can be the proper bearers of mental properties, such as sadness. And obviously artworks are not sentient beings. So artworks are only describable as sad metaphorically; they only possess their expressive properties metaphorically. This is a seductive argument, but in order to probe it effectively, we need to look at it in greater detail.

Stated more expansively, the argument contends:

1   If artworks (and parts of artworks) possess expressive properties, they do so either literally or metaphorically. (premise)
2   If artworks (and parts of artworks) possess expressive properties literally, they must the kinds of things that can bear mental properties. (premise)

3   Artworks (and parts of artworks) are not the kind of things that can bear mental properties. (premise)
4   Therefore, artworks (and parts thereof) do not possess expressive properties literally.
5   But artworks (and parts of artworks) do possess expressive properties. (premise)
6   Therefore, artworks (and parts thereof) possess expressive properties metaphorically.

For the purposes of argumentation, let us grant that the first premise is true – that, when we say an artwork has an expressive property, our attribution is either literal or metaphorical, and that these are the only two alternatives. Moreover, the fifth premise seems to be a matter of fact that every philosopher of art will accept. Consequently, if the conclusion of the argument is false, then that must be because either or both of the remaining premises are false. If there is a problem here, then it must lie in either the second or the third premise, or in both.

Premise #3 claims that no artwork nor any parts thereof belong to the class of things that can bear mental properties. A statue cannot be sad, nor can any part of it be sad. Stone is not sentient. If we attribute expression to stone, that can only be a metaphorical attribution, not a literal one. The case may seem to be an open and shut one, but it is not, especially if we attend to the way in which we often attribute expressive properties to artworks.

As we noted in the previous chapter, many artworks are representational. Episodes of the TV program the *X-Files* are representational. But also these episodes are often said to be deadpan. An expressive property often attributed to episodes of the *X-Files*, then, is *deadpan-ness*, a certain human quality of mind and manner. But why do we call the *X-Files* deadpan?

Isn't it because the major characters in the fiction – Mulder and Scully – are deadpan? Moreover, Mulder and Scully represent sentient beings. Mulder and Scully, then, do belong to the class of things that can bear mental properties literally. Thus, parts of artworks, notably representations of characters, are the sorts of things to which mental property terms are literally applicable. So if it is required that parts of artworks be proper bearers of mental properties in order to bear expressive properties literally, then some parts of artworks may (and quite frequently do) meet that requirement.

Furthermore, entire artworks, like Dostoevsky's *Notes From the Underground*, can be devoted to the representation of a character and his mentality. Likewise, the representational resources of entire artworks, such as *Lord of the Flies*, can be devoted to presenting the content of human situations that through group interaction manifest distinctively anthropomorphic properties like barbarity (call this a *social* anthropomorphic property). Thus, the content of entire artworks can be the kind of thing to which mental-property terms can be applied. So premise #3 looks false.

Perhaps the attempt will be made to reject these counterexamples on the grounds that these are cases of fictional representations and fictional characters, so the attribution of expressive properties to them is not really literal. But this objection fails for two reasons. First, there can be expressive artworks that are nonfictions (histories, biographies and documentaries) whose principal subjects are not fictional characters. And second, and more importantly, when we apply mental-property terms like "deadpan" to fictional characters, our usage is no less literal than when we apply them to real people. When we say that Fox Mulder is deadpan, we are not using "deadpan" in any extended or figurative sense of the term. We are using it in the same sense that we say that "Al Gore is deadpan." That is, the criteria for applying "deadpan" to Fox Mulder and to Al Gore are the same.

The distinction between literal versus metaphorical does not coincide with the distinction between fictional versus nonfictional. What is literal in fictional discourse abides by the same linguistic rules as what is literal in nonfictional discourse. Therefore, even though our counterexamples two paragraphs ago were drawn from fiction, that does not entail that they are not literal. So the objection against premise #3 stands.

Our objection here relies upon pointing out that some of the representational contents of some artworks are proper bearers of mental-property terms. Perhaps the exemplification theorist will respond that the relevant representational contents of these artworks are only parts of artworks. Consequently, we have only shown that mental-property terms are applicable to parts of artworks, not that they are applicable to whole artworks. Even if this were correct, it would not be much of a victory for the exemplification theorist, since generally when we attribute an expressive property to an artwork, we are directing attention only to parts of the work, not every inch of it.

And even when we use an expressive term to summarize an entire work, we are generally referring only to its dominant or most salient property, which if it involves the representation of a character can be connected to a proper bearer of a mental-property term. We call the *X-Files* deadpan because this property in large measure attaches to its major characters and, since they dominate the story, the expressive properties that attach to them suffuse the story as a whole, giving it its pervasive affective coloration. And this, among other things to be discussed below, is what prompts us to call the *X-Files* deadpan.

Undoubtedly, the exemplification theorist will object that these sorts of examples confuse representation with expression. Representing a character who is angry is different from being expressive of the property of anger. But King Lear is not only represented as a man who is mad; he is portrayed as behaving, on the moor, in a mad manner. His behavior expresses madness – it manifests the characteristic appearance of madness. If the same behavior expresses madness in everyday life, then so does Lear's. The actor expresses madness through Lear who, as a human being (albeit it a fictional one), is the right sort of entity to take on a mental-property term like madness. Thus, the actor's performance, an artwork, can be said to express madness literally.

Of course, the representation of characters and groups are not the only loci of expressivity that we need to consider in refuting premise #3. Artworks may not only contain characters who possess mental states literally. Artworks also contain points of view where the possession of a point of view presupposes the kinds of entities that can possess mental states literally. To see what is meant here by a point of view, recall that many artworks have viewpoints that diverge from the viewpoints of the characters in its story.

In the beginning of the film *Pulp Fiction*, the viewpoint of the young men who are about to be shot is that of high anxiety, but the film regards their plight as amusing. The point of view of the film is detached, cool, and sardonic. And this leads us to attribute the quality of irony to the film. Moreover, when we apply the terms ironic, detached, and cool to the point of view of *Pulp Fiction*, we are doing it in the same literal way that we might describe the attitude of a friend.

Point-of-view talk, of course, assumes that there is someone whose point of view it is. And points of view are proper bearers of mental-property terms, because points of view belong to or are attached to persons. In the case of a film like *Pulp Fiction*, the ironic point of view may belong to the director of the film, Quentin Tarantino. Of course, it may turn out that Quentin Tarantino is really a very forthright and feeling type of guy, and that the point of view of the film is not actually his – that he's only wearing the mask or playing the role of being detached and ironic. Nevertheless, the point of view still belongs to the right kind of entity, since even if Tarantino is only playing a role, there is a character, the implied author or narrative persona, whose point of view he projects, much in the manner of an actor performing a character.

As we've seen, fictional characters bear mental properties literally. The implied author or narrative persona is also a fictional character – the "voice" who tells the story from a certain point of view. Since there is no problem in saying that fictional characters bear their mental properties literally, there is no problem saying that fictional characters who are implied authors or narrative personas bear their mental properties literally. Moreover, since their points of view are connected to the right sorts of entities (fictional sentient beings), expressive properties are attributable to them literally.

Artworks may have points of view, and these may belong either to their actual creators or to implied authors (or even sets of actual creators or implied authors) where the latter are to be understood on the model of fictional characters. Thus, artworks with points of view are the kinds of things that can bear mental properties. An entire artwork can articulate the point of view of its actual or its implied author. Thus, artworks and parts of artworks can be the bearers of mental properties in virtue of their points of view. Artworks can express human qualities literally through the points of view of their actual and/or implied authors.

Lyric poems are an excellent example of this. They are exercises in elaborating points of view. Lyric poems articulate the attitudes and emotions of a speaker, who may be the actual author or a persona. The poet gives us access to the speaker's inner life in such a way that a picture of the speaker's emotional state emerges – that is, the distinctive feel of the speaker's attitude about such and such is rendered manifest. It is not simply stated. Rather, its ingredients – the desires, beliefs, intentions, perceptions and values – that give rise to it are presented so that the properties of the relevant feeling become available to the reader for reflection. With lyric poems it is generally the speaker's address that comprises the poem. But the speaker, whether the actual author or a fictional invention, is a suitable bearer of mental properties. So, it is false that artworks are never suitable bearers of mental properties. And for the same reasons, it is generally the case that lyric poems are literally expressive of human qualities.

We have been arguing against the third premise of the exemplification theorist's argument. Now it is time to turn to the second premise – that if artworks possess expressive properties literally, then they must be the kinds of things that can bear mental properties. This is offered as part of the definition of what it is to possess expressive properties literally. The premise presupposes that it is a necessary condition of the literal possession of a property that the alleged bearer of the property be the kind of thing that can have a mental state. That is, "x possesses expressive qualities literally only if x possesses mental states."

We can begin to examine this assertion with an uncontroversial example, the face of a St. Bernard dog. It is expressive of sadness. Of course, this is not a counterexample to the claim under examination, since presumably St. Bernards possess mental states. But why do we say that the face of the St. Bernard is expressive of sadness? The face of the St. Bernard is still expressive of sadness, even after the dog has eaten all the chow it wants, a point in time when it is as happy as dogs get. Its face is sad, independently of its mental state.

What leads us to attribute sadness to a St. Bernard's face is its configuration, which we call "sad," the dog's mental state, if it has any, notwithstanding. The face simply looks sad to us. We do not mean to make a metaphor when we say that the St. Bernard's looks sad. We are reporting how the face literally looks to us. The configuration of the dog's face is sad-looking, where "sad-looking" is a literal description of its appearance.

Undoubtedly, we call such configurations sad (or sad-looking) because similar facial configurations in humans are associated with psychological states of sadness – that is, similar configurations are characteristic of sadness. They strike us as sad. So, sometimes we attribute expressive properties to things because of their configuration – the way they look or sound – irrespective of whatever, if any mental states, they possess. In fact, we attribute expressive properties to things on the basis of their configuration, even when they are not animate objects.

Recall, for instance, the example of the weeping willow tree. Like the face of the St. Bernard dog, it strikes us as doleful. That is why we call this particular member of the genus Salix a *weeping* willow tree. When we say that the weeping willow tree is sad, we are doing that in virtue of how it looks; we mean that the tree is sad-looking; it gives the appearance of sadness. This is probably due to the fact that certain features of the tree resemble certain perceptible features of sad people – for example, sad people often slump.

A person with her head and shoulders drooped exhibits one of the characteristic appearances of sadness. Such a person is sad-looking. When we say she is sad-looking, we are not speaking metaphorically, but literally. We are offering a literal description of the way in which she looks to us. Similarly, when we call the weeping willow tree sad (sad-looking), we are offering a literal description of its perceptible configuration. Somehow, probably by resemblance, the tree reminds us of the characteristic appearance of sad people. Thus, when we say the weeping willow tree is sad, we are saying that it is sad-looking.

Human beings manifest certain outward, physiognomic features that are typically expressive of their psychological states – in the way that frowns and slumped shoulders are associated with sadness. Moreover, nonhuman things, like dogs and trees, can remind us of these features. Perhaps we are prone to see human physiognomic features in nature so readily because detecting the emotional states of others is so important to our survival. Thus, natural selection has invested us with such a hair-trigger capacity to recognize the "shape" of emotion in others that it often kicks in even when we are attending to nonhuman things. But, be that as it may, it is the case that we do tend to see features of nonhuman and even nonsentient objects as exhibiting the physiognomy of human feeling states. That is just how they look to us. Literally.

We see the gnarled branches of barren trees and call them anguished because they call to mind the twisted appearance of human suffering. Of course, if we call the tree anguished, we do not literally mean that it is suffering. But that does not entail that we are not speaking literally. For we are not saying that the tree is suffering (that it possesses a psychological state), but rather that it is anguished-looking – that it exhibits characteristic aspects of the physiognomy of anguish. And that attribution is literal; the tree does look anguished, however psychologists finally explain why it strikes us so.

The premise (#2) that "If artworks possess expressive properties literally, then they must be the kinds of things that can bear mental properties" presupposes that "If anything possesses expressive properties literally, then it must be the kind of thing that can bear mental properties." But our tree examples call this underlying assumption into question. For sometimes expressive-property terms are ascribed literally to the configuration or appearance of things that do not bear mental properties. Moreover, this opens up the possibility that sometimes we attribute expressive properties in this way to the configurations of artworks which, in turn, would undermine premise #2.

At this point, the defender of premise #2 is likely to say that when we refer to the willow tree as weeping, we are still trading in metaphors – still not speaking literally – even if we are referring to the configurational appearance of the tree. But this seems specious. For even if "weeping willow" was a live metaphor once upon a time (which is open to doubt), it is now a dead metaphor, and dead metaphors are metaphors that have become literal. When we speak of the "hands of a clock," "hands," if it ever was a metaphor, is no longer. Now it serves to describe literally certain features of clocks. Similarly, when we speak of "weeping willow trees," "weeping" is no longer metaphorical. It has become part of the literal description of a member of the genus Salix. It pertains to the look of the tree literally.

Likewise, when we speak of a furious storm or of nasty weather, though we do not mean that the climate is literally angry or mean-spirited, we are not speaking metaphorically. Rather we are saying that they remind us of the characteristic observable behavior of angry and mean-spirited people. A furious storm reminds us of how the behavior of a furious person appears. If this ever was a metaphor, now it is not. "Furious" is a literal description of how certain storms appear to us.

But if this talk of trees and pounding waves is persuasive, then we sometimes apply anthropomorphic terms as literal descriptions of inanimate configurations. That is, expressive properties are some-times applied literally to things that are not the bearers of mental states. This conclusion, moreover, is supported by the St. Bernard's unhappy frown as well, since frowns don't have mental states, but we have no difficulty describing the configuration of the St. Bernard's face as "unhappy."

So, sometimes we attribute expressiveness literally to things that lack mental states as descriptions of their configuration. Moreover, this conclu-sion, if correct, has significant implications for artworks. A great deal of orchestral music is described in terms of expressive properties. We say that the second movement of Beethoven's *Eroica* is sad. Perhaps that is like our description of the St. Bernard's frown – a literal description of a configuration.

Music often sounds – due to its dynamics, tempi, and tensions – in ways that remind us, almost automatically, of characteristic human feeling states, and we use the relevant feeling terminology to describe literally the configurations that we hear. We say certain chords sound ominous or cheerful as a way of describing literally the way in which they strike us. Not only is calling the *Dies Irae* foreboding a dead metaphor; it is how the configuration of notes and cadences actually sounds to us. It is literally foreboding. It is foreboding-sounding music.

Similar observations can be made with respect to other genres of art that, along with orchestral music, do not possess human characters – such as abstract painting, sculpture and architecture. Often we use expressive terminology in order to characterize their configurational properties. To say the prison looks sinister is not only a dead metaphor, it is how the building appears to us, even if we do not know it is a prison. To describe a standard prison as sinister-looking hardly seems metaphorical. Likewise, the steeples on a Gothic cathedral might be said to be expressive of aspiration, since they remind us of the look of human prayer, stretching upwards toward heaven.

There is, then, a configurational use of expressive terminology that applies literally to the appearance of inanimate objects, including art objects, which objects do not possess psychological states. The supposition (premise #2) that if artworks possess expressive properties literally, they must be bearers of mental states, therefore is false. We can literally attrib-ute expressive properties to artworks in virtue of their perceptible configurations.

Artworks can be sad, sinister, aspiring, or joyous in virtue of their con-figurational appearance. In many cases, this may be the result of the way in which they resemble how certain human qualities characteristically feel, look, or sound. Sad music may be low and slow because that is how we feel when we are sad, or the way sad people usually sound. In this manner, sad music may serve to exhibit, manifest, and bring to our attention distinctive human qualities.

To sum up: the argument that expressive properties *must be* attributed to artworks metaphorically fails to go through for two reasons. First, since there are some artworks that are the sorts of things that can be said to support the application of mental state language literally, then, even if it were the case that expression requires the capacity for mental states, some (indeed many) artworks would meet the requirement. But second, given the configurational use of expressive terminology, it is not the case that the application of expressive terminology restricts its genuine applicability only to objects that possess mental states. Orchestral music can be literally expressive in the configurational sense, though orchestral music lacks a mental life.

Moreover, the notion that expressive properties can only be ascribed to artworks metaphorically seems unlikely since in many cases, the basic way that we have to refer to certain of the configurational properties of artworks (such as the spriteliness of a painting) is to use anthropomorphic terminology. That is, there is no better, more straightforward way of talking about the artworks in question. Thus, ascribing anthropomorphic terms to such artworks should not be misunderstood as a matter of an optional, ornamental, metaphorical description. Rather, it is literal.

We have spent quite a lot of time criticizing the argument that the attribution of expressive properties to art is always metaphorical. However, the fruits of our labor have not been purely negative, since in the course of refuting premises #2 and #3 of the argument for exclusively metaphorical attributions of expressive properties to artworks, we have learnt quite a lot about how we go about saying justifiably that artworks are expressive of some human quality.

First, we have learnt that there is not only one set of considerations that come into play when we attribute expressive qualities to artworks. Sometimes we make such attributions on the basis of characters – individual characters, including implied authors, and characters collectively interacting. Sometimes the attributions are made in virtue of the points of view artworks exhibit. In these cases, expressive properties are often intimately related to that which the artwork represents. But we can also justifiably attribute expressive properties to nonrepresentational artworks, like orchestral music, by virtue of their configurational features.

We have argued that all these ways of attributing expressive terms to artworks are quite literal. So attributing expressive properties to artworks is not always metaphorical. But perhaps sometimes it is; perhaps sometimes it even involves homologies. So, one lesson of this chapter is that there is a plurality of ways that we go about attributing expressive properties to artworks.

Moreover, certain of these ways seem to figure more prominently with regard to some artforms rather than others. The attribution of expressive properties to artworks in virtue of characters and points of view seems dominant in the narrative arts, including poetry. With respect to non-representational arts, notably music, but also abstract painting, sculpture, architecture and so on, there is probably greater reliance on the attribution of expressive properties in virtue of configurational features.

Of course, this is not an absolute difference, but a proportionate difference. Literature, film, video, drama, narrative painting, dramatic dance, and so on have configurational features too (such as rhythm, composition, rhyme, and so on) and quite often these configurational features contribute to our ascription of expressive properties to them. And even abstract works can sometimes be connected to points of view that support attributions of expressive properties. Thus, though some artforms customarily gravitate toward certain primary routes for eliciting expressive uptake, other artforms, grossly speaking, exploit other avenues, or, at least, exploit different avenues with different emphases. Each artform probably shares the same general strategies for expression with other artforms, but some combine them in proportionately different ways. If literature employs character and points of view primarily, with configurational features usually in a subservient role, pure orchestral music relies far more heavily on configuration, with points of view and representational elements, where such works contain them, usually playing a far lesser role.

Chapter summary

The relation of art to expression is an especially central one. Art presents the world to us replete with expressive properties. We are shown events, like deaths, love affairs, and victories, swathed in human feeling. Art makes the world emotionally accessible, often in an immensely perspicuous way, showing us things with their human qualities manifest or foregrounded. Metaphorically speaking, art humanizes the world for us – it presents things to us in a humanly approachable way. It enables us to explore the world feelingly while at the same time we explore the world of feeling, its contours and its possibilities. Undeniably, this is one of the great attractions of art for us. Moreover, this is reflected in the way we talk about art – so much of our discourse is about the human qualities that art brings to our attention, such as the hopefulness of a piece of music, the stateliness of a painting, or the poignancy of a dance.

Theoretical awareness of the importance of feeling in the arts became especially pronounced at the end of the eighteenth century, perhaps as a result of Romanticism and the rise of absolute music. This influence resulted in a notable subjective turn in artistic practice throughout the nineteenth and early twentieth centuries that continues today. Philosophers, probably reflecting on that practice, developed what in this chapter we have called expression theories of art.

The main idea of expression theories is that all art is expressive of emotion. The transmission theory and the solo expression theory are two of the leading versions of the expression approach. Both theories see art as essentially involved with the expression of emotion. In this, expression theories of art provided a useful corrective to prevailing representational theories of art. However, like representational theorists, expression theorists overstated their case. Much art is expressive, but it is not the case that all art is expressive of emotion. A great deal of twentieth-century art is preoccupied with ideas, rather than emotions. And a great deal of art, past and present, is aimed at provoking perceptual pleasure, rather than exploring emotional possibilities.

Thus expression theories of art fail as universal theories of all art. Nevertheless, even if expression theories of art are false, since expression is so central a feature of art, we still need to address it theoretically. We need to ask, for example, not only what we mean by calling an artwork expressive but also how we go about justifiably attributing expressive properties to artworks.

One view is that such attributions are always essentially metaphorical. But we have seen that there is not one, but rather a number of ways in which we ascribe expressive terms like sadness and joy to artworks, and, furthermore, that several of them are literal, not metaphorical. Moreover, the discovery that there is more than one way to apply expressive terms to artworks is itself a worthwhile finding, since it gives us a clearer picture than is commonly available of one of our most pervasive activities with respect to art.

Annotated reading

For students interested in expression theories of art, two classic positions are represented by Leo Tolstoy and R.G. Collingwood. Tolstoy presents a version of what we have called a transmission theory in his book *What is Art?*, translated by Almyer Maude (New York: Macmillan Publishing Company, 1985). Collingwood defends a version of the solo expression theory in *Principles of Art* (Oxford: Clarendon Press, 1938). Another highly influential statement of an expression theory of art is Susanne Langer's *Feeling and Form* (New York: Scribner's, 1953).

For material on Romanticism, consult M.H. Abrams, *A Glossary of Literary Terms*, 6th edition (Fort Worth, Texas: Harcourt Brace Jovanovich College Publishers, 1993); and Aidan Day, *Romanticism* (London: Routledge, 1996).

An introduction to theories of expression can be found in Chapter 7 of Monroe Beardsley's *Aesthetics: Problems in the Philosophy of Criticism* (Indianapolis, Indiana: Hackett Publishing Company, 1981). Nelson Goodman advances a view of expression as metaphorical exemplification in Chapter 2 of his *Languages of Art* (Indianapolis, Indiana: Hackett Publishing Company, 1976). For criticism of the view that expression is metaphorical exemplification, see: Guy Sircello, *Mind and Art: An Essay on the Varieties of Expression* (Princeton, NJ: Princeton University Press, 1972); and Peter Kivy, *Sound Sentiment: An Essay on the Musical Emotions* (Philadelphia: Temple University Press, 1984). *The Concept of Expression* by Alan Tormey (Princeton, NJ: Princeton University Press, 1971) also contains a major discussion of artistic expression.

There are many articles on expression in the philosophical literature. Good places to start reading are: Robert Stecker, "Expression of Emotion in (Some of) the Arts," *Journal of Aesthetics and Art Criticism*, Vol. XLII, no. 4 (Summer 1984), pp. 409–418; Bruce Vermazen, "Expression as Expression," *Pacific Philosophical Quarterly*, vol. 67, no. 3 (July 1986), pp. 196–224; and Ismay Barwell, "How Does Art Express Emotion?" *Journal of Aesthetics and Art Criticism*, Vol. XLV, no. 2 (Winter, 1986), pp. 175–181.

CHAPTER 3
Art and form

3
Art and form

Part I
Art as form

Formalism

Like the expression theory of art, formalism arose as a reaction to representational theories of art. And also like the expression theory, it was prompted by striking shifts in artistic practice. The artistic practices that were particularly relevant to the emergence of formalism were the developments in painting and sculpture that have come to be known as modern art or modernism. Including Cubism and Minimalism, this art gravitates toward abstraction. Modern artists eschewed pictorial illustration, composing paintings out of often nonrepresentational shapes and masses of color. Their aim was not to capture the perceptual appearances of the world, but often to make images noteworthy for their visual organization, form, and arresting design.

Undoubtedly, one important cause of the evolution of this type of modern art was the advent of photography. Photography facilitated the production of pictures of remarkable verisimilitude both automatically and cheaply. Families could obtain portraits easily without the expenses in time and money incurred by posing for a painting. By the late nineteenth and early twentieth century, photography looked like it might put painting as imitation out of business. Artists had to find a new occupation, or at least a new style, in order to survive.

Abstraction was one of the ways they found to adapt to changing circumstances. From the turn of the twentieth century onwards, more and more painters became involved in the creation of nonobjective paintings that are primarily concerned with the articulation of the surface of the painting rather than with reference to "nature." Instead of treating the picture as a piece of glass – a mirror or a transparent windowpane onto the world – painters began to explore the very texture of the glass itself. Rather than looking into it or through it, they turned their attention *at* it. This was painting for the sake of painting – painting that experimented with the possibilities of shape, line and color – not painting for the sake of showing the world.

The evolution of modern art occurred gradually. At first, impressionists "dissolved" the solidity of the picture plane, though one could still recognize objects in their paintings. But stand up close to an impressionist canvas and it becomes a pure surface on which the play of colors interacts delightfully. Then Cézanne carried the experimentation further, reducing objects to their underlying, geometrical shapes, like squares, spheres and cubes, until still lifes of recognizable fruits showed forth their basic visual structure. Cubism was not far behind. And with Cubism there dawned the era of abstract art, which has dominated much of twentieth-century painting.

As we saw in previous chapters, the representational theory of art ill-suited this sort of painting, since much abstract art represents nothing at all. Modern art, therefore, required a new sort of theory in order to be enfranchised as art. In the English-speaking world, perhaps the most influential theorist of the new art was Clive Bell. His book, *Art*, taught generations of viewers how to understand modern art. If nothing else, this book heralded a revolution in taste.

According to Bell, what determines whether or not a painting is art is its possession of *significant form*. That is, a painting is art if and only if it has a salient design. Though the importance of form was made especially apparent by the tendency of modern art toward abstraction, significant form was a property said to be possessed by all artworks, past, present and future. Significant form is comprised of arrangements of lines, colors, shapes, volumes, vectors, and space (two-dimensional space, three-dimensional space and the interaction thereof). Genuine art, on this view, addresses the imagination like the figures of Gestalt psychology, prompting the viewer to fill the artwork in such a way that we apprehend it as an organized configuration of lines, colors, shapes, spaces, vectors, and so on.

To see what Bell was getting at, consider a painting like David's *The Oath of the Horatii*. Though representational, the painting is particularly notable for its structure. It is centripetal, pulling the viewer inwards toward the center of the image where the arms and swords of the Horatii form a veritable X, a virtual target toward which all the rest of the force lines and vectors in the composition drive the eye. For Bell, it is the unified structure of paintings like this one that make them art. Its Gestalt properties compel our attention and encourage us to dwell on and contemplate the ways in which the composition interacts with our perceptual capacities, thereby serving as pretext for us to explore our sensibility – to take note, for example, of how a particular diagonal line draws our attention to the foreground.

Clearly, this view of the art of painting is well suited for discussing modern abstract art. With its emphasis on structure, it tracks what is valuable in nonobjective and nonfigurative art more accurately than representational theories of art. As a theory of new directions in twentieth-century painting, it was obviously superior to the representational theory of art. Moreover, formalism also had the advantage of showing Europeans the value (the formal values) inherent in much of the nonimitative and "distorted" artworks from non-Western cultures which were beginning to appear with increasingly greater frequency in the museums of North Atlantic societies. Thus, formalism recommended itself not only because it identified what was important about modern art, but also because it provided a way to appreciate much otherwise inaccessible tribal art as well. That is, the relevant tribal artifacts, even if they deviated from the canons of strict verisimilitude, like modern abstract works, were art because they possessed significant form.

However, theorists like Bell did not argue simply that formalism was the best theory for newly emerging and newly acknowledged forms of art. Their claims were more ambitious. They maintained that formalism revealed the secret of all art for all times. They advanced formalism as the comprehensive theory of the nature of all art. They claimed that where the historical works, like *The Oath of the Horatii*, were artworks it was because they too possessed significant form.

Of course, most of the work in the tradition was representational. But the formalists claimed that where those works were genuine artworks, it was not, contra to the imitation theory of art, in virtue of their representational features that they enjoyed art status, but in virtue of their formal properties, such as unity. Thus, a consequence of formalism was that our idea of art history needed to be reconceived. Supposed works of art that had been counted as such merely because they were representational were to be dropped from the canon, while nonrepresentational or "distorted" works, like tribal carvings, that possessed significant form, had to be incorporated into art history.

From the formalist perspective art could be representational. But unlike the representational theorist, the formalist regarded representation as an incidental rather than as an essential property of artworks. Significant form was the hallmark of art. Indeed, formalists worried that representation could even get in the way of the appreciation of the formal interpretation of artwork – swamping it in floods of anecdotal observation.

This did not lead the formalist to declare that representation automatically disqualified a candidate from the order of art. Works like *The Oath of the Horatii* would be classified as artworks, but not in light of their representational content, only in terms of their formal properties. For the formalist, the representational content of an artwork is *strictly irrelevant* to its status as art. Form is all that makes the difference.

Formalism found its natural home in the realm of painting. Nevertheless, it was easy to extend the view to other arts. Obviously, most orchestral music is not representational. This was always a vexation for the representational theory of art. But it is scarcely controversial to describe music in terms of the temporal play of aural forms. Listening for the recurring themes and variations and the sequencing of audio structures is ground-zero for musical appreciation. In fact, formalism provides an even more comprehensive approach with respect to music than the expression theory, since as we saw in the last chapter, not all music is expressive. However, arguably, it all possesses form. Could it even be music, the formalist might ask rhetorically, if it did not have form? Formless sound, so it might be said, just is not music.

The tenets of formalism were also extended to dance, due to the influential criticism of theorists like André Levinson, while the notion of form became a shibboleth in modern architectural theory. Literature might appear to be a more difficult artform to explicate exclusively in terms of form. However, not only could formalists point to the centrality of features of poetry like meter, rhyme and generic structures (such as the sonnet *form*); but stories too possess formal features such as narrative structures and alternating points of view that theorists could claim lay at the heart of the literary experience. Formalists, of course, could not deny that most literature possessed representational content. Instead, formalists, notably the Russian Formalists, argued that such content only serves to motivate literary devices, and ultimately it is the play of literary devices that accounts for the art status of poems, novels and the like – at least in those cases that are truly artistic.

In certain ways, formalism is a very egalitarian doctrine. Previously, certain pictures were classified as artworks in virtue of their possession of certain highly valued representational content – historical subjects, religious subjects, mythological subjects, and so on. But under formalism, anything could be art – anything could play in the game – so long as it possessed significant form. Formalism revised how one thought about art. Some amorphous works which were nevertheless representational were cashiered from the order of art, while other hithertofore lowly, disenfranchised works, such as ingenious decorative art, could assume their rightful position alongside artworks with uplifting subject matter. Thus, formalism can acknowledge the artistry of the work of women quilters, for instance, that the representational theory of art ignores.

But formalism is not simply attractive because it is open to a greater range of achievement than representational theories of art. It can also claim several powerful arguments in its favor. The first of these can be called the "common denominator argument." This argument begins with the unexceptionable presupposition that if anything is to count as a necessary condition of art status, then it must be a property had by every artwork. So much is built into the definition of what it is to be a necessary condition.

Next the formalist invites us to consider rival claimants for the role of necessary conditions for art status. Form, of course, is one. But as we've seen, so is the possession of representational and/or expressive properties. Yet, not all artworks are representational. Think of many string quartets, as well as purely decorative abstract designs, such as the work of a Josef Albers, Dan Flavin, or a Kenneth Noland. Nor are all works of art possessed of expressive qualities; as we saw in the previous chapter, some artists even aspire to remove expressive qualities from their work, striving to create works of pure formal interest, such as many of the abstract ballets of George Balanchine. Thus, not all works of art are expressive.

That leaves us with form as the most viable candidate. Moreover, though we have arrived at this conclusion indirectly by negating competing alternatives, the result rings true directly, since all artworks do seem at the very least to possess form. Form is the common denominator among all artworks, the property that they all share – whether they be paintings, sculpture, drama, photography, film, music, dance, literature, architecture or whatever. At least at first glance, formalism seems to be the most promising hypothesis we've seen so far – one that is much more comprehensive than the representational or expression theories of art.

Stating the argument schematically, then:

1 Only if x is a feature of all artworks is x a plausible contender to be an essential (necessary) feature of art.
2 Either representation or expression or form is a feature of all artworks.
3 Representation is not a feature of all artworks.
4 Expression is not a feature of all artworks.
5 Therefore, form is a feature of all artworks.
6 Therefore, form is a plausible contender to be an essential feature of all artworks.

This argument suggests that form is the most plausible contender (out of the best-known competitors) to serve as a necessary condition for art. So, x is an artwork only if it possesses form. The common denominator argument, however, does not provide us with a sufficient condition for art status, since many things other than art also possess form. Indeed, the condition is too broad as stated, because, in some sense everything might be said to possess form.

Thus, the formalist needs to say that "x is art, only if it possesses *significant* form," though this, of course, will still not differentiate art from many other things, since it is the case that a well-made speech on the economics of dairy farming and a mathematical theorem may, as well, possess significant form. In order to establish that the possession of significant form provides a sufficient condition for art status, the formalist needs another argument. Standardly, the formalist attempts to meet this challenge by adverting to the *function* of artworks in contrast to other things.

Speeches and mathematical theorems may possess significant form, but it is not their primary purpose to display their form. The primary function of a speech about dairy economics is to report on a situation. A mathematical proof is undertaken in order to come to a conclusion. These activities may result in products that are remarkable for their form, but exhibiting their form is not what they are primarily about. If they lacked significant form, they could still be eminently serviceable vehicles for discharging their functions. Art is different from these other activities insofar as it is, so the formalist suggests, uniquely concerned with displaying form.

No other human activity, the formalist alleges, has the exhibition of form as its special or peculiar province of value. It is its primary preoccupation with the exploration of form that demarcates the dominion art from other human practices. Whereas representational content is not irrelevant to economics speeches or mathematical theorems, representation is always strictly irrelevant to artworks.

Art may be concerned with religious or political themes, moral education or philosophical world-views. But so are many other things. Indeed, many other things like sermons, pamphlets, newspaper editorials, and philosophical treatises generally do a better job of conveying cognitive and moral information than art does. What is special about art is that, above all else, it is concerned with discovering formal structures that are designed to encourage our imaginative interplay with them. In fact, many formalists would argue that artworks ultimately contain cognitive, moral and other types of representational content solely in order to motivate the display of formal properties. A sloppy sermon will be accounted a satisfactory one, so long as it moves an audience to divine adoration; but nothing will count as art if it fails to display form significant enough to intrigue us.

The doctrine of formalism accords nicely with many of our intuitions about art. We regard much of the art of the past as worthwhile, despite the fact that the ideas it represents are now known to be obsolete. This contrasts with physics, where discredited theories are long forgotten and rarely consulted. This is so because the primary function of physics is to give us information about the universe. But the information about the universe contained in many past artworks is believed to be wrong. So, why is it that we still read Lucretius's *On the Nature of Things* or Hesiod's *Theogany*? The formalist can explain this; it is due to their formal virtues, as is also the case with the architecture of Angkor Wat, whose representation of the cosmos is known to be false.

Moreover, it often transpires that we criticize certain films for being too message-oriented, while commending other films as being good of their kind. Why is this? The formalist has a ready answer: a dumb, amoral film may be formally interesting – it may deploy its formal devices (editing, camera movement, color schemes, and so on) – in ways that address our sensibility in a compelling manner. In many such films the thematic content is negligible, even silly, but its formal organization is riveting, whereas a film with a big idea, however important and earnestly expressed, may strike us as altogether, as they say, uncinematic.

We may feel with such a big-idea picture that "it's not really a movie, is it?" Or, as the adage goes among film-makers and film viewers: "If you want to send a message, use Western Union." A film with a heartfelt theme may be some kind of sermon, but it is not cinematic art, unless it exhibits significant form. Thus, formalism appears in tune with certain of our intuitions about art, especially about the centrality of formal inventiveness. And this is a tempting consideration on its behalf.

The preceding considerations suggest an argument for the view that a sufficient condition for art is that an artwork is something designed with the primary function of exhibiting significant form. We can call this the function argument.

1   Only if x is a primary function that is unique to art is x a sufficient condition for art.
2   The primary function unique to art is either representation, expression or the exhibition of significant form for its own sake.
3   Representation is not a primary function unique to art.
4   Expression is not a primary function unique to art.
5   Therefore, the primary function unique to art is the exhibition of significant form for its own sake.
6   Therefore, the exhibition of significant form for its own sake is a sufficient condition for art.

Here, it is important to note that by function is meant the purpose that the work is intended or designed to discharge. This qualification is required for two reasons. First, if the notion of an intention is not added, then natural beauties may be counted as artworks, since they may possess significant form, though they are not artworks.

And second, if the simple possession of significant form were the litmus test of art status, then many works of art would have to be discounted just because the artist fails to invest her work with significant form. But artwork is still art, even if it fails to discover a significant form – that is, many artworks are formally inadequate, and bad for that reason, yet they are still artworks. One must allow space in the world for bad art; a theory cannot render bad art nonexistent.

If one counts only work that achieves significant form as art, then only what we now call good art will count as art. But, at the same time, we classify bad art as art too which presupposes, of course, that bad artworks are art. To categorize only good art as art results in a commendatory theory of art, one where art = good art. However, that leaves us at a loss as to where to place bad art. Consequently, in order to avoid making formalism into a commendatory theory, rather than a classificatory theory, we need to add to the formula that an artwork be such that it is *intended* primarily to exhibit significant form. It may fail in its intention. Such should be the story of bad art, according to the formalist.

Representation is not a sufficient condition for art status, since representation is not a function unique to art. Ordinary cereal boxes wear representations on their faces, designed, as they are, to convey information. Nor is expression a function unique to art. Hate-speech is expressive, but almost never art.

On the one hand, representation and expression are too exclusive to serve as necessary conditions for art status. On the other hand, they are not sufficient to distinguish artworks from other things. Consequently, insofar as representation and expression are each both too inclusive and too exclusive, they afford neither necessary nor sufficient conditions for art status. Therefore, formalism appears to offer the most plausible theory of art. That is:

> x is a work of art if and only if x is designed primarily in order to possess and to exhibit significant form.

This theory accords neatly with our experience of much modern art, where we attend primarily to such things as the way in which one block of color advances on the picture plane while another recedes. And formalism does an excellent job of explaining why we still appreciate past art whose representational content is outmoded. The formalist says that we still appreciate its organization – for instance, its compositional unity.

Objections to formalism

Formalism is the doctrine that something is an artwork just in case it is designed with the primary intention that it possess and exhibit significant form. This does not entail that artworks cannot be representational, since representations can have significant form. However, such artifacts are not art because they are representational, but because of the significant form they display or attempt to display. That is, representational content is always strictly irrelevant to the determination of whether or not a candidate is an artwork. Thus, Picasso's *Guernica* is not art because it depicts an aerial bombardment, but because its juxtaposition of figures is arresting.

Unquestionably, formalism picks out what is important with much art. But is it an adequate, comprehensive theory of all art? We can begin to investigate this question by asking whether the *primary* intention to exhibit significant form is a necessary property of all art.

A casual review of art history would suggest that it is not. Much traditional art was religious or political, designed primarily to glorify gods and saints, important religious events, military victories, the coronations of kings, the signing of covenants and treaties, and so on. The primary purposes of the stained glass windows in cathedrals and of illustrations of the life of Buddha are educational – they are meant to enable viewers to recollect important religious doctrines and morals. A great deal of traditional art commemorates events – it is designed to recall to the mind of the viewer historic moments and to remind them of the commitments that such events have bequeathed to them as members of a common culture, race, or nation.

This much is obvious, and such intentions can generally be read off the surface of the works in question. The Arch of Triumph in Paris is primarily designed to celebrate victories; the Lincoln Memorial is designed to observe emancipation. Who could think otherwise? But if many artworks are primarily designed to discharge broader social agendas, then the primary intention to exhibit significant form cannot be a necessary condition for all art, since it should be fairly evident that much art (most art?) is primarily designed with other functions in mind.

To this objection, the formalist may reply that our problem comes from interpreting her requirement in the singular rather than the plural. An artifact, it might be said, can have more than one primary function and these may co-exist. The idea is this. An altarpiece may be designed to observe the resurrection of Jesus and to recall to the viewer the lesson of his sacrifice. That is one of its purposes. However, another purpose of equal weight is that the viewer appreciate the design of the work. The artist has two purposes: to celebrate the resurrection of Christ and to make a beautiful object. Both are simultaneously in the forefront of the artist's intention.

The formalist might add that this latter intention is why we visit churches of denominations of which we are not members – to appreciate the obviously intended beauty and subtlety of the work. The formalist will argue that such works had to be designed with the intention that the work be so appreciated, lest the artist would not have lavished such care in the execution of its design. Thus artifacts that have been made with the primary intention to acquit some social function will, if they are genuine artworks, also be made with another equally motivating and, therefore, primary intention, namely the intention to exhibit significant form for viewers to appreciate.

Or, if the notion of two or more *primary* intentions sounds virtually self-contradictory to you, the formalist may accommodate your misgivings by weakening his view so that it claims no more than that something is an artwork only if the artifact in question has been made with an intention (which may or may not be the primary intention, but only a secondary, tertiary, or even more remote intention) that the work exhibit significant form. Surely that does not appear unreasonable. Why would the artist have taken the pains to create a significant formal arrangement, unless she intended it to be exhibited and engaged?

However, this conceptual maneuver is inadequate. For example, in cultures all around the world, certain demon figures are common. The primary function of these figures is protection – they are supposed to ward off intruders and trespassers. They tell outsiders "Beware of the demon," or they are intended to cause the illusion that the demon is already on the loose. These figures are meant to scare people off.

Furthermore, we typically count such sculptures as artworks. They populate museums worldwide and are coveted pieces in private collections. Yet it is immensely implausible to suppose that these works are designed with any intention to exhibit significant form. They will not frighten anyone away, if they simultaneously invite the appreciation of significant form. Their creators must know this. So they cannot have intended the works to exhibit significant form.

Now it may be the case that these demon figures possess significant form, but it is not part of the artist's intention – primary or otherwise – to display it, since if the artist exhibits significant form successfully, he risks cancelling out the terrifying aspect of his work, thereby defeating, or, at least, compromising his purposes. Thus, it cannot be the case universally that the intention to exhibit significant form underwrites every artwork.

Counterexamples such as these are likely to incline the formalist to rethink the way in which this necessary condition is framed. Problems seem to be erupting with respect to the requirement that the exhibition of significant form be designed or intentional. So, why not avoid the problems by dropping the expectation that the display be intentional and merely require that the artworks possess and exhibit significant form? But, as we have already seen, that way lies trouble.

On the one hand, there is the aforementioned problem of bad art. Art may be bad because it lacks significant form, but it is still art. The imagined revision of the significant form requirement leaves us with no way to speak of bad art, but only of nonart. But bad art is not nonart; Antarctica is nonart. Bad art is still art, though art of an inferior sort. So the revision of the condition is too exclusive; it cannot serve as a necessary condition for art status.

On the other hand, there is also the problem of nature. Nature can have significant form – just study the play of color of country foliage in autumn or listen to the rhythms of a rippling brook. But nature is not art. Where the requirement is that the possession and exhibition of significant form be designed, the formalist can exclude nature from the corpus of art, since the beauties of nature have been intended by no one. But once the intention requirement is dropped, then the formalist's definition must count nature as art, and this is too inclusive. So by jettisoning the requirement of the relevant intention, the revised formulation fails to provide a sufficient condition for art status.

Thus, the formalist appears trapped in a dilemma. Either she regards the intention to display significant form as a necessary condition of art status or she does not. If she does, then her condition will be too exclusive, discounting the art status of demonic sculptures. But if she does not regard the pertinent intention as required, then she must confront the problem of excluding bad art, while including nature under her conception of art. None of these alternatives seem particularly savory ones.

Nor is the intention component the only unstable part of the formalist's theory. The notion of significant form itself is regrettably indeterminate. What is it exactly? The formalist has given us no way to discriminate between significant form and insignificant form. We have been given some examples, but no principles to tell the difference. What makes one juxtaposition of shapes significant, and another not? We have no way to decide. Thus, obscurity lies at the heart of formalism; the theory is useless, because its central term is undefined.

The formalist might say that a work has significant form, if it is arresting. But that is not enough, since a work can be arresting for reasons other than formal ones, or even in virtue of formal properties that are not significant in the formalist's sense – such as its unusual monotone color. How, without a characterization of significant form, will we know whether a work is arresting because it possesses significant form, rather than for some other reason?

Often formalists attempt to repair this shortcoming by saying that significant form is such that it causes a special state of mind in viewers. But that is an unhelpful suggestion, unless the formalist can define that state of mind. Otherwise we are left with one undefined concept posing as a definition of another – which is effectively equivalent to having no definition at all.

Nor can the formalist say that significant form causes that peculiar state of mind in percipients that is the apprehension of significant form, since such a definition is circular. We would have to already possess the concept of significant form in order to tell whether a mental state was indeed an apprehension of significant form.

In the next chapter, we will look at further attempts to develop the idea that artworks evoke certain distinctive states of mind. Until then we cannot fully foreclose this possible way of defining significant form. However, at this point, the burden of proof falls to the formalist, since, on the face of it, it appears unlikely that there is a distinctive state of mind elicited by all artworks. That is, since there are so many different kinds of artworks that require all sorts of different kinds of mental responses, it is doubtful that there is just one mental state that they all share. Does a feminist novel really engender the same kind of mental state that a Fabergé egg does? Until such hurdles can be crossed, the suggestion that significant form can be defined in terms of the distinctive mental state it provokes is moot.

But perhaps the formalist will say that we really don't need a definition of significant form here. Everybody knows what it is. Everyone can pick it out. It involves proportions, notably ones like the Golden Section, symmetries, asymmetries, balances, striking imbalances, tension, unity, contrast, and the like. In ordinary language we can pick out examples of significant form with a surprising degree of convergence. We may not call them significant form. But if asked to pick out examples of works of art with strong formal qualities – especially unity – we can do it with a very high ratio of agreement. We know what to look for: repeating motifs, equilibria, strong contrasts, symmetries, and so on. We can apply the notion of significant form without a definition. Therefore, the formalist suggests, the lack of a characterization of significant form is not the huge impediment that we have made it out to be.

But if we take the formalist at his word and use our ordinary language intuitions to apply the concept of significant form, there are many counterexamples to the thesis that significant form (and/or the intention to exhibit it) is a necessary condition for art. The composer John Cage created a piece called 4' 33" which is generally regarded as a major work of twentieth-century art. It is comprised of a set of instructions: a pianist is to sit at a piano and open a score, but not to strike the keys. The performance consists of all the ambient sounds that occur within the ensuing interval of four minutes and thirty-three seconds. If someone coughs and scrapes their chair along the floor, that is part of the piece. If a cellular phone rings, or a moving van rumbles past outside, that too is part of the piece. Likewise if someone turns on a radio and we hear Howard Stern preening. Then the pianist closes the score and the piece is over.

Obviously, what is heard from performance to performance will vary with locations. The sounds that make up 4' 33" have no predetermined formal order; the composition is aleatoric in that regard. The point of the piece is to draw our attention to the often neglected sounds of everyday life – to contemplate them at least for four minutes and thirty-three seconds.

This is an artwork, but if we use our ordinary language intuitions, we will not say that it possesses significant form. Indeed, it will appear formless to us – as formless as the array of everyday sounds that accost us on a daily basis. Nor is it plausible to attribute to Cage the intention to exhibit significant form. He has contrived a situation where formlessness is the designated object of our attention. But if with respect to the criteria inherent in ordinary language it is possible, as in the case of 4′ 3″, to make an intentionally formless artwork successfully, then neither significant form nor the intention to exhibit it is a necessary condition for art.

Moreover, Cage is not the only artist to explore formlessness – in our ordinary language sense – intentionally. The sculptor Robert Morris is another. His piece *Steam* emits steam from under a bed of stones, and the resulting "figure" is as formless as fog. Likewise his 1968 sculpture *Untitled (Threadwaste)* is made up of threadwaste, asphalt, mirrors, copper tubing and felt, scattered over the floor, while, in the same year, he composed *Untitled (Dirt)* where, on a bed of dirt, he distributed grease, peat moss, and pieces of brick, steel, aluminum, brass, zinc and felt with apparent randomness. Employing ordinary language, I predict that the first thing that comes to mind upon encountering these pieces is "What a mess!" If we found identical collections of debris on our living room floors, we'd want them cleaned up. And if asked to describe them, I suggest that we'd say they were formless, as formless as garbage heaps (which is what they look like).

Morris's works can be defended as art on several grounds. One can argue that they are about exploring the question of "What is art?" Or, an expression theorist might propose that they are meant to arouse feelings of disgust, or revulsion and to project the quality of abjectness so that audiences can contemplate this feeling, both in terms of its tones and its conditions. But both interpretations require that the works strike us as formless, in the ordinary sense of the word. Thus, contra formalism, there are formless works of art.

Perhaps the formalist will say that these works are not really formless. But the ambient sounds of 4′ 33″ are indiscernible from the ambient sounds of everyday life that we customarily call formless, while the steam and scrap piles that Morris has made are indiscernible from ordinary phenomena that is regarded as amorphous. They lack symmetries, balance, equilibrium, studied contrast and counterpoint, and every other criterion that we typically use to apply the concept of form in common discourse.

What lacks form in life must also lack form in art where the artworks in question are perceptually indiscernible from their real-world counterparts. If mounds of refuse are formless, so are Morris's sculptures. Thus, it is not the case that artworks universally possess and exhibit significant form, so it is false that significant form, as understood in ordinary language, or the intention to produce it is a necessary feature of all art.

As a last resort, the formalist may contend that these works by Cage and Morris actually do possess and exhibit significant form intentionally. For once one understands what these artists are up to, one can see that their choices were apposite. Form follows function. Where the artist wants to call attention to the vagrant sounds of everyday life, the design of 4′ 33″ is brilliant. It gets the job done with deliberate economy and verve. So, appearances notwithstanding, the work of Cage and Morris does exhibit formal virtues.

There is much truth in the preceding argument. However, it is not really available to the formalist at this point in the discussion. For in order to propose an interpretation like this of something like *Untitled (Dirt)*, one would have to know antecedently that it is an artwork and not an ordinary mess on the garage floor. That is, in order to attribute significant form to *Untitled (Dirt)* you would first have to be able to classify it as an artwork. But the formalist cannot do that, since the formalist needs to be able to identify significant form independently in order to classify something as art. He has not defined art, if we must first know whether the candidate is art – in terms of logical priority – in order to determine whether it possesses significant form. That would result in circularity.

In a gesture of desperation, the formalist may say "let's stopping talking about significant form and just talk about form," understood loosely as any relation between the parts of a whole. Something is art, only if it possesses and exhibits form. But this is extremely unhelpful. It does not provide a necessary condition for art, since there are artworks – like the monochrome paintings of Ad Reinhardt, Yves Klein, and Robert Ryman – that have no parts (they are blocks of single colors). Moreover, reading the formalist's theory in this way would defeat any hope of his securing a sufficient condition for art, since everything that has parts probably has form in the loose sense, and not everything is art.

Indeed, in his *Discourse on Metaphysics*, Leibniz notes that everything, no matter how apparently formless, has form in the sense that a mathematical equation can be devised to represent it. But if this is so, form, in the unqualified sense, is not a sufficient condition for anything in particular.

It should also be evident that even if we revert to the earlier statement of the theory – that x is art if and only if it is primarily designed to possess and exhibit significant form – the formalist has not secured a sufficient condition for art. For in our ordinary way of speaking, there are things that are primarily designed to possess and exhibit signifcant form that are not artworks. Consider a mathematical theorem where a proof already exists, but where it is a cumbersome one, involving many steps. A mathematician may decide to produce a more elegant proof of a truth already known. Her objective is not primarily to prove a conclusion, but to exhibit a more economical – as mathematicians say, "a more beautiful" – way of rendering the theorem. Her results have significant form, describable in terms of elegance. But a mathematical proof, even one like this, is never a work of art. Insofar as the formalist's theory forces him to accept it as one, the theory is overly inclusive. Nor is mathematics the only source of counterexamples here. Athletes and chessmasters can intend primarily to exhibit significant form in their activities.

But what of the earlier arguments on behalf of formalism – the common denominator argument and the function argument? By now we have assembled enough considerations to see what is amiss with each of them. We have seen that form, in the ordinary sense, is not a property of all artworks. Thus, the fifth step in the common denominator argument is false, even though it is a logically valid conclusion from earlier premises. That indicates that one of the earlier premises was false. The first premise seems true by definition, while third and fourth premises are the fruits of the preceding two chapters. So the problem, if there is a problem, is with the second premise.

The second premise states that "Either representation, expression, or form is a feature of all artworks." This premise is inadequate because it has not listed all the possible alternatives – both positively and negatively. Negatively, it has overlooked the alternative that there may be no feature that is a feature of all artworks. Positively, it has not enumerated other candidates, such as the ones to be explored in future chapters, that may identify a feature of all artworks. So, step five has been derived illegitimately from a premise that is incomplete. Moreover, as we have seen, when we examine the claim that form is a feature of all artworks independently of the rest of the argument, it is false. So the possession of form is not a necessary condition of art.

Parallel problems beset the function argument. There the fifth step – that the primary function unique to art is the exhibition of significant form for its own sake – is false. Certain mathematical theorems, athletic performances, and chess games may also be meant to exhibit significant form for its own sake. And once again the difficulty can be traced back to the second premise: that the primary function unique to art is either representation, expression, or the exhibition of significant form for its own sake. This premise is flawed just because it ignores the possibilities that there may be no primary function unique to art or that it resides somewhere other than in representation, expression or the expression of form. If the second premise were stated with proper closure (i.e., if all the alternatives were enumerated and explored), step five would not follow. Moreover, the notion that the primary function unique to art is the exhibition of significant form is false anyway. As we have seen, it is too inclusive. Therefore, formalism has failed to establish a sufficient condition for art.

Perhaps the most radical thought advanced by formalism is that representation, where it occurs in artworks, is always strictly irrelevant to art status. It is in virtue of this idea that formalists are often criticized for being politically incorrect, or, at least, insensitive. They regard fascist productions – like *The Triumph of the Will* – as art because it exhibits arresting formal structures cinematically, whereas many politicos are predisposed to classify it not as art, but as obscenity. That is, the politicos think that what *Triumph of the Will* represents is relevant to its art status, while the formalist regards the Nazi representational content as strictly irrelevant.

We cannot adjudicate this particular debate about *Triumph of the Will* here; perhaps the formalist is right in this case. But the deeper formalist supposition – that representation is always strictly irrelevant to art status – is mistaken. The reason for believing this is simply that in a large number of cases artworks possess and exhibit significant form just because of their representational content. That is, in many cases, the possession and exhibition of significant form depend upon the representational properties of the pertinent artworks. Thus, if significant form were, as the formalist alleges, criterion for art status, and if, additionally, in many cases significant form depends upon representation, it could not possibly be the case that representation is always strictly irrelevant to art status.

Consider an example. In Bruegel's *The Fall of Icarus* (see Figure 1), the foreground is dominated by a farmer plowing furrows; in the background, there is a seascape, stretching to the horizon, and some mountains on either side of the shore. As well, there are two ships riding the water. But if you look closely at the lower right-hand corner of the painting, there is also a leg, attached to a submerged body, splashing in the surf.

The leg, of course, belongs to Icarus, who flew so close to the sun that the wax fixative in his wings liquified, plunging him to earth. We know this because of the title of the painting. The painting is expressive of insouciance, observing the irony of the way in which everyday life goes on quietly and imperviously, while legendary events occur unnoticed. But the painting also has significant form – a delightful off-centeredness or asymmetry that underscores the contrast between the quotidian and the momentous.

That is, the narrative center of the painting – the fallen Icarus – is placed off to the side, where he goes almost unremarked; whereas everyday "background" details hold centerstage. Narrative structure and compositional conventions pull in opposite directions in a way that sets up a dynamic formal tension in the painting and in our perception of it. It bounces our

Figure 1 *Landscape with the Fall of Icarus*, Pieter Bruegel the Elder, c. 1558, oil on canvas, mounted on wood, 73.5 × 112 cm, Musées Royaux des Beaux-Arts de Belgique, Brussels.

eye back and forth between the farmer and Icarus. It initiates an interesting formal disturbance in the otherwise tranquil – or deceptively tranquil – scene.

But to appreciate this formal structure it is necessary to attend to the representational content of *The Fall of Icarus*. The pertinent formal tension could not be detected and appreciated – indeed, it would not be there – were the representational elements in the painting strictly irrelevant. From the formalist point of view, *The Fall of Icarus* has significant form and is art because of features like this interesting structural tension between "centers," both narrative and compositional. But it only possesses this structural tension in virtue of its representational elements. Thus, inasmuch as the possession of significant form often depends upon representation, and art status allegedly depends on significant form, it cannot be the case that representation is always strictly irrelevant to art status.

This problem is even more evident if we turn our attention to literature. Significant form in literature is generally inconceivable without representation. How can one discern tragic structure without taking heed of what is being represented? Even the reversal in the last two lines of an English sonnet depends on what is represented. Perhaps some aspects of literature are purely abstract – like alliteration – but even here the case is somewhat mixed, since a great deal of the form in poetry is what is called imitative form, and imitative form, as the very name implies, requires attention to what is represented in order to take hold. Thus, a great deal of form in literature is dependent on representation. So once again, if the formalist wants to maintain that only the exhibition of significant form is the sign of art, then he must concede that representation is not always irrelevant to art status. How could it be, if significant form frequently supervenes on representation?

Neoformalism

The utter neglect of the relevance of content to art status is the most glaring problem of formalist theories of art. Thus an obvious way to go about repairing formalism is to provide some accommodation for content. The neoformalist does this by making content a necessary condition for art. But, of course, content alone, even if it is traditional artistic content (such as the Madonna and Child), is not enough to secure art status; more is needed. A candidate must also possess form. But many things – such as multiplication tables – which are not art possess form and content. So it must be something about the way in which form and content are related in a work that makes it an artwork. Here, the neoformalist proposes that in an artwork, properly so called, form and content are related in a satisfyingly appropriate manner.

So, for neoformalism:

> x is an artwork if and only if (1) x has content (2) x has form and (3) the form and the content of x are related to each other in a satisfyingly appropriate manner.

"Form" and "content" are the two key terms in this definition. But what exactly do they mean? One popular way of construing this contrast is to think of it in terms of the analogy between a container and what it contains. Champagne has no form, unless it is placed in some vessel – a bottle or a glass. The container gives it shape. Similarly, form is often thought of as the container that gives shape to content. Content is the stuff of the artwork; form is what gives its contour and character.

This analogy – that form is to the content as container is to the contained – is very common. But it is also inadequate when applied to artworks, since, when it comes to art, it is generally impossible to distinguish between what is contained and a container. The content of Rimsky-Korsakov's *Russian Easter Overture* is elation and hope fulfilled. Presumably, the form is just the musical structures that comprise the work. But the content is not "contained" in the musical structures. The content would not exist apart from the musical structures. There is no elation here independent of the musical structures. The container/contained model presupposes that the two terms are separable. But the content of the *Russian Easter Overture* – elation – is not separable from the form in the way that the champagne is separable from the bottle.

One might say that the content of the *Russian Easter Overture* is really Easter and elation is the form. But elation doesn't sound like the sort of thing that we think of as form. If we employ the contained/container metaphor, elation seems more like the kind of thing that would be contained in something else. But then we are back to the problem of the previous paragraph, since the elation in the piece does not appear separable from the musical structure.

In order to avoid the problem of the container/contained analogy, the neoformalist may explicate the form/content distinction in another way. The content of an artwork may be said to be its meaning – its theme – or whatever it is about. Form, then, is the mode of presentation of its meaning, the way in which its meaning is made to appear, the way it is embodied, presented or articulated. Its mode of presentation is that which gives form (in the sense of embodiment) to meaning. One might think of the content of an artwork as its essence and form as the mode of appearance of that essence.

For example, the content, subject matter, meaning or theme of *The Fall of Icarus* is the way in which epoch-making history passes us by unnoticed. That is what the painting is about. The form of the work is how this theme is pictured. This theme is articulated by decentering the subject of the painting – Icarus's legendary fall – off to one side where it is likely to be missed (at least at first glance), thereby presenting and reinforcing the meaning of the work through its visual appearance.

The content of an artwork, then, is its meaning – what it is about; the form is the mode of presentation of the meaning, the way in which what it is about is made manifest or is articulated. Yet, every sentence has content and form in this sense, but not every sentence is an artwork. According to the neoformalist, what distinguishes artworks from other things that have form and content is that in artworks form and content are related in a satisfyingly appropriate manner. But what is "a satisfyingly appropriate manner?"

Let us consult *The Fall of Icarus* again. As we have seen, its theme is that history passes by unnoticed, a truth that strikes an arresting chord for many. Who knew in the late 1950s and early 1960s that we were living in the Golden Age of rock 'n' roll? *The Fall of Icarus* makes this point by placing the major event in the painting in such a way that it goes unnoticed. The decentered composition functions to provide an object lesson in the way in which legendary events can pass by unremarked, since the painting presents Icarus's fall in a way that we are apt to miss it.

Instead of looking at Icarus, we are likely to be wrapped up in the serenity of the overall composition of the painting, as inattentive to Icarus's plight as the farmer is. This is an extremely effective way of getting the point of the painting across. The very design of the painting brings its meaning home to us. It is a deftly suitable means for making us aware of what the painting is about. In that sense, the form is appropriate to the content.

Indeed, it is satisfyingly appropriate to the subject, since when we contemplate how Bruegel has articulated his meaning, we are disposed to say "How clever, how very suitable, how ingenious." The form fits or matches the meaning, and when we reflect upon the match between the meaning and the form, we feel satisfaction in seeing a job neatly done. The unity of meaning and form here abets a satisfying feeling of completeness that we might express by saying that in *The Fall of Icarus* meaning and form suit each other in a way that is "just right," or even "perfect."

Neoformalism has a number of advantages over formalism. According to neoformalism, the possession of a form that is satisfyingly appropriate to its content is necessary and sufficient for art status. Wherever an artifact matches its meaning with a suitably satisfying mode of presentation, it is art. Since this acknowledges that content can be relevant to art status, it avoids many of the most troublesome counterexamples to formalism. For instance, whereas *The Fall of Icarus* was an embarrassment for formalism, it can serve as a paradigmatic example for neoformalism.

That many artworks are intended to serve religious, political, intellectual, emotional and broader social purposes presents no difficulties for the neoformalist. Such work will count as art so long as those purposes are articulated and embodied in modes of presentation appropriate to their meaning. If the mode of presentation mismatched the purposes of a given work, the neoformalist might ask, why would we count it as an artwork anyway? A sermon that boringly recounted the tenets of a catechism is not art, but one whose rhythms raised hope might well be. Isn't this the kind of result we expect?

Neoformalism is also sensitive to the expressive dimensions of artworks. Where we say that the painting is lively or expresses liveliness, neoformalism counts the expression of liveliness as the content or meaning of the painting – as what it is about – and then asks whether the formal means of the painting – its lines, colors and choice of subject matter – are suitable for articulating that expressive property.

Formalism, in contrast, only attends to the structural forms of such paintings and ignores their relation to supervening human qualities. "Liveliness" does not sound like the name of a significant form. Thus, formalism is severely challenged by the fact that we often classify artifacts as art in virtue of their human qualities, their possession of expressive properties. But this liability does not confront the neoformalist.

Another advantage of neoformalism over mere formalism is that it can handle cases like Cage's 4′ 33″. If the meaning of Cage's work is that ordinary sounds are worth attending to, then he has discovered a strikingly effective mode of presentation for promoting that insight. He has arranged the performance situation in such a way that all one has left to listen to is ambient sound. This is a devilishly economical strategy for getting us to listen to what usually goes unnoticed – to what we customarily filter out as noise. It prompts us to contemplate noise for its own sake – to remark upon its texture and contrasts. The structure of the piece, in other words, functions to make its meaning manifest, almost unavoidable. That is, the neoformalist, unlike the formalist, can acknowledge that 4′ 33″ and other experiments like it are art. For according to the neoformalist, 4′ 33″ does have a form that is satisfyingly appropriate to its content.

A further strength of neoformalism versus formalism is that the notion of the satisfying appropriateness of form to content seems more informative and less obscure than the notion of significant form. Of course, one cannot antecedently list every type of appropriate form, since artists are always discovering new ones; that's what creativity is all about. But since the notion of appropriate form is tied to the meaning of the artwork, where we are able to identify the meaning of the work, we are in a position to determine whether it has been implemented effectively – whether the articulation promotes and reinforces it. Content, in other words, governs our determination of appropriate form. Knowing the content puts us in a position to isolate the elements that give rise to it and then to assess the suitability of those elements to advancing whatever the work is about.

But the case for neoformalism does not rest solely with its ability to recuperate the shortfalls of formalism. There are also independent considerations on its behalf. These do not take the form of deductive arguments, but rather arguments to the best explanation. That is, neoformalism is promoted on the grounds that it does the best job of explaining certain distinctive features of our artistic practices. So, if we expect our theories of art to make our artistic practices intelligible to us, then, the neoformalist argues, her view is attractive because it explains features of our artistic practices better than its predecessors.

What are some of the features of our artistic practices that neoformalism supposedly excels in explaining? One phenomenon is artistic change. Art is in perpetual motion. Styles mutate constantly. Why should this be? If the imitation theory of art were true, one would have expected the evolution of painting to halt, once artists discovered the pictorial secrets of realism. And if formalism were true, couldn't we predict a point in history when all the significant forms have been discovered? But we believe that art is restless; that it will always be developing new forms. How can this be?

The neoformalist explains this by pointing out that as history marches onwards, human situations change, and, as human situations change, new issues arise, people have new things to say, and artworks have new things to be about. New content mandates new forms – new forms of satisfying appropriateness are thus called forth. Form changes because content changes, where new content requires unprecedented, yet suitable modes of presentation. Artistic style is always transforming because new content impels the search for new forms of articulation. And this is exactly what one would expect, if neoformalism were true.

Connected to its explanation of why artistic forms change is the neoformalist's explanation of why we cherish art. New times call for new meanings, new ideas, new subjects, in short, for new content. Art serves to articulate this new content – to raise new questions and to reassess old verities – in the life of ever-changing communities. Art examines these issues and articulates them in ways that invite reflection. It gives body to the expression of new values, as well as to old ones in new times. And this is why art is important to social life.

Additionally, neoformalism makes sense out of our critical and appreciative practices. Characteristically, critics spend a great deal of their time interpreting artworks and calling attention to distinctive elements in the artworks that they interpret. They weave back and forth between disclosing the meaning of the work and then pointing to the parts of the artwork that are relevant to its meaning. A literary critic may call attention to the breathless pace of a poem like Tennyson's *The Charge of the Light Brigade* and then remind us that its subject is a relentless cavalry assault. What the critic is doing is relating a structural feature of the poem – its cadence – to what the poem is about. Her purpose is to show that the form of the poem, the way it is articulated, is appropriate to its meaning – that it is ideally suited, or, at least, well suited to expressing it.

Moreover, the neoformalist adds, this practice makes perfect sense, if what an artwork is essentially is a matter of fitting form to content. The critic, in such cases, is gesturing toward exactly what makes the relevant artifact art. She is revealing the *artistic* value in the work – the way in which the work works well as an artwork.

Of course, attending to the marriage of form and content is not just something that only critics do. This is often what we noncritics do as well. In this regard, critics are just special cases – exemplary, and frequently professional – representatives of what common folk do when responding to artworks. The critics help us by showing us where to look and how to understand what we find. But in this, their practices are merely a more refined extension of one of the central ways in which we all appreciate artworks.

Ordinary readers, viewers and listeners also ask why artworks are organized in the way they are and most frequently they answer that question by reference to the content of the work. And where the mode of articulation is fitting or particularly relevant or apposite to the work's content, we derive a satisfying sense of unity from the artist's craftsmanship in matching form with content.

This is how we go about appreciating artworks, whether we are critics or plain audience members. That this behavior lies at the heart of our appreciative practices accords trimly with neoformalism. For if what is special about artworks is the relation of fitness between form and content, then reflecting on that fitness would appear to be the natural way to respond to what is uniquely artistic about artworks. Thus, neoformalism offers a very illuminating account of our appreciative practices, whether we are critics or only nonprofessional or plain viewers, listeners or readers.

Neoformalism can also say something about what it is that artists do. What makes an artist different from a scientist, a doctor, or a lawyer? What is her special area of expertise? This is a question that Plato raised in several of his dialogues. The neoformalist answer is straightforward. The artist is essentially a specialist in matching modes of presentation and meanings, in marrying forms to content.

In sum, neoformalism is superior to formalism because it can acknowledge the importance of representational content for art. Conversely, it is superior to representational theories of art because it emphasizes that content alone is not sufficient for art status; form is at least equally indispensable. Neoformalism is also alert to the expressive dimension of artworks, regarding expressive properties as what the relevant artworks are about and form as their manner of embodiment. In addition, neoformalism can explain what artists are, why art changes, why we value art, and why critical and lay appreciation take the form they do. All in all, neoformalism is a powerful theory of art. It is the best candidate as a comprehensive theory of all art reviewed thus far. But even so, it has its problems.

According to neoformalism, x is an artwork if and only if (1) x has content; (2) x has form; and (3) the form and content of x are related in a satisfyingly appropriate manner. The requirement that x have content reminds us of the neorepresentational theory of art and it is susceptible to the same kind of objections raised against that theory in the first chapter of this book.

The neoformalist says that x is art only if x has content – a meaning, something that x is about. This is a necessary condition for art. But as we have already seen, not all art meets this condition. Some art has no meaning. Some art is exclusively devoted to producing an effect in audiences. Some art is designed to delight by means of its appearance. The abstract grillwork on a palace gate might be an example here. It possesses no distinctive expressive properties. It simply pleasures the eye with its look, and, moreover, this is all that it is intended to do. Therefore, meaning cannot be a necessary condition of all art; some art is "below" meaning. Such artworks may be simply beautiful. They are bereft of content; there is nothing they are about. Much pure orchestral music and pure dance might also be described this way.

But the neoformalist is not likely to take this objection lying down. He might argue that there is a way in which such art does have content. Though abstract painting and orchestral music do not appear to have content in the sense that they do not refer to perceptible events nor have themes nor express points of view about anything, they do have structures which produce effects in audiences – that cause pleasure and absorption.

The content of such works, the neoformalist then suggests, are the rhythms, aural and visual devices, and arrangements of elements that command audience attention, that pleasure us, or that absorb us. The artist puts these structures forward not only in order to move us in certain ways, but to enable us to reflect upon how we are moved by them. These structures address our human sensibilities, and, in that way, reveal the nature and contours of our sensibilities to us.

Such artworks show us, often to our surprise, that we are the kind of creatures capable of finding pleasure in, for example, having a bow drawn across taut cat guts (a.k.a. violins) in a certain way. Artists who manipulate appearances for the sake of delivering beauty and engendering pleasure are in fact also fundamentally involved in exploring human sensibility. Their works enable us to make discoveries about ourselves – about the kinds of creatures we are at the level of our perceptual sensibilities. These works are, then, about something; they are about the human sensorium – its capacities, its proclivities, and, perhaps, its limits. They have a meaning; they tell us about who and what we are.

Undoubtedly, this account of artworks is true in some cases. It does a good job describing the work of many Minimalist artists, such as the sculptor Donald Judd and the composer Philip Glass. These artists intend their works to have a reflexive dimension – they are about themselves in the sense that they encourage audiences to reflect upon their own experiences of the work in question (to reflect, for example, on the way in which various repetitive progressions affect one's temporal consciousness of the music). These works are meant to invite an apperceptive response in spectators – they extend an invitation to attend to the way that we attend to the artwork.

But not all abstract music and painting has this reflexive or apperceptive dimension. Much absorbs us without guiding us to reflect upon or to contemplate the conditions of our absorption. Much art engages us with its sheer beauty, without inviting us to stand back and ask from whence that sense of beauty springs. Minimalist art generally succeeds in educing a reflexive stance toward our experience of it by its austerity, by leaving us with little else to contemplate except the way the artwork addresses us along certain very restricted parameters of sensibility. The minimal (austere) structure of Minimalist art (that's why it's called *Minimalism*) compels us to take an apperceptive stance. But this is not the case with all abstract painting and music. It may engage our sensibilities – engage them richly – without encouraging us to interrogate the sources of that engagement. That is, it may be so rich and command our attention so overwhelmingly that we have neither the time nor the inclination to ponder the origin of its power. Much tap dancing is like this. Such works may and most frequently do lack the kind of internal structuring strategies that allow us to say of Minimalism what it is about or comments upon the nature of our human sensibilities.

But if such artworks do not encourage an apperceptive stance in audiences and do not possess the kinds of internal structures that invite it, what sense does it make to say that these works are about exploring our human sensibilities? Many artworks engage our sensibilities, even quite pleasurably, without being about our capacities for pleasure. To be about our capacities for pleasurable engagement surely requires more than just being pleasurable. A candy bar is pleasurable, but it is not about pleasure. It is not reflexive.

Similarly, unless they contain special internal structures that allude to or draw our attention to our capacities for absorption, there are no grounds to suppose that all "meaningless" artworks are really about our capacities for absorption. Most have the more mundane task of stimulating our senses in various ways, not the more recondite, reflexive goal of engendering reflection on the nature of human sensibility. This cannot be their "meaning" or content. Therefore, some works of art are not about anything. They have no subject or content. Therefore, content is not a necessary condition for art.

The neoformalist also contends that x is art only if it has form. This condition is a bit tricky; evaluating it depends on what we mean by "form." If we interpret "form" in some ways, it is clearly false. For example, if we mean by having form "having parts that are related to each other in some way or other," then, though the condition will hold for anything, including any artwork, that has discernible parts, it will not obtain for artworks that have no discernible parts, such as monochromatic paintings whose coloration is uniform throughout the picture plane.

But this, of course, is not the sense of form that we have attributed to the neoformalist. We have suggested that, for the neoformalist, form amounts to the way in which the meaning or content of an artwork is articulated – how meaning is embodied, its mode of presentation. However, this notion of form has at least one very obvious limitation. If form is necessarily correlative with meaning or content – if it requires content in order to subsist – then a work without meaning or content can have no form in this sense. And since there are some artworks bereft of meaning or content – artworks that are about nothing – then the neoformalist must concede that, in his sense of form, form cannot be a necessary condition of art.

One might try to find a more promising sense of form for the neoformalist. One candidate could be that the form of the work is nothing other than the appearance or shape of the work in the same way that the term "the human form" is interchangeable with "the human body." However, this usage seems inadmissibly broad with respect to artworks, since when we refer to the form of an artwork, we generally mean something less than its total appearance.

The third necessary condition in the neoformalist theory of art is that "x is an artwork only if the form and the content of x are related in a satisfyingly appropriate manner." Insofar as this condition depends on the concepts of form and content, it inherits the preceding objections. But the condition also raises new problems. It returns us, once again, to the issue of bad art.

Some art is bad. A common reason for badness in art is that an artwork fails to find a satisfyingly appropriate form for its content. But something does not cease to be an artwork because it is bad. It is still an artwork, but only a bad *artwork*. We find ourselves frequently saying, "I saw that artwork [a play, for example] last night, but it was a bad artwork [a bad play]." We don't say, "I didn't see an artwork." But the neoformalist cannot account for this. For if something fails to find a satisfyingly appropriate form for its content, it is not, so neoformalism implies, an artwork at all. The upshot of neoformalism is that all artworks, properly so called, are good – all are salutary achievements, since anything that is an artwork has discovered a satisfyingly appropriate form for its content. And how could anything like that be bad?

Instead of a comprehensive, classificatory theory of art, neoformalism turns out to be a commendatory theory of art – a theory that tracks only good art, art worthy of commendation for its satisfying marriage of form and content. But this overlooks all the bad art which, in fact, probably outnumbers the good art exponentially. Thus, the satisfying appropriateness of form to content cannot be a necessary condition of art.

Needless to say, neoformalists are aware of this objection and they are quick to provide a remedy. It is this: there is bad art, as ordinary usage indicates, but badness in art is a function of possessing very low degrees of satisfying appropriateness. Bad artworks are art; they possess satisfying appropriateness, but in very low quantities.

There are several problems with this gambit. First, one wonders how anything that has found a *satisfyingly* appropriate match of form to content could be bad, in any straightforward sense. But second, and oddly enough, badness here seems to be nothing more than the absence of goodness (goodness to a minimal degree), insofar as satisfying appropriateness must always count as a good-making property in artworks. Yet aren't some defects in artworks absolute blemishes in their own right, not just substandard virtues (appropriateness below some stipulated threshold)?

An artwork can be unsatisfyingly inappropriate formally in every way; bad science fiction films and sidewalk paintings at art fairs are often like this. They are not bad because they are not formally appropriate enough. They are total disasters. The problem is not that they are insufficiently good; they are altogether bad. The neoformalist's redefinition of badness as diminished goodness thus seems dubious. Moreover, since there is positive badness and not merely negative goodness to be found in art, even with this reconstrual of badness, the requirement of satisfyingly appropriate form cannot serve as a necessary condition for art, since it excludes from the order of art positively bad art – art that is unsatisfyingly inappropriate formally with no quotient of satisfyingly appropriate form.

Possibly some will say that that's okay. Sometimes an attempt at art can be so bad that we should not count it as art as all. So maybe the neoformalist is onto something important. To create an artwork is an achievement of sorts. An artwork, thus, cannot be altogether bad. It must have some goodness. Perhaps that involves some minimal matching of form to content. Badness in art is just a lack of a sufficient amount of satisfyingly appropriate form.

But there are two problems here. The first is obvious, namely: what is a sufficient amount of appropriateness and how do we measure it? Can this be done without courting arbitrariness? But there is also a deeper problem. Appropriateness or satisfying appropriateness is a matter of degrees. We might call appropriateness a degree concept. But being an artwork is not a matter of degrees. Rather, something is art or it is not art. Let's call this an either/or concept. For example, someone is either a virgin or not; one can't be a little bit of both.

Moreover, one cannot use a degree concept, except stipulatively, to define an either/or concept. You can't be 85 per cent virgin and 15 per cent innocent. Virginity is a done deal, not a matter of degrees. But if this is so – if degree concepts are ill-suited to define either/or concepts – then there is a deep problem with the neoformalist's attempt to define art in terms of satisfyingly appropriate form. Appropriateness – or satisfying appropriateness – are degree concepts, not either/or concepts, and, therefore, they are not the right sort of concepts logically for defining art. Artness or arthood or art status is not a matter of degree.

But suppose the neoformalist attempts to resolve this inadequacy by stipulating a cut-off point – a threshold below which a work's amount of formal appropriateness is not sufficient to count as art. It is hard to imagine that the results of such a gesture could be satisfactory. For any such boundary will appear arbitrary to anyone whose work falls below it. Constant disputes will arise along the border between art and nonart. And the disenfranchised will have good reasons on their side, since the disputed works will have at least some admitted degree of formal appropriateness. For satisfying appropriateness to provide a litmus test for art status, some nonarbitrary principle must be found for determining what amount of degree of formal appropriateness is just enough. But that seems a hopeless task.

In our discussion of the neoformalist's problem with bad art, the reader may be surprised that it was not suggested that it be resolved by replacing the requirement of formal appropriateness with the more modest requirement that the formal appropriateness merely be intended by the artist. Thus, an artwork need not achieve a satisfyingly appropriate match of form to content, but only be intended to achieve it. Bad art then would be art where there was an intention to discover formal appropriateness, but where the intention went unrealized. Would this save neoformalism?

Not really. In order to see this, we need only shift our attention from considering the necessity of each of the conditions individually to asking whether the conditions are jointly sufficient for defining all and only art. They are not, since many artifacts that are not art have form and content that are not only related in satisfyingly appropriate ways, but which are intended to be so related.

The packaging of ordinary household products, for example, has a content, something they are about, namely the product that they contain, about which they say something through their carefully selected designs. Ordinary Brillo boxes, for instance, are about the product Brillo, about which they say something by means of their shapes and colors. They have a meaning that they communicate intentionally through their form. The bright colors associate Brillo with sparkliness and their wavelike shapes suggest cleansing qualities.

The formal articulation of an ordinary Brillo box is appropriate – even satisfyingly so – since it matches the intended meaning of its producers. There can be no doubt that Brillo boxes project Proctor and Gamble's idea of their product in an economical, appropriate, and even imaginative way. But ordinary Brillo boxes are not art, even if Andy Warhol's appropriation of them is.

Nor is this a rare example. Many cultural artifacts match their content with satisfyingly appropriate forms. That is what commercial design is all about. If campers express solidity, their squared-off shapes articulate it. If sunglasses are about coolness, their clean streamlines have a lot to do with it. The labels on bottles of mouthwash have content, have meanings, and are about something. The companies that sell them hire armies of graphic designers to articulate it – to find an appropriate form for the content. Sometimes they succeed. But have you ever seen a bottle of mouthwash in a grocery store that you would call art? Yet might not a neoformalist have to?

Cultural artifacts – including gestures and behaviors – of all sorts have content and are freighted with meanings. Maybe most are. And, additionally, quite of few of them articulate their meanings by means of appropriate forms, ones that we can stand back from and admire for their satisfying economy, unity, coherence, and so on. But not all such cultural productions are art; ordinary Brillo boxes are not. And yet, by the same token, it is hard to see how neoformalism can deny them art status. Thus, though an initially promising comprehensive theory of art, neoformalism appears ultimately too inclusive and must be rejected for that reason.

Part II
What is artistic form?

Different views of artistic form

Form is an important concept for talking about art. No one could deny that. However, as we have seen, it cannot serve as the defining feature of all art on a comprehensive theory. Formalists and neoformalists, like representation and expression theorists of art before them, are pointing toward noteworthy features of art. But they overplay their hand. Neither significant form nor appropriate form is an essential feature of all art. But much art possesses form and that, in large measure, is often why we appreciate it. Thus, even though form does not define art, we still need an account of it – a comprehensive theory of artistic form.

So, what is artistic form?

Perhaps the most common way of thinking of artistic form is to conceive of it as one half of a distinction – the distinction between form and content. The neoformalist tries to clarify this contrast by turning it into the distinction between meaning and mode of presentation. However, this makes the concept of form wholly dependent logically upon the artwork's possession of something that we would be willing to call a meaning. Thus, as previously noted, if there are artworks without meanings, as there seem to be, then this way of conceptualizing form entails that such artworks lack form altogether.

But this is wrongheaded. Often "meaningless" artworks – such as works of pure music – are what we typically take to be the greatest exemplars of artistic form. Therefore, the neoformalist's conception of form – as the mode of presenting content – cannot provide us with a comprehensive theory of artistic form.

This suggests that one might look for a broader way of crafting the contrast between form and content. One way of doing this is to say that content is whatever makes up the artwork, and form is the *way* that whatever makes up the artwork is organized. Content is the matter; form is the manner. Form operates on whatever comprises the content. Again, this makes our conception of the form of an artwork dependent on our conception of the content of the artwork. That is, one cannot determine the manner of its organization, until one knows what is being organized.

A problem arises here almost immediately. What we will call the artistic form of a work depends upon our conception of the content of the work. But the notion of content, as just stated, is excessively ambiguous, and this ambiguity is likely to infect whatever we say about artistic form in such a way that the border between form and content becomes shaky.

If we understand "content" to be "whatever makes up the artwork," consider all the diverse things we might have in mind. Imagine a historical painting of St. Francis and a donkey. What makes up this artwork? In one sense, it is made up of – it consists of – oil paint. At another level of description, it is made up of lines, colors and closed shapes. These components then give rise to representational figures that refer to certain subjects or referents, namely St. Francis and his donkey, which, in turn, may also be expressive of the human quality of kindness. Furthermore, the painting may take a point of view toward St. Francis, regarding him admiringly. It may, in addition, suggest a thesis about St. Francis: that he is kind to his donkey. Indeed, the painting may even advance a more general theme: that all people should be kind to animals.

An imagined painting, such as this one, may be made up of many things: oil paint (and canvas); lines, colors and shapes; representations and their subjects; expressive properties; points of view; theses; and themes. Moreover, this list could be even longer if our descriptions of these dimensions were more fine-grained. Which of all these sorts of things that can be said to make up the content of the painting is the content of the painting? The problem is that, at various times and in various contexts, any of these things or combinations thereof can be and have been identified as the content of such paintings. But that renders the distinction between form and content unstable.

For example, if we identify the content of the painting with its lines, colors, and shapes, then that is not only at odds with the way in which we typically identify these elements in painting, it also leaves little else for form to be. If the lines, colors and shapes of the painting do not constitute its form, what does? Is there a way of handling a line – its length or thickness – that is separable from the line? If the line is a content element of the painting, and it is a nonrepresentational painting, where is the form of the painting? One might say that the form of the painting is some emergent property of the line – an expressive quality, for example – but, then, expressive qualities are content elements of artworks, not formal elements. Similar problems beset pure music. If their musical structures are their content, what is their form? Their expressive qualities? Form becomes a moving target on this conception of content, and, at times, an altogether invisible one.

In fact, another reason that it is probably impossible to distinguish form from content on the supposition that content is whatever makes up the artwork is that, speaking this broadly, form is undeniably one of the things that make up the artwork. Some might, indeed, embrace the notion that there is no difference between the form and content in an artwork. But that is hardly a contribution toward characterizing the nature of artistic form.

In order to negotiate these difficulties, one may resort to ordinary language. In ordinary speech, we often restrict content terminology to what the artwork represents. The content of a work is what it represents – its subject (St. Francis) and whatever it says about that subject (its theses and themes, for example). Thus, we might say that the lines, shapes and colors of the painting are the formal elements that are deployed in a certain manner in order to articulate the content of the painting – to represent St. Francis and/or to represent him in a certain light or for a certain purpose.

But it is not clear that the invocation of representation will draw the distinction between form and content sharply. Think of point of view as a feature of artworks. It is a representational element of an artwork – one, for example, that is often connected to the theme of a work (what it says about its subject). Hatred of racism, for instance, might describe the point of view of a work. Since it is a representational feature of the work, it seems as though it should count as a feature of the content of the work. And yet isn't it a formal feature as well? Isn't it the result of how the representational material in the work is handled? Moreover, if we revert to the container/contained analogy, isn't the point of view that in which all the representational elements in the work are contained? Thus, invoking the concept of representation won't mark determinately the boundary between form and content for us.

And, of course, another problem, which we have already met more than once, with invoking representation in this context is that many works of art have no representational content. On the face of it, this entails that they can have no form, since there is no content upon which form can operate. But there are many examples of nonrepresentational artworks that have form. Moreover, if it is stipulated that those works do have content – for example, their lines, colors and shapes – then again we are left with no way to speak of their form. Either such works have content or they do not; but on either supposition, they appear to lack form. Thus, either way, the conclusion is unacceptable. Therefore, the alleged distinction between form and content still does not provide us with a comprehensive way of characterizing artistic form.

So far the difficulty has been with trying to characterize artistic form in tandem with content. Drawing the line between them in exactly the right way has turned out to be daunting. Thus, an alternative approach that naturally recommends itself to us is to attempt to define artistic form without reference to content. That, at least, reduces our problem by half.

If we reflect upon the way in which we describe artistic form, we note that often we refer to it as unified or complex. These are two frequently recurring comments about artistic form. They also provide us with a clue about the nature of artistic form. In order to be unified or complex, an artwork must be composed of parts. If an artwork's parts are related in such a way that they appear co-ordinated, or, if certain relations between a work's parts are iterated – like the A/B/A/B rhyme pattern of a poem – we call those unity-making features in the artwork. If there are many different kinds of relations between the parts of an artwork, or, if the relations between the parts are variegated and diverse, we refer to the artwork as complex. The common thread that runs through these formal descriptions are *parts* and *relations*.

Parts and relations, then, are the basic ingredients of artistic form. When we make statements about the form of an artwork, we are speaking of the relations between parts of the work. When we say that the figures on one side of the painting balance off the figures on the other side of the painting, we are talking about parts of the painting in relation to each other. It seems reasonable to conjecture that whenever we make statements about the form of an artwork, we are making statements about some relation or relations between its parts. Form-statements are always ultimately translatable as instances of the statement "x has such and such a relation to y." Even where x and y are not mentioned, genuine form-statements can always be cashed in by reference to parts and their relations. To say that a story or dance is unified is often supported by reference to recurring motifs – parts of the story or dance that resemble or echo each other. The artistic form here is just the structure of repeating themes, where the themes are the parts and the relation between them is repetition.

Artworks have many elements, and these can be related in many ways. Sounds in a poem can relate to other sounds, or to the meaning of the work. Different event descriptions can relate to each other in stories and this is the basis of narrative structure. Musical phrases may be broken up, redistributed, reworked, modified, amplified, truncated, and so on; this is musical form. Characters in a drama may stand in adversarial relations to each other. This is dramatic conflict, a formal feature of artworks. It is a relation between parts of the play – the characters – and what they represent (good versus evil, the Allies versus the Nazis, intellect versus might, and so on). Volumes in painting and sculpture can be either in equilibrium or disequilibrium. These too are formal relations. Or a novel may be complex because it has a wealth of different characters. The quantity of characters and their contrasting array of different qualities are formal properties of the artwork.

Artistic form, then, consists of relations between parts of an artwork. Artworks may have many different parts that are related in different ways. Some of these ways may be co-ordinated, such as the way in which the characters are related to the plot in most stories. Or they may be relatively uncoordinated. The color elements in the decor of a stage set, though related to each other, may not have any relation to the dramatic conflict in the story. But whether or not the sets of relations in an artwork are hierarchically organized, all the relations are formal relations. When we speak of the artistic form of an artwork, then, we may take that to refer to *all the webs of relations* that obtain between the elements of an artwork.

This is a very democratic view of artistic form. Any relation between elements of an artwork counts as an instance of artistic form. This characterization is comprehensive. It obviously can apply to any artwork which has discriminable parts. They will all have form, though not necessarily commendable form. This notion of artistic form can even be applied to monochromatic paintings, since such paintings often derive their effect from the relation of their one color to the size or scale of the canvas. This view of artistic form will count relations between representational elements of a work – such as the contrast between good characters and bad ones – as a contribution to the artistic form of story. But that is not an untoward result. Contrasting characters contribute to both the coherence and complexity of the artworks that have them.

We can call this approach to artistic form the *descriptive account*. According to the descriptive account, any instance of a relation among elements of an artwork is an instance of artistic form. On this view, in order to provide a full account of the artistic form of a given artwork, one would list or summarize all the relations among the parts of the work. We call this approach the descriptive account because it classifies any relation among elements in an artwork as an instance of artistic form, irrespective of any principle of selection. On this conception of artistic form, the ideal analysis of the artistic form of a given artwork would be a long description of all the relations among the elements of an artwork. Some art criticism in the 1960s and 1970s actually aspired to this ideal.

In favor of the descriptive account is its comprehensiveness. It does not seem to leave anything out. Arguably it will track everything that one is likely to regard as an instance of artistic form. However, the descriptive account does not seem to accord with what we usually are talking about when we discuss the artistic form of an artwork. We rarely, if ever, encounter such exhaustive accounts of artistic form as one would expect if the descriptive account were our ruling conception of artistic form. Nor is it clear that we even desire such descriptive accounts. The accounts of artistic form we find are almost always more selective. Nor are they more selective simply because few would have the energy to read or to write up such exhaustive descriptions. They are more selective because typically we think of the artistic form of an artwork as comprised of only a subset of the relations among the elements of an artwork. But this raises the question "which ones?"

Form and function

The descriptive account of artistic form is very encompassing. It regards any relation among the elements of an artwork as an instance of its artistic form. This is a plausible and a coherent view of artistic form. However, it does not seem to match what we usually have in mind when we refer to the artistic form of a work. In such situations, we standardly only focus on some of the relations among elements of the work, but not all of them. The relations that concern us are the ones that contribute to the realization of the point of the artwork. On the descriptive account, a formal element of an artwork is anything that stands in some relation to another element. But on our ordinary conception of artistic form, an element is a formal element if it contributes to the point or the purpose of the artwork.

That is, our ordinary conception of artistic form is *explanatory* rather than descriptive. It does not aim at listing every relation in the total web of relations discoverable in an artwork. It selects out only those elements and relations in the work that promote the point or the purpose of the artwork. Our ordinary concept of artistic form seems to be functional. The form of the artwork is whatever functions to advance or to realize whatever the artwork is designed to bring about. The form of the artwork is what enables the artwork to realize its point or its purpose.

The American architect Louis Sullivan said, "Form follows function." What he had in mind, for example, was that the form of a garage door – its size and shape – was a certain way in order to discharge its function (to allow large vehicles to pass through it). The form of the garage door was related to what the door was intended to do. Similarly, the form of an artwork is ideally determined by what it is supposed to do – its point or its purpose.

This, of course, assumes that artworks can have purposes. However, this seems scarcely controversial, once we realize how diverse these purposes may be. In some cases, the purpose of an artwork may be to advance a theme or a point of view, or the purpose may be to display an expressive property, or it may be to arouse feelings, including feelings of pleasure, in audiences. An artwork may be about communicating ideas – ideas about the world or ideas about art – or it may have no ideas or meanings, but simply be devoted to engendering a certain sort of experience, such as repose, excitement, suspense, or delight. Artworks may make points, or they may merely have points – to encourage viewers, for instance, to use their discriminatory faculties delicately. It should not be difficult to concede that all or nearly all artworks have points or purposes – perhaps most frequently more than one – once we think of points and purposes in this broad way. And the form of the artwork is what enables the artwork to realize its purposes. A formal element is an element that contributes to or serves as a means to securing the point or purpose of an artwork.

The point or purpose of Edouard Manet's *Woman Playing a Guitar* is to present the woman in the painting as an agent or doer. Traditionally, women are often presented in paintings as objects of visual pleasure, charming figures for male delight. In *Woman Playing a Guitar*, Manet subverts the traditional approach by presenting his model with her back to the audience, thereby undermining her availability for ogling. She is intent on her task (guitar playing), rather than posing seductively for the male viewer. The orientation of the figure – with her back to the viewer – is a formal choice. It functions to realize the point of the painting – to portray women as doers.

An artwork is designed to perform some purpose (or set of purposes, co-ordinated or otherwise) and/or to make some point. Formal choices are elements and relations in the artwork that are the intended means to secure those points and purposes, in the way that the orientation of the figure in *Woman Playing a Guitar* articulates the point of the picture: that women are doers. A formal choice in an artwork is such that it has the design function to bring about or to facilitate the point or the purpose of the artwork. A formal choice has the intended function to advance the point or purpose of the artwork, if the point in question is the intended result of the formal choice and the formal choice occurs in the work in order to function to secure a point or purpose of the work.

The artistic form of an artwork comprises the collection of formal choices that enable the realization of the points or purposes of the artwork. Artworks, of course, may have more than one point and/or purpose, and these may be co-ordinated or not. In *Woman Playing a Guitar*, the theme of woman-as-doer is reinforced by the woman's glance which, rather than being coyly averted, seems absorbed in her music. Glance and figural orientation here are co-ordinated to implement the same point. But, in other artworks, formal choices may not be interconnected where they still nevertheless enable different artistic purposes. Nevertheless, whether co-ordinated or not, formal choices are always functional contributions to the purposes of the artwork. And the artistic form of the artwork is made up of all its formal choices – of all the formal articulations in the work that function to realize its purposes (its overall purposes, or the purposes of a particular part, like the scene of a play or a sequence in a film).

For blatantly obvious reasons, we will call this the *functional account* of artistic form. According to the functional account of artistic form, *the artistic form of an artwork is the ensemble of choices intended to realize the point or purpose of the artwork*. This approach to artistic form is different from the descriptive account. The descriptive account says that the artistic form of the artwork is the sum total of *all* the relations between the elements of an artwork. The functional account says that the artistic form *only* comprises the elements and relations that are intended to serve as the means to the end of an artwork.

This could include all the relations in an artwork, if they were all intended to serve the purposes of the work, but that occurs rarely, despite the flowery critical rhetoric that frequently commends artworks for being totalized organic wholes. Thus, almost all the time (if not all the time), analyses of the artistic form of an artwork that accord with the functional account will be far less exhaustive than the ideal that the descriptive account of artistic form encourages. And this, of course, conforms better to the way in which we usually discuss artistic form than does the descriptive account. The descriptive account is much broader than the functional account, and the former, logically speaking, contains the latter. But the descriptive account is far too broad to capture what we generally mean by artistic form.

The functional account also differs from the account of artistic form implicit in neoformalism, since the functional account defines artistic form relative to the point or purpose of the work, whereas neoformalism restricts artistic form solely to relations with respect to the content of the work. Speaking of the point or purpose of the work is a broader way of conceptualizing artistic form than speaking only in terms of content. Of course, where the point of an artwork is to advance something thought of as content (a theme, for example), the functionalist will attend to the same formal features of the artwork that the neoformalist does.

But, at the same time, functionalism is a richer approach than neoformalism, since it will also be capable of tracking artistic form where there is a point to the work, but no content. For example, works whose purpose is to instill a sense of beauty will still possess form according to the functionalist – whatever configurations engender delight – while the neoformalist has no way of speaking of artistic form where the correlative category of content is inoperative.

Thus, the functional account, logically, accommodates everything that neoformalism covers, while not being so restrictive. In this respect, the functional account lies somewhere between the descriptive account and neoformalism on the issue of artistic unity by being less inclusive than the former and less exclusive than the latter.

The functional account of artistic form regards artistic form as generative. Form is that which is designed to bring about the point or the purpose of the artwork. This account uses the notion of a function to explain why the artwork is the way it is. It enables us to say why the artwork has the shape and the structure it has. The form serves a function. It is designed to serve the purpose of the work; it is a means to securing the point of the work.

A formal element has been selected, according to the functionalist account, because realizing the point of the work is the intended function of the formal choice and the choice appears in the work in order to realize its point. Suppose a choreographer wants to project a somber mood. She chooses slow, weighty movements and advances with a measured gait, her head lowered. These decisions are formal choices – they give the point of the dance its outward manifestation, its artistic form. They embody the point of the dance. They function as the means of actualizing the purpose of the dance. Projecting a somber mood is the point or the *what* of the work; the form is the *how* of the work.

Moreover, these choices, like those in the preceding paragraph, are rarely completely isolated. Along with movement, the choreographer will also select accompanying music, generally with the idea of reinforcing the mood of the movement. Where the formal choices in a piece of choreography dovetail in this way, we refer to the form of the work as unified. To call the artistic form of a work unified is to say that its artistic choices are co-ordinated like this.

The formal elements of the work are referred to as choices, since when an artist contemplates the best way to articulate her point, she has an array of options before her. The choreographer can choose fast movements or slow ones. Manet could have oriented the figure of the woman guitarist toward or away from the viewer. Creating an artwork involves electing the forms that the artist believes will function optimally toward realizing the point or purpose of the work. Forms are formal *choices* because they are elected from arrays of options.

Forms are selected because they are intended or designed to perform certain functions. The notion of an intention needs to be included in the characterization of artistic form in order to allow for the possibility of failed artistic forms. Even a botched artwork still has a form, though its form may be defective. An artist may intend certain choices to have certain consequences, but they may not achieve those results. The point of a novel may be to engender mystery, but it may fail to do so. A formal analysis of it will pick out the elements intended to inspire mystery and then go on to explain how they were compromised either by other elements in the work or by being put in place incorrectly. That is, the formal analysis of even failed artworks will be functional.

In order to analyse the form of an artwork functionally, it is necessary to have some conception of the point of the work. Often the point can be isolated pretty easily in our experience of the work. But also quite frequently, the point of the work may be elusive. This is why formal analysis also usually comes hand-in-hand with interpretations or explications of the work. The interpretation of the work identifies the theme of the work as its point and uses the function of advancing the theme as a guide to the relevant formal choices.

Explication is broader in this respect. It may identify the point or purpose of the work in terms of some effect (rather than some communication) that work aims to bring about – like raising a certain feeling, such as awe – and then it goes on to point to the elements of the work conspiring to bring about this result. In this regard, the functional account of artistic form is explanatory. Unraveling the artistic form of the artwork in question explains how the artwork is capable (or, in some cases, is incapable) of making its intended points and actualizing its purposes.

We have granted that the descriptive account of artistic form is plausible and coherent. If there is nothing more to be said for the functional account than that it too is plausible and coherent, what reason is there to prefer the functional account over the descriptive account? Perhaps it is that the functional account is better suited to doing what we expect our concept of artistic form to do. Generally when we talk about the form of an artwork or the formal analysis of an artwork, we expect that learning about the form of the artwork will contribute to our understanding of it. If we are mystified by an artwork, we think that concentrating on its form may illuminate it.

Moreover, this intuition seems to fit better with the functional conception of artistic form than it does with the descriptive account. If the artwork as a whole is already confusing, enumerating the undifferentiated totality of its internal relations will not leave you any better off. However, if you approach the elements and the relations in the work asking what they are designed to do, you are far more likely to grasp the rationale behind the work.

Similarly, when we speak of the *form* of the artwork, this has overtones of the systematic – of there being some formula(e), or rule(s), or guiding principle(s) in operation. This connotation of systematicity is entirely lost in the descriptive account of artistic form, since it deals in the totality of relations of the artwork with no principle of selection. The functional account, on the other hand, connects artistic form with underlying motivations. In that sense, it preserves the intuition of systematicity, especially in cases where the forms are co-ordinated hierarchically to secure overarching purposes.

The functional account of artistic form, then, seems preferable to the descriptive account. But does it have certain limitations of its own? To round off our discussion of the functional account of artistic form, let us consider some possible objections to it.

According to the functional account, the form of an artwork is correlative to its purpose. But aren't there artworks without any purpose? Aren't there works that are simply about their form? The artwork just is its form, someone might say. But here the description seems elliptical. "The artwork just is its form" is shorthand for saying that the point of the artwork is to display its form, to bring its form to our attention so that we may contemplate it. The function of the form(s) of the artwork is to command our attention, to encourage us to take note of them, and perhaps to reflect on the way in which they mold our experience of them. And where the point of the artwork is not reflexive in this way, but where it only aspires to enrapture us with its beauty, the form of the artwork is still functional – it is comprised of those elements and relations that are designed to arrest us.

In the course of preceding discussions, we have spoken more than once about aleatoric art, art that employs chance procedures. In what sense are the results of these procedures "formal choices," since the "choices" appear random? But, of course, the relevant choice here is the chance procedure itself which is generally undertaken to make some point – such as: that art is not necessarily expressive, or that the artwork should be an open structure abetting the free play of the audience's interpretive powers, unfettered by the will of the presiding artist.

This response to the problem of aleatoric art may appear to have certain paradoxical consequences. It seems to imply that an avant-garde artist cannot make a truly formless work of art. Suppose an artist is bent on refuting the theory that significant form is a defining feature of all art. He makes an artwork, like the installations by Morris described earlier, in which he removes every vestige of pattern, repetition and salient contrast. He tries to make the result look as random and formless as possible. Can he succeed in making a formless artwork?

According to the functional account, he will not – for if he is successful in divesting his installation of significant form, his work will still possess artistic form. Artistic form is the ensemble of formal choices designed to articulate the point or realize the purpose of the artwork. Our avant-gardist has deliberately chosen and displayed a series of elements predicated upon frustrating our customary expectations about form. His strategies comprise the artistic form of the work from a functionalist perspective because his choices are designed to serve his ends. Thus, the avant-gardist dedicated to creating a "formless" artwork will in fact make a work with artistic form. His attempts to promote a sense of disunity at one level of experience will be surprisingly unified at the level of the relation of form to purpose.

Nor should this result be surprising, since one generation's revolt against the preferred forms of preceding generations (like Romanticism's revolt against Classicism) does not result in formlessness, but in new artistic forms. This result of the functionalist account of artistic form for the avant-garde, then, is not paradoxical, but what should be predicted on the basis of art history.

But if the avant-gardist cannot make a formless work of art, does that imply that there are no formless works of art? And if there are no formless works of art, should we reopen the possibility that artistic form construed functionally is a necessary condition for all art? No – because the functional account of artistic form can allow that there are formless artworks. These will be artworks where the creator, either consciously nor unconsciously, has no point or purpose, and makes choices willy-nilly with no idea where they are headed – not because she intends to make a formless artwork (since that would be a purpose), but because she has no sense at all of where the work is going. She simply slaps one thing on top of another thing in an act of desperation rather than intention.

I suspect that many artists find themselves in this situation. Suppose that the work that results in such circumstances is just an aimless jumble. The functionalist theory of art will say that it is formless. Functionalism, that is, can acknowledge the existence of formless art.

Thus, the functionalist account is not committed to claiming that there is no formless art. On the other hand, the proponent of the descriptive account would have to say that there is artistic form wherever there are elements in relation. This would suggest that there is no formless art. But that, then, is another reason to prefer the functionalist account of artistic form over the descriptive account.

The acknowledgment that there can be formless art also accounts for why the functionalist theory of artistic form is not a unintended reversion to or inadvertent revival of the formalist theory of art discussed at the beginning of this chapter, since the formalist cannot admit the possibility of formless art. Moreover, even if there was not this difference between the functionalist theory of artistic form and the formalist theory of art, there is another important distinction between the two views, since the formalist holds that art has a single, unique function (the exhibition of significant form), whereas the functionalist theory of artistic form allows for myriad nonconverging functional implementations of the point and/or purposes of artworks.

Form and appreciation

The concept of artistic form is intimately related to the notion of artistic appreciation. From some perspectives, such as formalism, artistic appreciation just is the appreciation of the form of the artwork. Any response, other than contemplating the form of the artwork, is, strictly speaking, inappropriate, according to the formalist. The only proper object of artistic appreciation is the form of the artwork. That is what makes something an artwork, so in order to respond to art as art, one must appreciate its form.

This view is too restrictive. Surely, it is appropriate to respond to works of social criticism – like Daumier's caricatures – by being moved to indignation by them. That is what they were designed to provoke, and so responding to them with indignation is responding to them in an appropriate way. Thus, formalism is far too extreme when it declares that responding to artworks by reflecting upon their form is always the only correct way of responding to them. We may appreciate artworks correctly by being aroused by them emotionally in the way they are designed to arouse us. But, at the same time, it is also true that one of the primary ways of appreciating artworks has to do with attending to their form.

In ordinary language, one common meaning of appreciate is "to like." When I say that "I appreciate what you did for me" that usually means "I like what you did for me." But art appreciation refers to a less frequently used sense of "appreciation." When a general asks his staff for their appreciation of a battle, he is not asking them whether they liked it. He is asking them to *size up* what happened during the battle – he is asking them about what maneuvers caused what countermoves, which ones worked and did not work, which initiatives succeeded and which failed, and why. He is asking his staff to recount the battle in a way that makes it intelligible. Similarly, an appreciation of a chess match involves explaining its results, showing how certain strategies led to checkmate and why they had to. Appreciating in this sense is a matter of discerning and understanding how and why a certain strategy was chosen.

When we attend art appreciation classes, the primary goal of the teacher is to enable us to understand how art works. If it is a class in opera appreciation, the teacher introduces us to the elements of opera, explaining what they are supposed to do and why they are put together in the ways they are. The teacher probably hopes that once we come to understand opera, we will like it. But that is not her bottom line. Her bottom line is getting us to understand operas.

The final exam is not made up of the question "Do you like opera?" It is made up of questions designed to determine whether or not we understand opera, usually in terms of whether or not we understand particular operas. We are asked why Wagner employs leitmotifs, not whether we like leitmotifs. The class could be called "Understanding Opera 101" as readily as "Appreciating Opera 101." It is intended to teach one how to appreciate opera, which means "listening to it with understanding."

But what are we supposed to understand? What is it that we need to be taught to understand? Almost anyone should be able to understand that *Carmen* is about the death of a gypsy. What else does the teacher have to teach? She can teach us how the forms – musical, narrative, and dramatic – are assembled to bring about certain effects. By informing us about how certain formal choices are often used, about the way in which they have been used, and by exposing us to a variety of different examples, the teacher hopes to equip us with a rudimentary understanding of how opera works. That way when we hear operas outside of class, we will be able to appreciate them, to size them up, to listen to them with understanding.

Presumably the teacher thinks that by enabling us to listen to opera with understanding, we will come to like it. But, be that as it may, her primary goal is that we come to be able to understand it – to appreciate it. And understanding it – appreciating it in this sense – involves primarily comprehending why the artists (composers, librettists, singers, conductors, set designers, and so on) have made the choices they have made. Appreciating it comes down finally to "getting" why it is designed the way it is.

Art appreciation, then, in large measure is *design appreciation* – knowing how the work works, seeing how its parts are intended to function toward the realization of the point(s) or purpose(s) of the work. Thus, a natural object of artistic appreciation is artistic form, where artistic form is understood functionally. What we appreciate in an artwork is how the forms function as means to bring about the ends of the artwork. Where these forms are well suited to the ends of the artwork, we generally take satisfaction in their design. But even where we do not feel pleasure in the design of the work, we may still understand it – "appreciate it" in the sizing-up sense of the word.

Critics enable us to appreciate artworks by providing exemplary insight into how the artwork under discussion works. They explain the presence of certain features in a work – like the disjunctive editing in a film – by disclosing the way in which it contributes to advancing the point and purpose of the work (such as projecting an aura of nervousness and uncertainty). Following their example, we can return to the film in question, and other films, equipped with an understanding of why such editing is mobilized. Critics enable us to see how parts of an artwork serve larger designs. Often this requires that the critics offer interpretations or explications of the larger aims of the work, but these overviews are often introduced, in large measure, in order to explain why the works have the parts they do – not only so that we will understand and appreciate the work at hand, but so that we can understand and appreciate why other works are similarly designed.

Much of our reflective life as art consumers is spent appreciating the way in which artistic forms have been adapted to serve their purposes. This is often what we argue about after a play – were the characters developed in a way suited to raising pity (how or why not?) These are questions about the design of the artwork. Was the artwork well made? – did the formal choices suit their intended function?

These are not the only questions that concern us with respect to artworks. But they are central ones. They reveal that, to a surprising extent, art appreciation is preoccupied with artistic form. Art appreciation is, to a large degree, design appreciation, a matter of understanding how formal choices realize or articulate the purposes of the artwork.

The functional account of artistic form obviously squares better with this picture of design appreciation than does the descriptive account. If the form of the work were merely all the relations between the elements of the artwork, it would be difficult to see the connection between artistic form and appreciation (in the understanding or sizing-up sense). Attending to all the relations in an artwork is an unlikely road to understanding the work. Why are some relations in the work pertinent and others not? The descriptive account provides no reliable clue here. However, conceiving the artistic form of the work functionally connects it directly to the issue of understanding, since, on the functional account, a formal element must be linked to a larger purpose, the disclosure of which yields understanding of the place of a feature in a broader context.

As we will see in the next chapter, some theorists identify design appreciation with the whole of artistic appreciation. This is too extreme. Art appreciation has dimensions other than design appreciation. Being absorbed in the representational content of a play or being moved by the theme of a novel may be appropriate forms of artistic appreciation as well. But design appreciation is a central aspect of art appreciation. That the functionalist account elucidates how artistic form is capable of serving in this capacity as a proper object of artistic appreciation is a major consideration on its behalf.

Of course, not all art appreciation is design appreciation. Following a story with understanding is a form of appreciation too. But design appreciation involves more; it involves reflecting upon how the story works. Following a story with appreciation is like driving a car correctly; appreciating the design of the story is like driving a car, noting how smoothly it corners and thinking about how the steering mechanism must have been made to facilitate that. Design appreciation is not the whole story of art appreciation. But it is such an important subcategory of art appreciation that we need an account of how it is possible – of what conditions make it available. And the functionalist account of artistic form does this better than its competitors.

Before closing this chapter, one complication needs to be noted. We have framed the functional account of artistic form in terms of the *intended* function that formal choices are meant to acquit. Some might suggest that talk about artistic intentions here might be best forgotten. Why not merely say that a formal element in an artwork is whatever serves to realize the point of the artwork, whether or not the artist had any awareness, conciously or subconsciously, of the relevant point?

Suppose the artist intended a comedy, but the results are tragic, tragic enough to move the audience to genuine tears. Why not say then that the artistic form of the work is whatever realizes the tragic effect of the work? Why tie the form of the work to the design the artist intended? Why not just talk about what the work actually does, as opposed to what it was designed to do?

These queries raise deep questions about the role artistic intention should play both with respect to the identity of artworks and our appreciation of them. Some of these issues will be addressed in subsequent chapters. However, for the time being, suffice it to say that whether we are talking about the intended function of an element or the function an element serves to perform irrespective of the artist's intentions, we are still talking about functions. In that regard, *some* type of functionalist account of artistic form still appears more promising than rival views. Perhaps that is the truth that Sullivan expressed when he said that "Form follows function."

Chapter summary

Artistic form is a major factor in our appreciation of artworks. So much of our reflection about artworks is preoccupied with their design. Taking note of how suitably an artwork is designed to acquit its purpose is a powerful source of the pleasure we find in artworks. Just as we appreciate tools for the way in which they implement the ends they are designed to serve, so reflection upon artworks is frequently gratified by contemplating the way in which their design functions to secure their points and purposes.

Impressed by the importance of form to appreciation, formalists proposed that significant form was the essence of all art. Formalist theories of art had the beneficial consequence of alerting spectators to what was of value in much twentieth-century art. Formalist theories of art were better attuned to acknowledging the accomplishments of modern art than representational theories of art. However, the formalist intends to theorize about the nature of all art, not just modern art. And as a comprehensive theory of all art, formalism fails.

A major failing of formalism is its tendency to regard content as strictly irrelevant to art status. This doctrine is very unpersuasive when one considers the history of art, since not only is most traditional art as concerned with content as much as it is with form, but also because in many cases it would be impossible to discern significant form in artworks, if content were irrelevant to art status.

Neoformalism attempts to remedy this shortcoming of formalism – and thereby to preserve the grain of truth in formalism – by replacing the notion of significant form with that of the satisfying appropriateness of form to content. However, neoformalism, like neorepresentationalism, confronts the problem that not all works of art possess content. Thus, neoformalism is unacceptable as a comprehensive theory of all art.

Nevertheless, even if form is not the defining feature of all art, it is a notable feature of much art. A large portion of art appreciation – what we called *design appreciation* – takes form as its object. Therefore, we need an account of artistic form, despite the fact that form may not be a feature of every artwork. It is a feature of so much art that we need a theory of what it is.

Several views present themselves. Two major contenders are the descriptive account and the functional account. The functional account – that the artistic form of an artwork is the ensemble of choices intended to realize the point or purpose of the work – illuminates perspicuously why artistic form is a natural object of one important dimension of appreciation, design appreciation. Why this should be so is far from obvious on a descriptive account of artistic form. Consequently, the functional account of artistic form appears superior to the descriptive account. Though we may argue about exactly how to frame the best account of artistic form – should it be keyed to artistic intentions or not? – still, functionalism of some sort seems our best bet as a comprehensive theory of artistic form.

Annotated reading

The most widely cited statement of formalism is contained in Clive Bell's book *Art* (London: Chatto and Windus, 1914). This book was a major contribution to teaching audiences in the English-speaking world about the way in which to appreciate modern art, especially painting. Roger Fry's *Vision and Design* (New York: Meridian, 1956) is also an immensely instructive exercise in formalism in regard to the visual arts.

One of the most important statements of formalism with respect to music is Eduard Hanslick, *On the Musically Beautiful*, translated by G. Payzant (Indianapolis, Indiana: Hackett, 1986). In terms of literature, the Russian Formalists are notably informative. See: Lee T. Lemon and Marion J. Reis (eds), *Russian Formalist Criticism* (Lincoln, Nebraska: University of Nebraska Press, 1965), and Ladislav Matejka and Krystyna Pomorska (eds), *Readings in Russian Poetics: Formalist and Structuralist Views* (Ann Arbor, Michigan: University of Michigan Press, 1978). For an overview, see Victor Erlich, *Russian Formalism: A History* (The Hague: Mouton, 1981).

Neoformalism is a view that is at least suggested by Hegel's writings on art. Recent defenses of neoformalism can be found in: Richard Eldridge, "Form and Content: An

Aesthetic Theory of Art," *British Journal of Aesthetics*, Vol. 25 (1985), pp. 303–316; and Arthur Danto, *After the End of Art* (Princeton, NJ: Princeton University Press, 1997). For criticisms of Danto's theory, see Noël Carroll, "Danto's New Definition of Art and the Problem of Art Theories," *British Journal of Aesthetics*, Vol. 37 (1997), pp. 386–392.

The *locus classicus* for the claim that form and content are identical is A.C. Bradley's "Poetry for Poetry's Sake," which is reprinted in Eliseo Vivas and Murray Kreiger, (eds), *The Problems of Aesthetics* (New York: Holt, Rinehart and Winston, 1960). This view is criticized at length in Chapter 4 of Peter Kivy, *Philosophies of Arts* (New York: Cambridge University Press, 1997).

A version of the descriptive account of form can be found in Monroe Beardsley, *Aesthetics: Problems in the Philosophy of Criticism* (Indianapolis, Indiana: Hackett Publishing Company, 1981), Chapter 4. Students interested in pursuing the topic of artistic form at greater length are advised to consult the philosophical literature on style, since "style" is often just another word for the artistic form of an artwork. A good place to begin studying philosophical conceptions of style is Berel Lang's anthology *The Concept of Style* (Ithaca, New York: Cornell University Press, 1987). In that volume, see especially: Richard Wollheim, "Pictorial Style: Two Views."

The conception of appreciation as a matter of sizing up is defended in Chapter 6 of Paul Ziff's *Semantic Analysis* (Ithaca, New York: Cornell University Press, 1960).

CHAPTER 4
Art and aesthetic experience

4
Art and aesthetic experience

Part I
Aesthetic theories of art

Art and aesthetics

The term "aesthetics" has a variety of meanings. In ordinary language, people often refer to so-and-so's aesthetics – for example,
Yeats' aesthetics. What this generally means is something like
Yeats' artistic principles, preferences, and/or his agenda. A reader, listener
or viewer can also have "an aesthetic" in this sense. Here it refers to her
convictions about art or her preferences. However, "aesthetics" also has a
theoretical usage.

With respect to our concerns in this chapter, there are several uses of
the term "aesthetics" that call for comment. One of these is very broad;
another is narrow; and a third is tendentious.

In the broadest sense, "aesthetics" is roughly equivalent to "the philosophy of art." On this broad usage, introductory courses to the topics
discussed in this book are often called "aesthetics." In this regard, this
book might have been entitled *Aesthetics* rather than *Philosophy of Art*.
Here "aesthetics" and "the philosophy of art" are interchangeable. Choosing one over the other is a matter of indifference. This is a loose sense, but
one that is frequent, even among philosophers.

However, for theoretical purposes, "aesthetics" also has a narrower
meaning. "Aesthetics" originally derives from the Greek work, *aisthesis*,
which means "sense perception" or "sensory cognition." In the middle of
the eighteenth century, this term was adapted by Alexander Baumgarten
as the label covering the philosophical study of art. Baumgarten chose this
label because he thought that artworks primarily address sensory perception and very low-level forms of cognition. The important thing to notice
about Baumgarten's usage of the term is that he looked at art from the
reception side of things. He conceived of it from the perspective of the way
in which art addresses spectators.

Thus, when philosophers talk about aesthetics in the narrower sense, that frequently signals that they are interested in the audience's portion of the interaction between artworks and readers, listeners and viewers. Commonly "aesthetics" is used as an adjective, modifying nouns that clearly refer to the audience's share. Some examples include: "aesthetic experience," "aesthetic perception," and "the aesthetic attitude." These phrases all refer to some mental state that a spectator brings to or undergoes either in response to artworks or to nature.

That is, you can have an aesthetic experience of a concerto or of a sunset. The task of a philosopher of aesthetics in this context is to attempt to say what is distinctive about aesthetic experience (aesthetic perceptions, attitudes, and so on) in contrast to other sorts of experiences (perceptions, attitudes, and so on). What, for instance, is the difference between an aesthetic experience and the experience of analysing a computer program? Here the emphasis is primarily on the experiencing subject rather than the object that gives rise to the experience.

However, in addition to "aesthetic experiences," there are also aesthetic properties or qualities. What are these? Expressive properties, which were discussed in Chapter 2, are a major subclass of aesthetic properties. But not all aesthetic properties are expressive properties, since not all of them involve anthropomorphic terminology. For example, we say of artworks and natural vistas that they are "monumental," "dynamic," "balanced," "unified," "graceful," "elegant," "brittle," and "disorganized." Unlike "sad" or "somber," these usages do not allude to mental states or to uniquely anthropomorphic properties. But like expressive properties, these properties too supervene on discernible properties and structures in artworks.

Moreover, whether aesthetic properties are expressive or not, these properties are nevertheless still different from properties such as being three meters long, because they are *response-dependent properties*. Being three meters long is a property that an object could have whether or not humans exist. In a peopleless universe, objects would still possess determinate length. However, the property of monumentality – ascribed to a mountain, for example – is dependent upon human perception. Mountains of certain scales and configurations strike creatures like us, given our sensibilities (our perceptual and cognitive make-up), as being monumental.

This is not to say that it is arbitrary that we call a given mountain monumental, since, as creatures of the sort we are, we can all agree that Mt. Cook is monumental. Nevertheless, it depends upon creatures built like us to detect its monumentality. The size and configuration of Mt. Cook raises a sense of monumentality in our kind on a regularly recurring basis. Godzilla, in all probability, would not be struck by the monumentality of Mt. Cook.

Insofar as aesthetic properties are respondent-dependent properties, they are also implicitly connected to the reception side of things. This is not to suggest that when we attribute the property of monumentality to Mt. Cook, we are referring to our experience. We mean to be referring to a property of the object – to some sensuous or structural property – but it is a property that the object possesses and discloses only in relation to the possibility of experiencers like us. We experience aesthetic qualities as qualities of objects, like Mt. Cook, rather than as properties of ourselves. But these properties of objects can only obtain in relation to subjects like us (I say "like us" rather than "humans," since other kinds of rational beings, such as E.T., may also be able to detect aesthetic properties).

Understood as a term indicating "audience-relatedness" or "receiver-relatedness," there is at least a possible distinction to be drawn between "aesthetics" and "art." In principle, a theory of art could be designed without reference to potential audiences. It might construe art solely by means of reference to the art object and its function, without alluding to an audience. Perhaps prehistoric peoples thought of what we now call art – the bisons cavorting in Neolithic cave paintings – as magical devices for populating their hunting grounds with an abundance of prey. What was important for them was not the experience the images raised in viewers or the properties it made available for viewers, but the function of the object for survival. If there had been a prehistoric theory of art, it might have identified art as a certain sort of technology.

Likewise, aesthetic investigation could proceed without reference to art objects. Natural objects and events, like the starry sky at night and storms at sea, provoke aesthetic experiences and possess aesthetic properties. A philosopher could develop a theory of the aesthetics of nature without ever mentioning art. Thus, at least in principle, "art" and "aesthetics" can be viewed as different theoretical domains of study: *art* is primarily the theoretical domain of certain objects (whose nature, for example, the representational theory of art attempts to define); whereas "aesthetics" is primarily the theoretical domain of a certain form of receptive experience, or perception, or of response-dependent properties which are not necessarily unique to artworks. This book is called a *Philosophy of Art* because its primary focus of attention is on art. It does not deal with the aesthetics of nature directly, and it treats as an open question the issue of the extent, if any, that a definition of art is dependent upon the aesthetic reception of artworks.

In the broad theoretical sense, briefly mentioned earlier, there need be no difference between the philosophy of art and aesthetics; they might be taken as interchangeable labels for the division of philosophy that investigates art. But in the narrow theoretical sense, the two terms, at least in principle, signal a different primary focus: the philosophy of art is object-oriented; aesthetics is reception-oriented. One can at least imagine a philosophy of art that renders questions of aesthetics peripheral, particularly in terms of the definition of art.

In principle, then, these two domains of investigation can be contrasted. Aesthetics is broader than the philosophy of art, since it studies nature as well. And a philosophy of art might define "art" without reference to aesthetic experience or audience reception. Such a philosophy of art would not regard aesthetic experiences or aesthetic properties as necessary ingredients in all art (although it still might recognize them as important).

However, to complicate matters, there is *also* one approach to the philosophy of art which maintains that any definition of art must necessarily involve notions of aesthetic experience. Such definitions, for obvious reasons, are called *aesthetic definitions of art*. On this view, to be refined in the next section, artworks are objects whose function is to engender aesthetic experiences. For aesthetic theorists of art, though the philosophy of art and aesthetics might have, in some sense, been independent areas of inquiry, *as a matter of fact*, they are not. As a matter of fact, art status is intimately and inseparably connected to aesthetic experience. Artworks just are objects and events predicated upon instilling aesthetic experiences in audiences.

This way of understanding the relationship between art and aesthetics is tendentious because it represents a particular theoretical bias; it makes a substantive claim about the nature of art. According to aesthetic theorists, "art" and "aesthetics" might, in some abstract sense, have turned out to be the names for different domains of inquiry; but in fact, once one studies the matter, it is discovered that they are not, because one cannot, so the aesthetic theorist alleges, say what art is without invoking the concept of aesthetic experience. Thus, on this view, the philosophy of art belongs squarely in the domain of aesthetics, along with the study of the aesthetics of nature.

For aesthetic theorists of art, calling this book *Philosophy of Art* is not a matter of indifference. It should have been called *Aesthetics*, because such theorists believe that questions about the nature of art are crucially reducible to questions of aesthetic experience. For aesthetic theorists of art, "aesthetics" and "philosophy of art" are not interchangeable because they are merely neutral, theoretically uncommitted labels for the same inquiry. Rather, they are interchangeable because art is essentially a vehicle for aesthetic experience. Thus, on the tendentious use of "art" and "aesthetics," the underlying theoretical viewpoint is that the two terms are inter-definable: specifically, art can be defined in terms of aesthetics. For the aesthetic theorist of art, the discovery that art can be defined in terms of aesthetic experience is akin to the discovery that water is H_2O.

The aesthetic definition of art

We have already had a brush with aesthetic theories of art in our discussion of formalism. Clive Bell defined art in terms of significant form. However, if you had asked him how to identify significant form, his answer would have been in terms of that which has the capacity to engender aesthetic experience, or, as he calls it, aesthetic emotion. Nevertheless, we did not treat Bell's version of formalism as an aesthetic theory of art, since he does not mention aesthetic experience in his definition explicitly. The difference between a Bell-type formalist and an outright aesthetic theorist of art is that the latter, one might say, "cuts to the chase," referring directly to aesthetic experience, without the intervening concept of significant form, in his definition of art.

The aesthetic theorist of art starts with the supposition that there is something special about our commerce with artworks. Artworks, she claims, afford a unique kind of experience. The experiences we have strolling through a gallery or seated in a concert hall are different in kind from other sorts of experience like completing tax forms, shoveling snow, buying groceries, building rocket ships, or writing news bulletins. Moreover, though different in kind from other sorts of experiences, there is also something uniform about our encounters with artworks. They abet a peculiar – that is to say, *distinctive* – type of contemplative state.

Though more will be said about this contemplative state in the next section, suffice it to say for the time being that, customarily, when encountering artworks, our attention is engaged by its sensuous forms, its aesthetic properties, including expressive ones, and its design. We peruse the object, we let our attention roam, but not aimlessly, since what we see and hear has been structured to guide our attention along certain pathways, rather than others. In the best of cases, the aforesaid features of the work are inter-related in interesting ways and detecting these correspondences is satisfying. This sort of contemplation or absorption is reputedly different in kind from what we experience when pursuing a practical task, like looking up a phone number. There we do not savor the experience for its own sake, but hurry through it to get the job done. With artworks, the aesthetic theorist argues, the contemplative state is its own reward; we do not enter it for the sake of something else.

This contemplative state is what theorists call aesthetic experience. Artworks are opportunities to undergo this special state. Artworks are devices that facilitate it. Moreover, it is for the purpose of having such states raised in us that we attend to artworks. That is, we seek out artworks in order to obtain aesthetic experiences. Artworks are primarily esteemed by audiences as potential sources of these self-rewarding, aesthetic experiences.

So far, we have only considered the reception side of things. We have spoken of the audience's interest in attending to artworks. But what of the artist? Presumably, if audiences are interested in artworks in order to obtain aesthetic experiences, and if artists are typically interested in acquiring audiences, then there will be some connection between what artists set out to do and what audiences expect to derive from artworks. What audiences expect to derive, according to aesthetic theorists of art, are aesthetic experiences. Therefore, it is reasonable to hypothesize that what artists intend to do by way of making artworks is to afford the opportunity for audiences to have aesthetic experiences – for example, by making objects replete with aesthetic properties.

To appreciate the aesthetic theorist's argument, consider this analogy. People buy nails to drive through surfaces in order that those surfaces will adhere to each other. Hardware stores stock nails so that people with this goal can find what they are looking for. Therefore, it is reasonable to conjecture that the manufacturers of nails, who supply the hardware stores, intend by making nails to provide the sort of implements that will facilitate the goals of nail-buyers. This is the best explanation we have of the social nexus among nail-makers, hardware-store owners, and nail-consumers. Similarly, if audiences typically use artworks to secure aesthetic experiences and seek out artworks for this very purpose, then it is a good bet that artists typically intend artworks to function in ways that are conducive to realizing the audience's goals of obtaining aesthetic experience.

That is, the aesthetic theorist argues:

1 Audiences use all artworks to function as sources of aesthetic experience; this is the reason audiences seek out artworks.
2 Therefore audiences expect artworks to function as sources of aesthetic experience (this is the reason they seek out artworks).
3 If artists are interested in having audiences, then artists intend their works to be serviceable for realizing the expectations that audiences have in seeking out artworks.
4 Artists are interested in having audiences.
5 Therefore, artists intend their works to be serviceable for realizing the expectations audiences have in seeking out artworks.
6 Therefore, artists intend their works to function as sources of aesthetic experience.

Furthermore, if artists intend their works to function as sources of aesthetic experience *and* this is what audiences expect from artworks, in addition to how they use them, then this suggests a thesis about the nature of art, viz., that artworks are things produced with the intention of possessing the capacity to engender aesthetic experiences. Support for this theory derives from the fact that it ostensibly gives us the best explanation available of the characteristic activities of the creators and consumers of the objects and performances we call artworks. That is, postulating that artworks are things designed with the capacity to afford aesthetic experience makes the most sense of the activities alleged to be central to our artistic practices – both the practices of artists and spectators, and the relation between the two.

Or, perhaps another way to say it is: we supposedly know what the characteristic behaviors of artists and audiences are with respect to artworks; hypothesizing that artworks are objects that are intentionally designed to function as sources of aesthetic experience is the posit that coheres best with what we think we know about the behavior of the creators and consumers of art. The aesthetic definition of art, then, is supposedly the most intelligible account of the artwork – the account that is maximally consistent with and fits best with the rest of what we believe about our artistic practices.

Stated precisely, the aesthetic definition of art maintains:

> x is an artwork if and only if (1) x is produced with the intention that it possess a certain capacity, namely (2) the capacity of affording aesthetic experience.

This is a functional definition of art, since it defines art in terms of the intended function that all artworks are alleged to have. It is an aesthetic definition of art, since it designates that intended function in terms of the capacity to afford aesthetic experience. The aesthetic definition of art is a rival theory of art to the representational theory of art, the expression theory and formalism, since it is advanced as a comprehensive theory of all art. It proposes two necessary conditions for art status that are conjointly sufficient.

The aesthetic definition of art has several components. It is instructive to review them one at a time in order to see why they are included in the theory. One component of the theory is the artist's intention. We can call this an aesthetic intention, since it is the intention to create something capable of imparting an aesthetic experience.

The first thing to notice about this theory is that it merely requires that the work be made with such an intention as at least one of the motivating factors in the creation of an artwork. The aesthetic definition does not require that the aesthetic intention be the only intention, nor does it require that it be the dominant or primary intention. It simply requires that an aesthetic intention be one of the intentions operative in the production of the work.

This allows that an artwork might also be produced in order to realize certain religious or political intentions. It will be an artwork just so long as there is, in addition, an aesthetic intention behind it. Indeed, an artwork might be created primarily with the intention to realize some religious or political goal. But it will still count as an artwork, insofar as there is also an aesthetic intention motivating it. Portrayals of Christ's crucifixion, even if primarily intended to instill adoration, will count as art inasmuch as there is also a co-existing intention to promote aesthetic experience.

This aesthetic intention may only be secondary. However, something is an artwork, only if it numbers an aesthetic intention among its intentions. Some artworks may be motivated solely by aesthetic intentions; others may have dominant intentions other than aesthetic ones. However, the possession of an aesthetic intention is a necessary condition for art status. Nothing shall count as an artwork unless it implements an aesthetic intention.

Moreover, it is important to note that the relevant intention is an intention to afford aesthetic experience; it is not an intention to create art. If it were an intention to create art, then the definition would be circular, since in order to tell whether a work was motivated by an intention to create art, we would have to know antecedently what counts as art. And in that case, we would be presupposing knowledge of the nature of the very thing the theory is supposed to define.

Some may fear that by alluding to aesthetic intentions, the definition is impracticable. How can we know whether or not there is an aesthetic intention behind a given work? Isn't any intention something that exists in the mind of the artist and isn't the mind of the artist remote from spectators? How can we know that the artist had such an intention?

Actually, this is not so hard to determine. If a painting, for example, exhibits care in its composition, harmony in its color arrangements, and subtle variations in its lighting effects and brushstrokes, then that is evidence that it is intended to support aesthetic experience. Here we infer the presence of an aesthetic intention on the same kind of grounds that we infer everyday intentions – as the best explanation of the behavior of agents.

In this case, the agent is the artist; her behavior is the way in which she handles her materials. On these grounds, that she had an aesthetic intention is the most probable explanation of her behavior. Furthermore, with artworks, additional evidence for hypothesizing aesthetic intentions includes the genre of the work. If a work belongs to an artistic genre in which the promotion of aesthetic experience is a standard feature of works in that genre, then it is likely that anyone working in that genre shares this generic intention.

By including the requirement of an intention in the definition of art, the aesthetic theorist succeeds in drawing a distinction between artworks and nature. Earlier we noted that aesthetic experiences also accompany many encounters with nature. If the aesthetic definition of art were framed only in terms of the capacity of an object to afford aesthetic experience, the theory would be too broad; it would not differentiate artworks with the capacity to engender aesthetic experiences from majestic waterfalls that share that power. This would make the theory too inclusive, thereby undercutting its claim to provide sufficient grounds for discriminating artworks from other things. But by requiring that artworks be under-written by aesthetic intentions, the aesthetic theorist segregates artworks from nature in general, since nature, even natural objects possessed with aesthetic capacities, is not the result of anyone's intention.

Similarly, by incorporating reference to intentions in the definition, the aesthetic theorist is able to accommodate the existence of bad art. Bad art comprises works intended to afford aesthetic experience which fail to real-ize their intentions. If the aesthetic definition only spoke of a capacity to promote aesthetic experience, the theory would only count successful works as art – i.e., it would only count as art works that actually stimulate aesthetic experience. This would leave us no way to classify bad art as art. But, as we saw in the previous chapter, this would be a very counterintui-tive result. Nevertheless, it is not a problem for the aesthetic definition of art, since by referring to artistic intentions, the theory allows for failed intentions, and, thereby, for bad art.

One might fear that by relying so heavily on the notion of intention, the aesthetic theorist of art renders his definition virtually toothless. That is, if all that is required for art status is the mere intention to provide aesthetic experience – rather than the realization of said intention – that makes it too easy for a candidate to count as an artwork. If a work need not deliver on its aesthetic intention to any degree whatsoever, then anyone can claim that any artifact is underwritten by an aesthetic intention and, therefore, that it is art. Thus, the aesthetic definition of art appears too broad. It really possesses no means to exclude anything from the order of art.

But this worry is misplaced. The aesthetic definition of art has resources to deny large numbers of artifacts art status. These resources reside in the notion of what it is to have an intention and, by extension, an aesthetic intention.

An intention is a mental state that is itself comprised of at least two constituent types of mental states: beliefs and desires. In order to intend to take the bus to Baton Rouge, I must not only desire to go to Baton Rouge, I must also possess certain beliefs, such as: that Baton Rouge exists and that it is a place that one can reach by taking a bus. Before you ascribe to me the intention to go to Baton Rouge by bus, you must satisfy yourself that I possess the relevant beliefs and desires. If I tell you that I intend to go to Baton Rouge by bus, but you see me in an airport without bus service, and I tell you sincerely that I know there is no bus service connected to the airport, then you will be very reluctant to attribute the intention to go to Baton Rouge by bus to me. Maybe you will think I am just ribbing you, or trying to cover something up.

Why will you refrain from attributing to me the intention to go to Baton Rouge by bus? Because I do not seem to have the beliefs appropriate to that intention. My behavior, including my verbal behavior, doesn't support an intention to go to Baton Rouge by bus; indeed, my behavior appears to be at odds with such an intention. To ascribe to me the intention to go to Baton Rouge by bus, you need to satisfy yourself that I have the right sort of beliefs. If your best explanation of my behavior blocks the hypothesis that I have the right sort of beliefs, then, all things being equal, you are ready to override what I say and to deny that I intend to go to Baton Rouge by bus.

A similar story may be told about the desire component of intentions. If my behavior indicates that I do not possess the right kind of desires, then you refrain from attributing to me an intention to go to Baton Rouge. If I sit in an airport for two months without making any effort to get from there to Baton Rouge, then you discount what I say and surmise that I don't really desire to go to Baton Rouge, and, therefore, that I don't intend to, either.

What does this story about Baton Rouge have to do with art? According to the aesthetic theorist, an intention to afford aesthetic experience is an essential constituent of art status. Consequently, in order to attribute an aesthetic intention to an artist, we must be satisfied that he has the beliefs and desires requisite for that kind of intention. If his behavior, notably his work, fails to indicate his possession of the relevant beliefs and desires, the aesthetic theorist of art has grounds to deny that the artist has an aesthetic intention, and, thereby, the grounds to deny that his work is art.

Consider an example – Edward T. Cone's musical composition "Poème Symphonique." The piece involves one hundred metronomes running down. Can it be said to be motivated by the intention to promote aesthetic experience? According to at least one aesthetic theorist of art, it cannot. For it does not seem likely that someone like Cone, a professor of music steeped in the tradition, could believe anyone would be able to derive an aesthetic experience from the aural spectacle of one hundred metronomes clicking to exhaustion. Undoubtedly, Cone, like everyone else, realizes that the effect of his work is more likely to drive listeners batty than it is to engender contemplation. Cone would have to be a lunatic to think that this piece could possibly afford aesthetic experience. But he is not a lunatic, and the principle of charity in interpretation encourages us to presuppose that Cone, like everyone else, does not believe that "Poème Symphonique" has the capacity to afford aesthetic experience.

Moreover, for the same reasons, we will not attribute to Cone the desire to stimulate aesthetic experiences in his audience. Undoubtedly, he desires to engender some other sort of state, for other reasons, in his auditors. A music critic, or Cone himself, might be able to tell us about the identity of this other state, and Cone's reasons for wanting to induce it. But, in any case, we will not attribute to Cone the intention to afford, by means of "Poème Symphonique," the opportunity for aesthetic experience, because we find it vastly improbable that Cone could really have the beliefs and desires required to form such an intention.

But if the aesthetic theorist of art has the conceptual wherewithal at her disposal to deny that an artist has the relevant aesthetic intention with respect to a given work, then the aesthetic definition of art has teeth. It can filter out certain prospective candidates from the order of art because there are grounds for denying that the relevant works are genuinely underwritten by aesthetic intentions. The aesthetic theorist can do this wherever she is able to argue that it is not plausible – indeed, that it is wildly implausible – to attribute to the pertinent artist the sorts of beliefs and/or desires that are the constituents of aesthetic intentions.

Thus, some aesthetic theorists of art exclude readymades, like Duchamp's *Fountain*, from the realm of art proper on the grounds that it is ridiculous to attribute to someone as savvy and as informed as Duchamp the belief that an ordinary urinal could afford an aesthetic experience. Perhaps, they will admit, he was up to something else. But, additionally, they will argue that he was clearly not intending to engender aesthetic experience, and, therefore, that *Fountain* is not an artwork.

Consequently, one can fail to make an artwork according to the aesthetic definition of art. Admittedly, it may be the case that it is not that difficult to make a work of art according to the aesthetic theory. But two things remain to be said. First, it is not really too difficult to make a work of art in the classificatory sense (even though it is difficult to make a *good* one). Thus, the aesthetic definition of art, appropriately enough, reflects the way things are. And, second, though it is easy to make a work of art, according to the theory, it is not so easy that one cannot fail to make one. One could fail to create an artwork if one's intentions were not aesthetic. Thus, the aesthetic definition of art is not too broad. It can exclude candidates from the order of art.

In addition to the intention component, the aesthetic definition of art also contains a function component. The function component is nested inside the intention component. It is the requirement that the relevant intention be the intention that the work have the *capacity* to afford aesthetic experience. Here, capacity-talk is ultimately function-talk. That is, the artwork is designed to function as a source of aesthetic experience. But this intended function of the artwork is described merely as a capacity to afford aesthetic experience, since with artworks the artist only proposes, while the audience deposes.

The artist makes something capable of supporting an aesthetic experience. But it is up to the audience to take advantage of this opportunity. Christian audiences, for example, refused to engage the possibilities for aesthetic experience richly afforded by the internal structures of Martin Scorsese's film *The Last Temptation of Christ*. But the film is still a work of art, since it is structured in a way that affords aesthetic experience, even if this capacity was ignored by many.

Thus, rather than saying that an artwork is designed with the function to cause aesthetic experiences invariantly, the definition is stated in terms of an intended capacity, which may remain latent; even if audiences are not disposed to be receptive, a work is still an artwork. The fact that the audience, for some reason, refrains from using a work to serve the function it was fashioned to discharge does not compromise its artistic status.

The aesthetic definition of art is particularly attractive because of the way in which it suggests systematic answers to many of the leading questions of the philosophy of art. It enables us to say why artworks are good, when they are good. Specifically, artworks are good when they realize their presiding aesthetic intentions – when they indeed afford aesthetic experiences. They are bad when they fail to deliver the goods, i.e., aesthetic experiences.

The aesthetic theory also suggests a criterion for what counts as a critical reason when commenting on artworks. A critical reason for or against an artwork pertains to comments about whether and/or why an element of an artwork or the artwork as a whole contributes or fails to contribute to the potential production of aesthetic experiences. Saying that a work is unified, for example, is a critical reason, since unity is a feature of artworks that is conducive to having aesthetic experiences.

And, finally, the aesthetic definition of art puts one in a position to say why art is valuable. Art is valuable because it affords aesthetic experience. Thus if we can say why having aesthetic experiences are valuable, then we are also on our way to saying why art is valuable. The value of art will be derived from the value of having aesthetic experiences.

If the aesthetic definition of art is true, then it can serve as the cornerstone of a systematically unified theory of art that can explain why artworks are good (and bad), what counts as a critical reason, and why art as an organized form of human practice is valuable. Providing such a remarkably unified account of art with this scope is certainly a large consideration on behalf of the aesthetic theory of art.

Of course, the component of the theory that enables it to explain so much in a systematic way is aesthetic experience. It is the central theoretical term in the edifice of such theories. Since artworks are intended to function to afford aesthetic experience, they are said to be good when they possess the capacity to do this. Critical reasons are ones that remark upon features of artworks that facilitate or inhibit this function. And art as a practice has value because aesthetic experience has value. Undoubtedly, the notion of aesthetic experience is the fulcrum upon which the aesthetic definition of art and its various systematically inter-related, explanatory bonuses are balanced. Thus, in order to assess the aesthetic theory, we need to get clear on what is involved in its central notion.

Two versions of aesthetic experience

As we saw in the previous chapter, a major problem with Bell's theory of significant form was the failure to specify exactly what it is. He maintained that it is whatever provokes aesthetic emotions, but since he did not clarify the nature of the aesthetic emotion, the concept of significant form remained disastrously undefined. "The capacity to afford aesthetic experience" performs an analogous task in the aesthetic definition of art to that of significant form in formalist theories. Thus, if the aesthetic definition of art is to avoid the same kind of objections leveled at formalism, some conception of the notion of aesthetic experience must be supplied.

There are many diverse conceptions of aesthetic experience. Entire books have been devoted to discussions of different characterizations of aesthetic experience. Thus, we must be selective in our discussion here. Let us look at two major accounts of aesthetic experience – what we may call respectively the *content-oriented account* and the *affect-oriented account*.

The content-oriented account is very straightforward: an aesthetic experience is an experience of the aesthetic properties of a work. Here it is the content of the experience – what we attend to – that makes an experience aesthetic. Aesthetic properties include the expressive properties of a work, the properties imparted by its sensuous appearance (elegance, brittleness, monumentality), and its formal relations. For convenience's sake, these properties can be sorted under three broad headings: unity, diversity and intensity. On the content-oriented account, attending to the unity, diversity and/or intensity of a work (or of its parts) amounts to an aesthetic experience of the work.

The unity of a work depends on its formal relations. Where the elements of the work are co-ordinated in part or throughout, the work is unified. It may be unified by virtue of repeating motifs and themes (its parts may resemble or recall each other in pertinent respects), or it may build to a singular, coherent effect, like the plot of a story where most of its elements led to closure. When we attend to the unity-making features of a work and their mode of inter-relationship, our attention to the piece is an aesthetic experience, an aesthetic experience of unity. That is, unity is the content or object of our experience that makes our experience aesthetic.

Works may also possess various properties – like sadness and gracefulness – in varying intensities. A work may be extremely joyous or only mildly so. It may appear hectic or delicate, implacable or strong in different degrees. Attending to the aesthetic properties of the work, discriminating their variable intensities, is an aesthetic experience of the work. It is an experience of the qualitative dimension of the work as it offers itself in appearance. And since these qualities will always appear with some degree of intensity – whether high, low or somewhere in between – experiences of the aesthetic qualities of a work will always be experiences of the intensity of the work.

A work that foregrounds certain aesthetic properties relentlessly – that, for example, projects sadness in every register (as in an opera where the plot, music and gestures are all sad) – is highly unified and, therefore, affords a very unified experience of sadness. But not all works aspire to this sort of unity. Many are designed to project a variety of different feeling properties. Some of these may contrast with each other. But many different feeling tones may also be enlisted by a work to suggest the overall effect of richness. Many of Shakespeare's plays are like this. They juxtapose many different and sometimes opposing expressive properties in order to hold our attention by alerting us to the stunning variety of things.

Diversity can be secured in artworks not only by projecting a wide variety of expressive properties, but also by multiplying the range of characters, events, or vocabularies (words, musical structures, visual forms, and so on) deployed in a given artwork. Obviously, unity and diversity are co-varying terms here. As the work becomes more complex in its different elements, its unity may diminish, while, as its themes and elements recur or blend into each other, it becomes less and less striking for its diversity. Monochrome paintings exhibit a low degree of diversity, whereas large-scale novels, like *The Brothers Karamazov*, appear sprawling rather than unified. Nevertheless, few works are altogether diverse, with no unity whatsoever. Rather, diversity is standardly a feature of works that have some unity – that is, diversity typically is a matter of variety amidst unity. When a work is notable for this type of diversity, we often refer to it as complex.

Speaking roughly, then, an aesthetic experience, according to the content-oriented account, is an experience of unity, diversity and/or intensity, where it is understood that these very features of a work may be inter-related in various ways. It is the possession of features like these that make aesthetic experience possible. That is, a work has the capacity to afford aesthetic experience – experiences of unity, diversity and intensity – inasmuch as the work has features of this sort. An artwork is something intended to present features like these for the audience to apprehend.

Plugging the content-oriented account of aesthetic experience into the aesthetic definition of art, then, we get: x is an artwork if and only if it is intended to present unities, diversities and/or intensities for apprehension. Something not intended to present these features to audiences is not an artwork. Artworks that succeed in presenting such features for audience attention are good; ones that fail in this regard are bad. A critical reason on behalf of an artwork takes note of its possession of unity, diversity, and/or intensity; a critical reason that counts against an artwork points out its lack of unity, diversity and/or intensity. In addition, art, as an organized form of human activity, is said to be valuable because it is valuable for human life to have experiences of unity, diversity and intensity. Who could deny it?

This is the content-oriented account of aesthetic experience. It is not the only account of aesthetic experience, and, in all probability, it is not the most popular one. In discussions of aesthetic experience, *affect-oriented accounts* usually dominate. Indeed, the affect-oriented account, in all likelihood, can claim to be the canonical account of aesthetic experience.

The content-oriented account relies on aesthetic properties to define aesthetic experience; aesthetic properties are what aesthetic experiences are experiences of. This says nothing at all about the special modalities of such experiences; it says nothing about what such experiences are like. That is, it does not offer a phenomenology of such experiences. Speaking very crudely, the content-oriented account characterizes such experiences in terms of what they "contain." It does not inform us about the nature of the "container." Affect-oriented accounts, metaphorically speaking, attempt to do just that.

According to one very well-known version of the affect-oriented account, an aesthetic experience is marked by the disinterested and sympathetic attention and contemplation of any object of awareness whatsoever for its own sake alone. Aesthetic experience is a form of attention. What sort of attention? Disinterested and sympathetic attention.

Disinterested attention, here, is not equivalent to noninterested attention. Attending to an artwork with disinterest is not the same as attending to it without interest. Disinterest is compatible with being interested in the artwork. What disinterest amounts to here is "interest without ulterior purposes." With respect to the law, we want disinterested judges – judges who do not have personal interests in the case (such as standing to gain, if the plaintiff loses), or ulterior motives (such as wanting to send a message to the electorate). We want judges to make rulings disinterestedly – to judge the case impartially and on its own merits, rather than on the basis of issues and purposes external to the case.

Similarly, aesthetic experience is allegedly disinterested in this way. We attend to the artwork on its own terms. We do not ask whether it will corrupt the morals of children. Rather, for example, we attend to whether or not its formal organization is suitable. If we are Muslims and the work concerns Islam, we do not ask whether the work is good for our people. We ask whether it is unified, complexly diversified, or intense. A film-producer who watches her movie trying to calculate whether it will draw large audiences into the cineplexes is not viewing the film disinterestedly. Her viewing is connected to her personal interests – to the amount of money she hopes to make.

In attending to something disinterestedly, we feel a release from the pressing concerns of everyday life – from our own concerns, such as our monetary interests – and from the issues of society at large – such as the moral education of children. Some authors speak of aesthetic experience as freedom from the pressures of ordinary life. We leave life outside when we enter the concert hall and listen to the music.

When we attend to an artwork disinterestedly, we appreciate it for its own sake, not for its connection with practical issues. Are its structures unified, is it pleasingly complex, what are its noteworthy aesthetic properties, and are they intense or not? These are the questions that occur to disinterested viewers – not "Is this good or bad for society?", "Will it make money?", or "Will it arouse me sexually?"

Attending to something aesthetically is disinterested. But it is also sympathetic. The relevant sort of sympathy involves more than simply not allowing ulterior motives to influence our attention. It involves surrendering to the work – allowing ourselves to be guided by its structures and their purposes. Sympathetic attention is directed at the object and willingly accepts the guidance of the object over the succession of our mental states by the properties and relations that structure the object. Sympathetic attention presupposes playing by the object's own rules, rather than importing our own – for example, going along with the convention of people singing to each other in operas, instead of saying people don't behave like that, or accepting the notion of warp-drive while reading a science fiction story. Attending sympathetically involves placing yourself in the hands of the maker of the object – going wherever she bids you, and attending to whatever she makes salient.

Aesthetic experience is also described as a form of contemplation. This should not be understood as a passive state. When contemplating an object, we do not simply receive its stimuli passively. It is not a matter of a cow-like, vacant gaze, nor is it a state of distraction or inattention, as in the expression "lost in contemplation." It is not aimless wool-gathering. To contemplate an object is to be acutely aware of its details and their inter-relationships. Contemplation, in this sense, calls for keen observation. It also involves exercising actively the constructive powers of the mind, of being challenged by a diversity of often initially conflicting stimuli and of attempting to make them cohere. Contemplation here is riveted on the object of attention, is closely observant of its discrete elements and proper-ties, and strives to find connections between them.

This process of contemplation, when supported by the object of our attention, can be a source of immense satisfaction. The active search for details and connections itself can be exhilarating, and the success of such activity, where it occurs, can bestow a kind of self-rewarding pleasure on the activity as a whole. With aesthetic experience this sort of pleasure is said to be valued for its own sake. Just as we value the pleasure that accompanies employing the powers of our minds (irrespective of whether we win or lose) in a chess match for its own sake – and not because it might make us better military strategists – similarly the mental and emotional workout afforded by aesthetic experience is its own reward.

We do not enter such experiences for the sake of becoming smarter or more sensitive, even if this might result from such encounters, but because the active exercise of our constructive powers, perceptual skills, and emo-tional resources is exciting in and of itself. Just as we enjoy fairground rides for the fun of it, and not because they prepare us for being astronauts (though some of the rides might), aesthetic experience is something we pursue for its own sake.

According to the affect-oriented account, aesthetic experience is the disinterested and sympathetic attention to and contemplation of any object whatsoever for its own sake. This way of putting it allows that anything could be an object of aesthetic experience. Nevertheless, some objects are more conducive to this sort of experience than others. Clouds are more conducive to being attended to and contemplated than are water-logged construction sites.

Moreover, certain objects can be intentionally constructed in such a way that they are eminently suitable for disinterested and sympathetic attention and contemplation. They will contain structures that guide attention and contemplation – that encourage it by means of their inten-tionally designed features of unity, complexity and intensity – and that reward such attention and contemplation. The aesthetic experiencer will not have to do all the work herself. The object itself will be structured intentionally to invite, sustain and, optimally, reward disinterested and sympathetic attention and contemplation. Such objects, of course, are artworks.

Plugging the affect-oriented account into the aesthetic definition of art, then, x is an artwork if and only if x is intentionally produced with the capacity to afford the disinterested and sympathetic attention and contemplation of x for its own sake. Natural objects are not produced with this capacity, and, therefore, do not count as artworks. Nor are the majority of human artifacts created with this intention either; so they are not artworks either. It may be that many human artifacts can be contemplated disinterestedly and sympathetically, but they are not designed to be conducive to this mode of attention, and, in many cases, the question of design notwithstanding, many human artifacts are not conducive to the relevant form of contemplation – they neither invite, sustain nor reward it. Autobody repair shops, for example, typically do not.

Employing the affect-oriented account, we can identify artworks as artifacts (both objects and performances) designed with the intended capacity to invite, abet, and repay disinterested and sympathetic attention and contemplation. This is the affect-oriented version of the aesthetic definition of art.

This approach also suggests grounds for pronouncing an artwork to be good: it is good where it indeed has the capacity to encourage, support and remit disinterested attention and contemplation. It is bad when it fails to do so. A critical reason in favor of an artwork is one that comments upon its capacities to realize its intended function, whereas negative critical evaluations will rest on showing how a work lacks these capacities.

The importance of art in general resides in the value of developing our powers of disinterested and sympathetic attention and contemplation. Here there are a variety of advantages to be had from cultivating these human powers, though we do not seek out aesthetic experiences in order to enhance these powers, but rather simply for the sake of having these powers exercised. That our human powers are augmented by aesthetic experiences is a concomitant value aesthetic experiences happen to possess. We would seek out artworks and the aesthetic experiences thereof, even if they were not beneficial for human life. However, that they are so beneficial, through their exercise of our powers of observation and construction, helps explain why art is such a valued province of social life.

Unlike Bell, the aesthetic theorist of art need not remain silent about what she means by aesthetic experience. Thus, her theory cannot be rejected because it provides no instruction about its central terms. Indeed, we have seen that the aesthetic theorist has at least two ways to define aesthetic experience: the content-oriented account and the affect-oriented account. These accounts, in turn, yield two different versions of the aesthetic definition of art. Thus, to assess the aesthetic definition of art, we need to examine each version respectively.

Objections to the aesthetic definition of art

The aesthetic definition of art can be construed either in terms of the content-oriented account of aesthetic experience or the affect-oriented account. These two accounts, of course, could be connected. However, for analytic purposes it is more convenient to consider them one at a time. And, in any case, if neither is convincing on its own, it is unlikely that they will be convincing when added together.

Reading "aesthetic experience" after the fashion of the content-oriented account, x is an artwork if and only if x is intended to present unities, diversities and/or intensities for apprehension.

But this formula is far too broad to provide a sufficient condition for art status, since virtually every human artifact will present unities, diversities and/or intensities for apprehension. A loaf of bread possesses unity in virtue of being a single object, and the baker presents it to us with the intention that we apprehend it as such. Most human artifacts have different parts – telephones have numerous buttons, for example – and they are diverse to that extent, while, in addition, the telephone company wants us to apprehend the parts and believes that we will. Likewise, everyday artifacts and their parts possess properties of varying intensity – perhaps they are color-coded – and their designers intend us to discriminate these signals by virtue of their varying intensities. But none of these examples are artworks, though they seem to satisfy the conditions of the aesthetic definition.

In response to these observations, the aesthetic theorist is apt to say that we have misunderstood what he means by unity, diversity, and intensity. These are to be conceived of as *aesthetic* properties, not as brute properties of objects. They are properties of the appearance of objects. Hills covered with green trees may strike us as soft and downy as we drive past them; this is how they impress us and creatures like us. But such hills and trees are not soft – when you get close to them, they are rough and scratchy. Rather, they appear to be soft and downy.

Similarly, when speaking of unity, diversity and intensity aesthetically, we are talking about the way in which such objects strike us and people like us. Artworks are objects intended to present unities, diversities and/or intensities for apprehension where these are understood to be aesthetic properties.

But this still results in a theory that is far too broad to be an adequate definition of art. For many human artifacts, notably, for our purposes, myriad nonart objects, are designed to present aesthetic properties for apprehension, including the properties of unity, diversity and intensity. Motor boats are designed to exhibit many expressive properties intensely. They connote aggressiveness and strength, and their possession of these intensely projected properties give them a compelling unity of appearance. We might say they look very "macho." This may not be the only intention behind the design of speed boats, but it is undeniably one of them.

On the other hand, children's playgrounds are often laid out to suggest a pleasing diversity. But neither power boats or playgrounds are art. The problem here is that human artifacts of all sorts are intended, among other things, to present aesthetically unified, diverse, and intense arrays for apprehension. But only a subset of such artifacts are artworks. The presentation of aesthetic properties intended to be apprehended is not enough to qualify an object as an artwork. Something stronger is required. But what?

The aesthetic theorist might be tempted to say that the aesthetic unity, diversity and/or intensities intended for apprehension must be artistically relevant. And it is true that features like unity, diversity, and the intensity of their aesthetic properties are characteristically artistically relevant properties of artworks. That is, they are generally relevant to our appreciation of the artworks that present them. However, the aesthetic theorist cannot invoke the notion of artistic relevance in his definition, since that would presuppose that he already knows how to identify art (in order to say what is *artistically* relevant) and that is what his definition is supposed to be elucidating. Thus, to speak of artistically relevant properties here would be circular.

Indeed, very often we look for properties like unity, diversity and intensity in certain objects just because we know that they are artworks. We apprehend diversity as a significant feature of Cage's 4′ 33″ because it is an artwork; we are not struck by the diversity of everyday ambient sounds, and we rarely, if ever, suppose that they are intended to foreground the property of diversity for our apprehension. It is the fact that 4′ 33″ is an artwork that leads us to attribute the aesthetic property of diversity to it. But if art status is what makes the intended presentation of aesthetic properties for apprehension possible, it seems wrong to attempt to characterize art status in the way the aesthetic definition does. The definition appears to get things the wrong way around.

The aesthetic definition of art, construed in light of the content-oriented account of aesthetic experience, does not give us a sufficient condition for art status. But is the intention to present unities, diversities and/or intensities for apprehension a necessary condition for art? Certainly artists can intend to make works bereft of each of these properties individually. Some artworks, like Luis Buñuel's film *Un Chien Andalou*, appear intended to subvert any sense of unity – images are deliberately cut together with no apparent narrative logic. Many of Sol LeWitt's sculptures – repetitions of a simple geometric shape – seem scarcely diverse at all, and they look as though they were intended to be that way. And many readymades are chosen for the absence of any striking aesthetic properties in them, and, therefore, they lack intensity altogether. Aren't these counterexamples to the theory?

Perhaps the aesthetic theorist will say "no." He may grant that a work may lack either unity, or diversity, or intensity, but deny that there could be an artwork that was intended to present none of the preceding properties for apprehension. The argument might go like this: unity and diversity co-vary. So if an artist presents a work remarkable for its intended lack of unity, then the work will inevitably impart a sense of diversity. Conversely, a work that downplays diversity will automatically yield a sense of unity.

Consequently, any artwork will have to be presented with the intention to present either unity or diversity for apprehension, since the absence of one will entail the presence of the other for apprehension. Therefore, the intentional presentation of *either* unity or diversity for apprehension is a necessary condition of all artworks. There is no way of getting around it.

Whether one accepts this argument partly depends on one's understanding of the terms "unity" and "diversity." If presenting the property of diversity for apprehension means that we are struck by the variety of the work amidst its unity, then surely there are artworks, like some Abstract Expressionist paintings, where the perceptible array strikes us as confused, rather than diverse. Moreover, confusion may be what the artist is after, rather than a sense of variety amidst unity. Historically, artists have had a number of reasons for intending to provoke confusion. Thus, an artwork that lacks unity may not be intended to present the relevant sort of diversity for apprehension. The artist may be interested in exploiting disunity in order to sow total confusion and disorientation.

Furthermore, if an artist intends to engender confusion, it does not follow that she intends to present diversity for apprehension. It may be the incredible wealth of different things in the work that brings about confusion and disorientation, but the artist may not present the work with the intention that we locate our confusion in the diversity of elements in the work. The purpose of the work may not be to encourage us to contemplate the diverse elements of the work, but to overwhelm and bewilder us by it. Some of Robert Morris's installations, which were discussed in the previous chapter, are pertinent examples to think about here.

Likewise, a work that downplays diversity need not be intended to present unity for apprehension. Andy Warhol's film *Empire* – an eight-hour view of the Empire State Building – is hardly describable as diverse or complex. It is intentionally minimal in its content and its execution. One could call it unified, but it is not the intention of the film-maker that we apprehend its unity. Rather, it is the implications of the experiment for common notions about the nature of film that Warhol ultimately wants to explore by means of *Empire*. It is a *reductio ad absurdum* of certain claims about film realism and of the view that what is important about film is the mechanical reproduction of the world. To respond to the film by saying "Ah! How aesthetically unified!" would be to miss the intended point of *Empire*. Thus, an artwork that underplays variety need not be intended to present unity for apprehension. It may have very different fish to fry.

At the same time, *Empire* is intentionally unemphatic in the manner in which it shoots the Empire State Building. It does not invest its subject with intense aesthetic properties, nor does it underline any of the aesthetic properties for which the building is duly famous. The film is intentionally as mundane as mundane can be. Thus, if *Empire* is an artwork, then there are artworks that are not intended to present unities, diversities, or intensities for apprehension. They may be underwritten by altogether different intentions. Consequently, the aesthetic definition of art, stated in terms of the content-oriented account of aesthetic experience, does not identify a necessary condition of all art.

But what if we read the aesthetic definition of art in terms of the affect-oriented account of aesthetic experience? Will that improve matters? On that view, x is an artwork if and only if x is intentionally produced with the capacity to afford disinterested and sympathetic attention and contemplation for its own sake. Is it plausible to believe that all artworks are necessarily produced with such an intention?

It seems unlikely. The biggest problem here is the notion of disinterestedness. As we have already noted more than once, many artworks are produced with religious and political purposes in mind. They are not designed to be contemplated disinterestedly, but are connected to practical affairs. A feminist novel may be intended to rouse readers – both women and men – to change their lives. Here the personal may be political, and the novel may address interests of readers that intertwine the two. Such a novel is not designed to be perused disinterestedly. Indeed, a disinterested reading might subvert the intention of the novel. That is, it is hard to imagine that a disinterested reading is even a secondary goal of such a novel, since any such reading is antithetical to its primary purpose. Thus, not all artworks need be underwritten by the intention to invite, sustain and reward disinterested contemplation. Some enjoin interested contemplation and application to one's interested, practical affairs.

Of course, the aesthetic theorist may claim that such works are not really art, but that just seems to beg the question, especially since there are so many examples of this sort that are considered to be canonical works of art. Nor does it make much sense to argue on the grounds that such works have aesthetic properties and formal structures that the works have a secondary intention to invite disinterested contemplation, if those features are all rhetorically in the service of moving readers to an interested consideration of personal and political oppression.

Indeed, cases like this one suggest an even deeper problem with the aesthetic definition of art. The theory may be fundamentally incoherent. The definition requires that an artwork be intended to have the capacity to afford a disinterested *and* a sympathetic response. But in many cases, this may be an impossible combination. Surely, a sympathetic response to a social protest fiction about racism – like a dramatization of *Cry the Beloved Country* – involves being moved to indignation. The drama calls for readers to change their society and to change their lives. A sympathetic response to *Cry the Beloved Country* should predispose the spectator toward certain practical actions, or, at least, toward thinking about such practical actions. And some of these practical actions may even be connected to possible actions in the spectator's everyday life.

Cry the Beloved Country addresses practical problems that may be connected to the spectator's personal and political interests, and it endorses certain solutions that anyone worth calling a sympathetic viewer should take seriously. Being a sympathetic viewer (or reader) in this case is bound up with broader social and even personal interests (especially if one is a victim of racism, as both black and white spectators may be). So in what sense can the sympathetic viewer also be disinterested? The disinterested stance and the sympathetic stance are in conflict here. If one genuinely places oneself under the guidance of artworks like *Cry the Beloved Country*, it is difficult to see how one's attention and contemplation of the work can be simultaneously disinterested. Furthermore, it is hard to understand how an artist can rationally intend such a work to have the capacity to promote both of these modes of attention and contemplation, since each cancels out the other.

Art history provides many examples of works that are bound up with personal and social interests. Artworks frequently function to forge personal identities and to advance practical projects. If we suppose that the makers of these works intend them to possess the capacity to afford disinterested *and* sympathetic attention, must we not then agree that the makers of the relevant works have self-contradictory intentions? But it is a very dubious definition of art that entails that so much of art history is made up of self-contradictory works.

Of course, it is open to the aesthetic theorist to claim that where works possess only the capacity to afford sympathetic responses that somehow preclude disinterested responses, then we are not dealing with art. A work is art only where both intended capacities can be realized. But this would result in a radical gerrymandering of art history. So many works regarded as paradigmatic would drop out of the tradition.

Or, the aesthetic theorist might bite the bullet and say that the creators of engaged artworks are self-contradictory, but they just don't realize it. However, ascribing irrationality to artists on such a large scale seems quite unpalatable, especially since so many artists are self-consciously explicit about their opposition to the concept of disinterestedness. A more obvious solution to the dilemma is to admit that the aesthetic definition of art, framed in terms of the affect-oriented account of aesthetic experience, does not provide a necessary condition for art status.

Needless to say, the aesthetic theorist can remove the incoherence in his theory by dropping the idea that the artwork is intended to have the capacity to afford both a sympathetic *and* a disinterested response. Instead he may require only that artworks have the capacity to afford disinterested attention and contemplation. That gets rid of the incoherence, but it only questionably makes the definition more attractive, since there are many artworks that are not intended to encourage or to afford disinterested responses.

For example, the shields of the Sepik and Highlands warriors of New Guinea have a fair claim to art status. They are replete with representational, expressive, and formal properties, and they belong to an intelligible tradition of making. And yet the horrific faces on them are intended to frighten their enemies, not to promote disinterested attention and contemplation. They are not meant to release onlookers from the oppression of practical interests, but to give them a practical interest in running away. Fetishes of all sorts are intended to serve practical interests that are inimicable to a disinterested stance. The discussion of statues of demons in the previous chapter raises another case in point. If any of these examples are artworks, then it cannot be the case that an intended capacity to afford disinterested attention and contemplation for its own sake is a necessary condition for all art. That we citizens of other cultures choose to peruse these objects in our museums with what is called disinterested attention does not indicate that these works were produced with the intended capacity to afford such responses.

Nor can the aesthetic theorist drop the requirement that the capacity here *must be intended* in favor of saying merely that x is an artwork only if it affords distinterested attention, since that will lose the distinction between good art and bad art. That is, a work that fails to afford disinterested attention and contemplation – that fails to afford aesthetic experience – will not count as art at all. But a definition that does not cover bad art does not adequately capture our concept of art.

Does the aesthetic definition of art, read in terms of an affect-oriented account of aesthetic experience, supply a sufficient condition for art? No, and for reasons with which we are already very familiar. Many nonartworks are intended to have the capacity to promote the kind of attention and contemplation that the aesthetic definition of art ascribes to all and only artworks. High-priced cutlery often has intended aesthetic properties that warrant attention and contemplation, independently of their practical purposes. A Sabatier knife can be a thing of beauty – so much so that we would prefer to look at it rather than to use it.

Cars too often afford occasions for aesthetic experience. We may stand back and appreciate their lines for the aesthetic properties they impart. Undoubtedly, these lines are also intended to serve practical functions. But they are also intended to project an aesthetic profile. A car may connote elegance by its design.

Perhaps part of the reason for this is that car manufacturers hope that buyers will purchase such vehicles in order to say something about them-selves to the world. But one can attend to the shape of a car and dwell upon its dashing curves without having any personal interests in owning the car or buying stock in the company. Moreover, the intention to appeal to the eye in this way by means of arresting appearances undeniably numbers among the intentions of car designers. But our highways are not jammed with artworks. That is, *most* cars are not artworks, but it would appear that the aesthetic theorist would have to count most of them (and not just the custom-made ones) as such. And this indicates that the affect-oriented aesthetic definition is too broad.

On neither the content-oriented nor the affect-oriented account of aes-thetic experience, does the aesthetic definition of art provide necessary or sufficient conditions for art. Some readers may feel that the problems we've encountered here are really the result of the limitations of the accounts of aesthetic experience that we've inserted into the aesthetic defi-nition of art. They may suspect that if we just stated that x is an artwork if and only if x is intended to have the capacity to afford aesthetic experience – using our ordinary language notions of this concept – the aesthetic theory of art would have a better chance of succeeding.

Of course, there is a real question about whether we have any ordinary language intuitions about the phrase "aesthetic experience." The concept really seems primarily a technical one. But if we do have some ordinary sense of the notion, then it still seems that the theory is doomed. The aesthetic definition does not pick out only artworks, since ordinary lan-guage recognizes that things other than artworks can be intentionally designed with the capacity to afford aesthetic experiences – Fords, for example.

Moreover, not all artworks are designed to afford aesthetic experiences in any "ordinary" sense of the phrase. The capacity to afford aesthetic experience is not a necessary condition for art. Some artworks, like Duchamp's *Fountain*, are idea based, rather than experience based. One can derive satisfaction from thinking about *Fountain* without even experiencing it, let alone experiencing it aesthetically. One can read about it and think about it without knowing what exactly it looked like in terms of its form and its perceptible properties. Arguably, Duchamp would have subverted his own intention to provoke thinking about the nature and future of art, if *Fountain* had the capacity to afford the disinterested contemplation of its form and perceptible properties.

Thus, the aesthetic theorist of art was mistaken earlier in the first premise of his argument. It is not the case that audiences use *all* artworks to function as sources of aesthetic experience, nor is this the reason they seek out *all* artworks. Some artworks are sought for their ideas, not for the aesthetic experiences they afford.

Another generic problem with aesthetic definitions of art is that they treat art status as dependent upon the intended function to promote aesthetic experience. But whether or not a candidate has this capacity is frequently dependent on whether or not it is an artwork. Duchamp presented a vial of fifty cubic centimeters of Parisian air as an artwork. Called *Paris Air*, it is *impish* (and affords an aesthetic experience of quality of impishness) just because it is an artwork. It offers a satirical comment on the artworld's obsession with all things Parisian.

An ordinary vial full of Parisian air, even one perceptually indiscernible from Duchamp's, would not afford, nor is it intended to afford, a comparable aesthetic experience. It is the fact that we know that Duchamp's vial is an artwork that enables us to appreciate its impishness; indeed, it wouldn't be impish if it weren't an artwork. But if aesthetic experience is sometimes dependent on art status, then art status cannot be defined noncircularly in terms of aesthetic experience.

Many of the preceding counterexamples to the conjecture that the intended capacity to afford aesthetic experience is a necessary condition for art status have been drawn from the avant-garde. This may seem unfair, since earlier it was noted that often aesthetic theorists of art deny that works of the avant-garde are artworks. We reviewed the case against Cone's "Poème Symphonique," for instance. So if aesthetic theorists of art do not regard such works as artworks, is it legitimate to introduce avant-garde works as counterexamples to the aesthetic definition of art?

Inasmuch as a great deal of avant-garde art is avowedly anti-aesthetic, it should come as no surprise that the aesthetic definition of art cannot accommodate it. Aesthetic theorists of art are aware of this, and, as a result, they deny that so-called anti-aesthetic art is genuinely art. Doesn't it simply beg the question, then, to cite it against aesthetic definitions of art?

And yet we expect definitions of art to track our practices of classifying art. Anti-aesthetic art has existed for over eighty-five years, and it has been classified as art by art historians, critics, collectors, and a great many informed viewers. Nor is it a marginal movement in twentieth-century art. It has often commanded the limelight. Names like Duchamp, Cage, and Warhol are generally regarded as central figures of twentieth-century art, and they exert a continuing influence on artmaking and criticism today. This is not to say that there are no dissenters. But they have not deterred the unflagging interest in anti-aesthetic art among impressively large numbers of artists, experts, historians, critics, and art lovers. That presents a *prima facie* case that anti-aesthetic art warrants inclusion under our operative concept of art. It is difficult to explain the practices of modern art, unless our concept is inclusive enough to countenance anti-aesthetic art.

It seems that the existence of anti-aesthetic art is a fact of the artworld and has been for some time. The aesthetic theorist of art cannot define it away. If that is a consequence of the aesthetic definition of art, then it seems that the definition's proponent, not the critic, is begging the question. A comprehensive theory of art must accommodate the facts as she finds them revealed in our practices. Where, indeed, should we look for our facts, except in our practices? The aesthetic theorist cannot stipulate what she will count as facts in the face of massive amounts of countervailing evidence, which continues to grow daily. We have every reason to believe that anti-aesthetic art is art on the basis of our evolving practice, which, in turn, gives us compelling grounds to deny that the aesthetic definition of art is a comprehensive theory of all art.

Part II
The aesthetic dimension

Aesthetic experience revisited

Aesthetic experience is not definitory of all art. There is nonaesthetic and even anti-aesthetic art. Thus, the aesthetic theory of art is not a comprehensive theory of all art. However, the notion of aesthetic experience pervades our discussion of art. Therefore, we must ask what sense, if any, can be made of it.

As already noted, the most popular conception of aesthetic experience claims that it is the disinterested and sympathetic attention and contemplation of any object whatsoever for its own sake. We have pointed out that there may be some problems in this view with wedding the notions of disinterest and sympathy with regard to many artworks. But that tension may only be an issue when we are attempting to use aesthetic experience to define all art. The problem may appear to be less pressing when we are merely trying to characterize aesthetic experience, allowing that the affordance of aesthetic experience is not a feature, let alone a defining feature, of all artworks. Our responses to artworks – let us call them art-responses – may encompass things other than aesthetic experience. Yet what is it when we experience an artwork aesthetically? Is it disinterested and sympathetic attention and contemplation for their own sake?

We can have what we call aesthetic experiences of artworks, or of every-day things, like nature. These experiences involve attention and contemplation as their most characteristic elements. We look at, listen to and/or read the objects of aesthetic experience and we peruse them thoughtfully. Kicking around a copy of *The Blithedale Romance* like a football, no matter how enjoyable, is not what we usually think of as an aesthetic experience. Of course, there are interactive artworks, and aesthetic experiences of nature often involve doing things, like wading through a warm, placid pond. But generally these experiences are only called aesthetic when we attend to the these interactions and reflect upon them. Attention and contemplation are at least the most frequent modes of experiencing something aesthetically.

Moreover, what are called aesthetic experiences are sympathetic, at least in this sense: that we take cognizance of the object in question and we attempt to let it guide us where it will. It may turn out that the object is a poor guide. If it is an artwork, it may be ineptly constructed. Or, it may be intended to lead us where we do not wish to go. It may alienate our sympathies. However, our experience can still be called aesthetic so long as we approach the work openly, even if the object eventually makes our continued sympathetic attention impossible. The relevant sort of sympathy here only requires that we enter the experience with a willingness to see where it will take us. We would not call it an aesthetic experience if before encountering the object we were completely closed to it.

An Islamic fundamentalist who reads Salman Rushdie's *Satanic Verses*, unwilling to explore it with openness and predisposed to deem its every word blasphemous, does not undergo what is typically called an aesthetic experience of the work. On the other hand, the reader who gives the book a shot, but finally puts it aside, finding it too prolix, can be said to have had an aesthetic experience, at least in terms of the requirement of sympathy, even if his is ultimately a mistaken construal of the book. Sympathy, here, just requires a reasonable amount of openness to the book, even if it is withdrawn in the last instance. We would not typically call an experience of a work aesthetic that altogether ignored the structures of the work and what they were intended to do.

Attention, contemplation, and sympathy seem like reasonable components of the notion called aesthetic experience. But what of disinterestedness? Disinterestedness is generally regarded as the most important element of aesthetic experience. But is aesthetic experience really disinterested?

Disinterested attention is supposed to be the mark of aesthetic experience. The existence of such a state is often inferred by considering certain examples and by proposing disinterestedness as the best concept for explaining them. For instance, if someone goes to a school play because her daughter is in it, and she spends all her time nodding beamingly at her offspring's performance, proponents of disinterestedness will suggest that we all agree that her experience is not aesthetic. What is wrong here? The proponent of disinterestedness explains: her attention is guided by her personal interests; it is not impartial; it is not disinterested.

Likewise, if a patron of the arts admires his recently acquired painting because he is sure it will make him world famous, his attention is motivated by his personal interests; his experience is not what is called disinterested. And that is why we will refrain from calling his responses aesthetic experiences.

Finally, where a Bolshevik commissar reads a novel solely to confirm that all the references to Stalin are adulatory, he was not reading in a manner that most would call aesthetic. Why not? Because his attention was guided by practical, political interests, and not by disinterestedness.

Surely in these cases, there is something wrong or deficient about the way in which the audience members in question are responding to the relevant artworks. The friend of disinterestedness offers an explanation that covers all these cases, and many others like them. In all these examples, the problem is that these "art-lovers" bring the wrong sort of attention to the pertinent artworks. Their attention is interested, rather than, as it should be, disinterested.

This account, however, makes a significant presumption, namely that attention and contemplation are the sorts of things that are interested or disinterested. But if attention is not the sort of thing that can be interested or disinterested, then, the notion that aesthetic experience is necessarily defined in terms of disinterested attention is unacceptable. This is the possibility that we must now explore.

Disinterestedness is supposed to pick out a certain kind of attention. But does it? Is a woman who is only concentrating on her daughter's performance attending to the play interestedly (rather than disinterestedly)? Or, is she not paying attention to the play at all? Similarly, the art patron who fantasizes about incipient glory has not failed to pay disinterested attention to his painting. As he dreams of fame, he is just not attending to the painting, period. He is off in never-never land. Nor is the commissar paying attention to the novel as a whole; he is reading it incompletely, heeding only the references to Stalin.

These aren't failures to mobilize a peculiar kind of attention called disinterested attention. Rather, these are examples of inattention. That is, what the friend of disinterested attention calls interested attention may just not be attention of any sort. It may be more accurate to call it distraction or inattention.

Commonly a distinction is drawn between disinterested and interested attention. Allegedly, these are two contrasting forms of attention. But is that contrast a real one, or is it rather a misleading way of framing another contrast – the contrast between attention and nonattention? Surely it makes more sense to describe the mother, the art patron, and the commissar in our preceding examples as being inattentive, rather than in terms of their failure to enlist some special kind of attention called disinterested attention. Shouldn't we be talking about attention versus nonattention in these cases rather than disinterested versus interested attention?

To determine whether or not there is some special form of attention worthy of the title disinterested attention, consider the case of Sydney and Evelyn. Both of them are listening to Beethoven's *Emperor Concerto*. Sydney is listening to it for pure pleasure. She attends to its aesthetic properties and follows its structures carefully. Evelyn listens to it in the same way. She takes note of its aesthetic properties and strains to notice its every structural variation.

But there is this difference between Sydney and Evelyn. Tomorrow Evelyn has an exam in music theory in which she will be expected to discuss the aesthetic properties and musicological structures of the *Emperor Concerto* at length. Evelyn is listening to the concerto with a personal interest, her desire for a good grade, motivating her attentiveness. But does the fact that Evelyn is motivated in this way entail that the manner in which she attends to the concerto need be any different from the way in which Sydney listens to the music?

Sydney and Evelyn listen to all the same notes, phrases and movements. Both apprehend the same aesthetic properties. Both follow the same musical structures as they evolve over time. Indeed, it is even possible that Evelyn takes notice of more aesthetic properties and structures in the concerto than Sydney does. Surely, Evelyn is paying attention to the concerto in a way that is appropriate to what the artist intends. She may be doing exactly what Sydney is doing, and even then some. What sense does it make to say that Evelyn's mode of attention must be different in kind than Sydney's?

Attention is a matter of concentrating the mind on something. Evelyn is certainly concentrating her mind on the *Emperor Concerto*. There is no reason to suppose that the quantity, quality, and focus of her concentration here are any different from Sydney's. What difference should it make that Evelyn's motives differ from Sydney's – that Evelyn's motives are to get a good grade, while Sydney's are to be entertained? Attending to something is concentrating on it, irrespective of one's motives.

The bank robber and the rescue team may have different reasons for attending to the combination lock on a vault: the safe-cracker wants to steal the money inside; the police officer to save the people trapped behind the door. But both attend to the clicks of the tumbler in the lock mechanism in the same way. Similarly, if we imagine some third party, solely concerned with opening the lock for the fun of it, we would not say that the mode of attention he lavishes on the combination lock is different in kind from the thief's or the policeman's. There are not two kinds of attention here – two different ways of concentrating – one called interested attention and the other called disinterested attention. There is just plain attention.

An act of attention is identified in terms of its object. Acts of attention can be undertaken for different motives. The critic scrutinizes a sculpture with an eye to writing a review; the gallery-goer contemplates it for sheer enjoyment. Suppose both of them like the sculpture. Does it seem credible to say that the critic's mode of attention – what she looks at, or how she considers it imaginatively – need be different than the plain gallery-goer's, just because she has to file an article?

Think of Sydney and Evelyn again. Now add to their company Jerome. Jerome is also playing a recording of the *Emperor Concerto*. But Jerome is playing the recording to impress his lover with his highbrow culture. He barely listens to the music, and when he does he spins into reveries of how it will persuade his lover to hold him in awe. Shall we call his attention to the concerto interested?

But is Evelyn's attention in any way like Jerome's? She, like Sydney, is attending to the qualities and structures of the music. Doesn't it seem right here to say that Jerome isn't paying attention to the music, whereas Sydney and Evelyn are, rather than saying that Sydney is attending disinterestedly whereas Evelyn and Jerome are attending to it interestedly?

That is, there is attention and there is nonattention, here, instead of disinterested and interested attention. The notions of attention and inattention do as well as, if not a better job of, explaining the cases of the mother, the art patron and the commissar as do the notions of disinterested and interested attention. Moreover, the couplet attention-and-inattention does a better job than the couplet disinterestedness-and-interestedness in describing what is going on with Sydney, Evelyn and Jerome. So perhaps it is better to dispense with the notions like disinterested attention completely.

This also appears to accord with what we mean by attention. Attention is concentration. This can be done intensely and well, in a slipshod fashion, or not at all. We can concentrate on any object in any of these ways, irrespective of our motives. Motives are not part of the activity of attention proper. They cause acts of attention, but they do not qualify them as particular kinds of acts of attention. We can be personally motivated to attend to a painting, but attend to it distractedly nevertheless; while we can be paid to listen to a piece of music, and follow its every twist and turn with the *élan* of a musicologist. Our motives do not determine the quality of our attention.

"Disinterestedness" refers to our motivation with respect to certain acts of attention. Thus, it is not a part or kind of attention proper. At best it alludes to certain causal factors, or the lack thereof, that may prompt certain acts of attention. It is not a constituent of attention, nor a way of attending. Therefore, we have grounds to suspect that process of disinterested attention that is said to define aesthetic experience does not, in fact, exist. There is only attention and inattention, not some rarefied animal called "disinterested attention."

Furthermore, as we have seen, the concept of disinterested attention does not have the explanatory power that we initially thought. It is not really the best explanation of what went wrong with the mother, the art patron, and the commissar. Their way of responding to their respective art objects was not defective because they failed to attend disinterestedly, but because they failed to attend to them at all. The notions of distraction, inattention and nonattention – in their ordinary language usages – are far more accurate, serviceable, and appealing than the concocted, technical notion of disinterested attention for explaining why certain kinds of responses to artworks – like the art patron's – are flawed. Thus, from an explanatory point of view, we can dispense with the notion of disinterested attention.

The preceding discussion of disinterested attention, of course, indicates that there is no such thing, at least where it is intended to designate a special mode of attention. However, if disinterested attention (and contemplation) do not exist, then they cannot be invoked to define aesthetic experience. Thus, one account of aesthetic experience – the account of aesthetic experience as disinterested attention – must be abandoned.

The consequences of this are at least twofold. First, with respect to Part I of this chapter, if there is no such thing as disinterested attention (and contemplation), then that is yet another reason why the aesthetic definition of art, construed in terms of the affect-oriented account, cannot be correct. If there is no such thing as aesthetic experience of the relevant sort – namely, disinterested experience – and artists are aware of this (as the majority seem to be), then it appears unlikely that artworks are essentially objects produced with the intended capacity to afford aesthetic experiences of the allegedly disinterested variety.

The second implication of this exercise is that if there is no such thing as disinterested attention, then the most common account of aesthetic experience goes by the board. There is nothing that the account refers to, if there is no such thing as disinterested attention. However, people, or at least philosophers (they're people too), have been talking about aesthetic experience for two centuries. Did the concept mark nothing at all? Can it be that they were talking about something totally imaginary?

Probably not. But in order to see what people were getting at, we need to get rid of the popular conception of aesthetic experience as necessarily disinterested. We need to return to what in the last section was called the content-oriented conception of aesthetic experience. That conception calls an experience aesthetic in virtue of what it is an experience of. An experience is aesthetic, if it is an experience of the sensuous properties, aesthetic properties, and formal relations of its objects of attention.

In this regard, what in the previous chapter was called *design appreciation* is a major subcategory of aesthetic experience. Design appreciation focuses upon how a work works. It is preoccupied with the ways in which the means employed in an artwork suit (or ill-suit) its purposes. This is not the only response that we can have to an artwork, nor even the only appropriate response. But it is one very common response. Indeed, we often read books and attend art appreciation classes in order to learn how to do this, since it can be very satisfying.

Design appreciation is one thing that people often mean by the phrase "aesthetic experience." Moreover, it is easy to see how attention to the design of the work could have been mistaken for and misdescribed as "disinterested attention." When we focus on the design of a work, we batten on its internal structure. We examine the parts in order to take note of the whole. Our attention is, so to speak, centripetal. We are not directly involved in assessing the consequences of the work for either ourselves or for society. We are simply concerned with how it works. Our attention is bracketed on its structure. It is this bracketing that people attempt to characterize by notions like disinterested attention, though it may be suggested that a more accurate way of describing it is to say that we are centrally focussed upon and attentive to the design of the work – the way in which the form of the work functions to realize its intended point and/or purpose.

When immersed in the process of design appreciation, we are involved in determining and assessing the form of the work. We attend to and contemplate its design. We generally put to one side questions about whether the point or the purpose of the work is ignoble or noble, useful or harmful (to ourselves or others), frivolous or important, and so on. Just as a pacificist can study the design of an armored car and note the suitability of its modifications for its purpose – even though she deplores the purpose – we can size up the design of an artwork, irrespective of the interests it serves. Indeed, where our response to an artwork is primarily to its design, dwelling on the point or purpose of the work in terms of a framework of broader interests is generally outside the purview of our concerns. Design appreciation is compartmentalized, attending to and contemplating (in their usual senses) the design of the work, while bracketing larger questions.

Perhaps it is this bracketing of broader interests for the sake of focussing on the design of the work that some have misnamed "disinterested attention." But design appreciation is not a matter of a special kind of attention. Rather it is a matter of focussing attention in a certain way – of limiting it in scope to the form of the work.

Design appreciation is not disinterested attention, nor should it be described that way. Disinterested attention allegedly names a kind of attention; design appreciation merely refers to the scope of our attention in certain circumstances. Design appreciation is just plain old concentration, directed and focussed upon a certain kind of object, namely the form of the artwork. If our attention is primarily engaged with the design of an artwork, then that is an instance of aesthetic experience, no matter the interests that motivate us to be so preoccupied. Design appreciation is simply one, albeit a major, form that aesthetic experience takes.

When people speak of aesthetic experience, they are frequently referring to design appreciation. When commenting upon the unity or complexity of an artwork, we are reporting the results of an aesthetic experience, often an experience of the form of an artwork. Aesthetic experience in this respect is attention to and contemplation of the design of the work, including features such as unity and complexity.

But the design of artworks is not the only object of aesthetic experience. Along with formal relations, aesthetic experiences are also experiences of aesthetic properties, including expressive properties, of varying intensities. Consequently, in order to continue this discussion of aesthetic experience, we need to say a bit more about aesthetic properties.

Aesthetic properties

Watching a dancer pirouette, we are struck by her gracefulness. Reading a novel, we sense its dark qualities. A great deal of our attention to artworks is devoted to detecting their characteristic aesthetic properties. When discussing artworks, a major source of interest is in comparing our descriptions of their aesthetic properties with those of others, including our friends and professional critics. One value of art, one value among many, is that it affords the opportunity for us to exercise our powers of discrimination. We enjoy clarifying the impression that the artwork has made on us, both during the experience and afterwards in recollection. Art calls for sensitivity, or, what was called "delicacy" in the eighteenth century. That is, artworks challenge and often reward our sensitive consideration of them.

Sometimes the detection of aesthetic properties blends into design appreciation – as in cases where we seek out the structures that give rise to the dark, brooding aura of the novel. But aesthetic experience also occurs where we simply apprehend the aesthetic qualities of a work, without searching for any subtending structures. We may simply note and savor the gracefulness of the dancer. To confirm the significance of this aspect of aesthetic experience, reflect upon how often your own descriptions of art-works are dominated by taking notice of the aesthetic properties of the works in question.

There are various different sorts of aesthetic properties. There are the expressive properties discussed in Chapter 2, including emotion properties ("somber," "melancholic," "gay") and character properties ("bold," "stately," "pompous"). But many aesthetic properties are nonanthropomorphic. Some are Gestalt properties like "unified," "balanced," "tightly knit," "chaotic." And others, because they are related to certain standards, may be called "taste" properties: "gaudy," "vulgar," "kitschy," "garish" and so on. Finally, there are also certain aesthetic properties that might be categorized as reaction properties because they are derived from the way in which certain artworks move us or arouse various mental states; these properties include the sublime, the beautiful, the comic, the suspenseful, and so on. The aforesaid categories, of course, are neither exhaustive, nor are they always mutually exclusive, but they do give one a sense of the wide range of aesthetic properties.

Moreover, we often have different grounds for ascribing aesthetic pro-perties to artworks. A film will be called suspenseful on condition that it raises a certain mental state in normal viewers, whereas a piece of orches-tral music expresses elation only if it *sounds* elated. Many aesthetic pro-perties are perceptible properties, but not all. A work of literature may express alienation by enabling us to entertain an estranged point-of-view on the world. Literature, of course, may also possess aesthetic qualities in virtue of its perceptible properties – such as its sounds and rhythms – but it also presents aesthetic properties through the organization of its fictional worlds.

Aesthetic properties are different from the properties that interest physicists. Physicists are preoccupied with the quantitative properties of things – their weight, mass, velocity, length, and so on. The aesthetic dimension is qualitative. The physicist's description of the universe is not dependent on human psychology. Creatures from other galaxies with biological and psychological make-ups different from our own – including different sense modalities – should, in principle, be able to understand our physics textbooks, stated in the language of mathematics. But it is unlikely that they will grasp the aesthetic properties of our artworks so readily, since aesthetic properties are, as we said earlier, response-dependent – their detection requires creatures with our kind of sensibilities.

But aesthetic properties are not free-floating. They depend for their existence on the kind of properties that physicists study. For a particular line in a painting to be elegant, it must still be a line of a certain length and thickness. In cases like these, the property of elegance is said to supervene on certain base-properties, including the length and thickness of the line. This term, "supervenience," signals a relation of dependence between aesthetic properties like elegance and their base properties such that were the base properties different, the aesthetic properties would be different also. But the elegance of the line is not reducible to its physical dimensions; it is also related to the way in which creatures like us typically apprehend the line.

Since aesthetic properties are response-dependent, the base in question includes not only the length and thickness of the line, but its relation to percipients with our sensibilities – percipients who view the line in standard conditions (in the right light, from the right distance, with no perceptual impediments, like uncorrected vision, and so on). In this way, aesthetic properties are very much like color properties, which also supervene on certain molecular structures. And, in turn, aesthetic properties can supervene on what are called secondary properties, such as color, as well as on primary properties – properties such as mass, weight, velocity, length, width, and so on. In this respect, aesthetic properties are sometimes called tertiary – or third-order – properties.

This account of aesthetic properties, however, raises certain skeptical worries which are relevant to any account we might offer of aesthetic experience as something involving, at least in part, the detection and discrimination of aesthetic properties. As noted earlier, we think of aesthetic properties as properties of the objects – whether artworks or things in nature – to which we predicate aesthetic property-terms. We think the sadness is an objective property of the music. But since aesthetic properties are response-dependent, can we be sure that they are not simply properties in us – really subjective properties, not objective properties? In addition, since aesthetic properties are not part of the universe that the physicist studies, do they really exist?

Thus, is what we call the aesthetic experience – the alleged discrimination of aesthetic properties – anything more than mere *projection*? We have called it detection, but perhaps it is nothing beyond the ascription to external objects of our own internal thoughts, attitudes, and feelings.

Detection or projection?

A major question about aesthetic experience is whether it is a matter of detection or projection, which question is related to the issue of whether aesthetic properties are real, objective properties of objects. Aesthetic properties are not real, objective properties, if by that we mean properties that exist independently of the possibility of any perceivers. Aesthetic properties are response-dependent. But is their response dependency sufficient grounds for denying that they are real, objective properties?

Typically, we regard color properties as real, objective properties of objects – as qualities of objects, rather than merely properties of experiencing subjects. But color properties are also response-dependent properties. Nevertheless, we believe that our responses with respect to color track real phenomena. One reason for believing that our color responses track real phenomena is that this explains why most humans, save the color-blind, tend to converge on their color judgments (where those are made in circumstances in which standard conditions obtain).

If color judgments were only subjective projections, we would not predict such uniformity. So, rather than saying that color perception is nothing but subjective projection, we argue that most humans, with normally functioning perceptual equipment, see blue under standard viewing conditions because the relevant stimulus *is* blue. If the stimulus were orange, they would not see it as blue (under standard conditions). This seems to be a more compelling explanation than the claim that each person subjectively just happens to experience blue on his own. But isn't aesthetic experience pretty much on all fours with color perception?

The detection of aesthetic properties appears to us quite like color perception. The experience of an aesthetic property, like the delicacy of a line, does not seem fundamentally different from perceiving the line to be a blue one. Thus, on phenomenological grounds, it would be arbitrary to say that color perception tracks objective qualities, whereas aesthetic experience does not. Color perception, though response-dependent, tracks objective properties of things. So response-dependency is no reason to categorize aesthetic experience as purely projective, if we do not treat color perception likewise.

Moreover, we believe that color perception tracks objective properties, because this hypothesis has explanatory power; it explains our observations of such things as blueness in objects. But so does a similar treatment of aesthetic experience. Most people, under standard conditions, will agree that the opening bars of Beethoven's *Fifth Symphony* are powerful. It is unlikely that this kind of convergence could be explained convincingly in terms of subjective projection. It would be an astounding coincidence if everyone just happened to have the same personal associations with the opening bars of the symphony.

And even if we accept coincidence in this one case, could *all* the other examples of overwhelmingly convergent aesthetic experiences – such as the pervasive finding that the opening of Mozart's *Twenty-Ninth Symphony* is beautiful – also be merely coincidental? This begins to stretch credulity, once one begins to think about how very much agreement there is between people with regard to the aesthetic properties of artworks. A better explanation is that these convergent responses are the result of real properties of the works in question – that is to say, of their aesthetic qualities, construed as objective properties of the artworks in question. Thus, the argument on behalf of the realism of aesthetic properties here is exactly parallel to the argument for the objectivity of color properties – which like aesthetic properties are also response dependent.

Regarding aesthetic properties as objective properties explains why artworks are the way they are. Beethoven arranged the notes of the opening of the *Fifth Symphony* in the way he did in order to present the appearance of forcefulness to an audience who he predicted would appreciate that very property because of the way in which it addresses their common perceptual apparatuses, not because of any personal associations that they each might bring to the music. That is, by citing the work's aesthetic properties, we are able to explain why the work has the features – the notes, time signatures, etc. – that it has as well as the audience's convergent, appreciative responses to the work.

It is true that aesthetic properties are not part of the physicist's universe. But that does not prove that they do not exist. Many properties, like mental properties, are not part of the physicist's universe either, but they exist. Mental properties are supervenient properties; they are not reducible to mere physical states. But supervenient properties, such as mental properties and aesthetic properties, call for explanation, not dismissal.

Moreover, aesthetic experiences are not explicable in the physicist's idiom; the physicist cannot explain why most find the *Fifth Symphony* powerful. The best explanation of that is that there are objective aesthetic properties that ground the relevant aesthetic experiences. This is a more scientific way of proceeding – in terms of our scientific commitment to explaining phenomena – than declaring that aesthetic experience is nothing but random personal association. For to an arresting degree, the relevant phenomena – aesthetic experience (like color experience) – scarcely appears random.

At this point, the skeptic about the realism of aesthetic properties is apt to object. He will argue that the analogy with color properties is exaggerated. There is not, he will claim, as much convergence in the attribution of aesthetic properties to objects as there is to color properties. There is, in fact, a great deal of disagreement. What one informed critic finds delicate, another will pronounce bland. This is not an eccentric exception. It happens very frequently. There is nowhere as much agreement with respect to aesthetic properties as we find with color properties, even where perceptual conditions are standard and the percipients are normal in every respect.

Furthermore, the skeptic adds, the explanation for what convergence there is with respect to aesthetic experiences is to be explained not by invoking chance but by claiming that it is the result of the common culture of the experiencers. They all say that the opening bars of Beethoven's *Fifth Symphony* are powerful, because that is what they have been conditioned socially to say. Thus, we need not suppose that aesthetic properties are objective in order to explain convergence; aesthetic experience is projective, but it is culturally mediated projection. This accounts for convergence wherever we find it. Or, in short, there is no call to resort to the objectivity of aesthetic properties in order to explain convergence.

The skeptic has two arrows in his quiver. The first is that there is too much disagreement over the attribution of aesthetic properties for the analogy with color properties to be persuasive. Second, what convergence there is can be explained by reference to the common culture of the percipients; there is no explanatory pressure to invoke the objectivity of aesthetic properties. Thus, we may presume that the so-called detection of aesthetic properties is nothing more than projection.

These are estimable objections. But they are not decisive. There is disagreement about the attribution of aesthetic properties. But this does not show that the properties are merely projections. For two people may disagree about the best way to describe a color. Both are well-sighted and stare at the pertinent object in the right viewing conditions. One says it's light beige; the other that it is light grey. The color may be somewhere in between. It may be taupe. The fact of disagreement is not explained by surmising that they are both projecting. There is a fact of the matter. But it hinges on subtle differences in shading which the disputants fail to articulate with complete precision. Disputes about aesthetic properties also revolve around subtle differences. Nevertheless, there may be a fact of the matter which they cannot characterize with exactitude. There is no reason to suppose that disagreement here is a function of projection.

Indeed, projection seems an unlikely hypothesis in the preceding color example. For in order to be really disagreeing, our two disputants must be disagreeing about the same thing. They are both referring to the same color, only describing it differently. If they weren't referring to the same color, there would be no genuine disagreement between them. They would merely be shouting at each other. If they are genuinely disagreeing, they must have something in common. Disagreement presupposes a background of agreement. They must agree to disagree about the same thing. But what are they disagreeing about? The best hypothesis is that they are disagreeing about the same color – which is an objective, response-dependent property of the object under observation. What point would there be to their disagreeing about their personal associations with the object?

Similarly, where one critic says that the drawing is delicate and the other says that it is bland, the most reasonable hypothesis is that they are disagreeing about the best description of a property of an object that they are both experiencing. Thus, the fact of disagreement, which is so important to the skeptic's case, need not compel us to adjudge cases of aesthetic experience to be mere projection. Disagreements about aesthetic properties are more intelligible when understood as pertaining to shades of difference in objective properties whose best description is open to debate and, often, to negotiation.

The important point to make against the skeptic is that disagreement always presupposes agreement of some sort. If two people are genuinely disagreeing about the state of the economy, they must have some common ground. They need to be referring to the same kinds of things – GNP, employment, and so on – and to share some criteria about how to assess those features. If they are both just free-associating about different things, it does not make any sense to say that they are really disagreeing.

Likewise, disagreements about aesthetic properties presuppose something in common between disputants. It cannot be their personal associations, since presumably there is no disputing personal associations. So it must be something else. The best posit here is that they are disagreeing about the objective aesthetic properties of the objects under contestation. If it were simply a matter of projection, then the disagreement would not be real. Thus, inasmuch as the skeptic points to genuine disagreement as an important consideration, he seems driven to admit that the supposition that aesthetic properties are indeed objective offers the best general account of such disagreements. Rather than counting towards the projection theory, genuine disagreement counts more in favor of the view that aesthetic properties are objective.

Among the things that must be shared for disputants to have a genuine disagreement about the aesthetic properties of an artwork is a common conceptual framework. If the rival viewpoints are using different sets of concepts, they will be talking past each other. If you mean "loose" where I mean "powerful," then we are not really having an argument. Words may be exchanged heatedly, but there is no genuine disagreement here.

Yet if this is correct, then at least some aesthetic qualities have to be objective properties of things. For how else could we learn to use aesthetic property-terminology consistently, unless this were so? If aesthetic property terms were just free-floating personal projections, how could anyone ever learn them in a way that permits communication with others? But we do use them to communicate with others, including in cases of disagreement. So projection seems unlikely.

That is, if you say "x is powerful" and I say it is not, we only disagree where we mean the same thing by "powerful." There can be no authentic disagreement where the parties involved do not agree on the application of the relevant aesthetic predicates to their observations. But how do we acquire this concept of "powerful" and its intersubjective criteria of application in a way that explains our consistent usage of it?

Undoubtedly, we learn it by ostension. People point to certain examples of powerful things, or we listen to pieces of music that are described as powerful, and we get the hang of the term. Yet in order for us to do this, people need to be picking out the same kind of thing by the concept; we need to be attending to the same feature of the relevant objects that our tutors are. If they were all simply projecting idiosyncratically, we would not acquire the concept. We'd simply be confused.

But we are not. So there must be something we share, and it can't be personal projections, since if they could be shared, they wouldn't be personal. Consequently, a more likely hypothesis is that we both have access to the relevant property *of the object*. A better account than the projection account of how we come to acquire the concept and its consistent intersubjective usage is that the concept refers to an objective property of the object to which we all have access. But this, of course, presupposes that aesthetic properties, at least in most cases, are objective properties.

We cannot debate with others unless we are talking about the same thing. Our concepts must be shared concepts. But the possession of shared concepts for the relevant aesthetic properties indicates that the concepts must refer to real, objective properties of objects, since otherwise it is difficult to explain how we come to share these concepts. Thus, once again, it seems that the fact of disagreement, upon which the skeptic rests his case, actually suggests the opposite of his conclusion.

That is, idiosyncratically projected properties would not explain the possession of the shared concepts required for genuine disagreement. On the other hand, the supposition that aesthetic properties are objective does a better job of explaining the shared, consistent usage of aesthetic property terminology requisite for disagreement. Therefore, genuine disagreement is really evidence that aesthetic experience is a matter of detection, not projection.

At this point, the skeptic may say that he agrees that there is convergent application of aesthetic predicate terms, but that this is to be explained by social conditioning. There is no reason to invoke the idea of objective aesthetic properties to explain shared, consistently used aesthetic concepts; enculturation will do the trick. However, how will enculturation proceed, if the objects used to introduce the relevant concepts do not possess common, objective properties? That is, how can we be trained to use aesthetic concepts consistently – to apply them appropriately to cases we have never encountered before – unless there is something about them, and not merely about us, that remains constant from case to case?

Moreover, it cannot be by virtue of only the properties in the physicist's vocabulary, since the relevant properties are not reducible to that idiom. They are supervenient. So cultural conditioning itself must presuppose that at least some of aesthetic properties are properties in the object that enable us to apply aesthetic concepts with intersubjective consistency. And if at least some aesthetic properties are objective properties, aesthetic experience need not be generally described as projection. Thus, as with the case of disagreement, so with the skeptic's appeal to cultural conditioning: the very facts the skeptic employs to explain away the objectivity of aesthetic qualities, ironically, lend credence to their status as real properties.

The enculturation hypothesis also has difficulty explaining what we might call the phenomenon of aesthetic revelation. Someone brought up in one culture may be moved immediately by artworks from an alien culture about which she has no relevant background training. Reference to cultural conditioning is of little use in such instances, since there is no pertinent conditioning. A better explanation is that the subject of aesthetic revelation is moved by the objective aesthetic properties of the work.

The supposition that aesthetic properties are objective also explains better how we talk about them than does the projection theory. For example, people involved in disputes over aesthetic properties act as though they think that they are disagreeing about the real properties of objects. They behave as though they think that there is a fact of the matter to be determined. They speak as if one side of the disagreement is right and the other wrong. So, they, at least, must believe that aesthetic properties are objective. That is the way of understanding their behavior that renders it most intelligible. On the other hand, if disputants are simply trading projections, we would have to say that their behavior is ultimately irrational. And it is far from clear that the skeptics' arguments are compelling enough to warrant such wholesale suspicion of irrationality.

Of course, the skeptic is right that there is disagreement about the attribution of aesthetic properties. Sometimes one critic will claim that an artwork is delicate, whereas another says it is insipid, and the debate may persist in a way that seems far more intractable than disagreements about color attributions. Isn't this at least somewhat odd? If aesthetic properties are objective properties, why do debates about aesthetic property ascriptions often seem more stubborn than debates about color attributions?

There are several ways of accounting for the persistence of critical debates over aesthetic properties that are compatible with the hypothesis that, generally, aesthetic qualities are objective properties of things. Let us look at two. The first calls attention to the fact that aesthetic property terms can be used in different contexts. In this section, we have been talking about the descriptive use of aesthetic property terms. When we say that a piece of music is powerful, we are reporting its aesthetic properties; we are not commenting on whether or not we like it.

However, aesthetic terminology also often figures in statements of personal preference. Consequently, one critic may say that the music is bombastic, rather than powerful, as a way of signalling her dislike of the music. This is not a disagreement about the aesthetic property of the music so much as a debate about how worthy of attention the critic finds it. Often when people appear to be disagreeing about aesthetic property ascriptions, they are really staking out personal preferences.

Disagreements about color ascriptions less frequently involve covert differences in preferences than do attributions of aesthetic properties. This is why disagreements about colors are not generally as unyielding as some exchanges of opinion about aesthetic properties. But the intractability of such exchanges only shows that people can be obstinate about their preferences, not that aesthetic property terms, used descriptively, do not refer to objective properties.

Some skeptics might challenge this sort of explanation of aesthetic disagreement by alleging that there is no descriptive use of aesthetic property terminology – that every attribution of an aesthetic property entails a preference, and, therefore, involves subjective projection. To say "x is unified" always implies a positive attitude toward x, whereas to say that "x is garish" always implies a negative attitude.

But this seems extravagant. There is no contradiction in saying that "x is unified, however, it is not to my taste," while a critic, commenting on a postmodernist pastiche, can say without inconsistency, "It's marvelously garish, and I love it." Perhaps some aesthetic property terms can only be used preferentially rather than descriptively. But most can be used descriptively and, where they are, the prospects for utterly intractable exchanges are vastly diminished.

Of course, there is still disagreement even where aesthetic property terms are used descriptively. One major source of this is that the attribution of aesthetic property terms is often genre (and/or tradition) relative. What counts as "reserved" and "sober" with reference to a horror novel may seem nevertheless "excited" in a less intense genre. Determining precisely which aesthetic properties an artwork possesses hinges upon situating the work in the right genre or category. Disagreements about aesthetic properties often revolve around implicit disagreements about the category to which the artwork belongs. Many of these disagreements can be resolved by locating the correct category for the work, or, where the disagreement emerges because the work inhabits more than one category, the disagreement can be at least explained.

Two ways, then, of explaining disagreements over aesthetic properties which are compatible with regarding aesthetic properties as objective are to attribute such exchanges to differences in preferences and/or to differences in categorization. Though these go a long way toward undercutting the skeptic's interpretation of aesthetic disagreement, undoubtedly some aesthetic disputes may remain. But, of course, this should be expected, since aesthetic properties are often subtle, and our language is not always equal to their shades of difference. And, in any case, that there is persisting disagreement over aesthetic properties should not be overestimated, since physicists also disagree, often quite vociferously, but skeptics do not take this to show that physicists are not referring to objective properties.

If the preceding arguments are convincing, then the skeptic is wrong. We have reasonable grounds for supposing that aesthetic properties are objective properties. Attributions of aesthetic predicates to artworks, when used descriptively, can generally be taken to refer to objective properties. Such attributions are not projections. They are, when true, reports about the aesthetic properties we have *detected* in the relevant artworks. Thus, there should be no problem in describing aesthetic experience as frequently a matter of discerning and discriminating the aesthetic properties of artworks.

We value artworks, in part, because they afford the opportunity for us to exercise our sensibilities, to recognize and to distinguish different qualities in the appearance of things. The aesthetic properties of artworks alert us to the qualitative dimensions of the world at large and improve our capacities for discovering them. Aesthetic properties enliven experience.

We are also interested in the aesthetic qualities of artworks – like the graceful movements of the dancer, or the sadness of the poet's lament – because we too invest our own activities with aesthetic qualities, and are thus fascinated by superlative displays of aesthetic prowess which enable us to reflect upon the nature, limits and possibilities of our own performances. Aesthetic properties give a humanly accessible shape to things, and, as shape-seeking animals, we are, therefore, naturally curious about aesthetic properties. That is why, with respect to artworks, the detection of aesthetic properties, along with – and sometimes in conjunction with – design appreciation, comprises the major portion of what we call aesthetic experience.

Aesthetic experience and the experience of art

There are many different ways of responding to or experiencing artworks. We can call these, generically, art responses. Being amused by a play is an art response, and, if the play is a farce, it is, all things being equal, an appropriate response. Similarly, if one is reading a social protest novel, then being angered by the oppression depicted is an art response, and probably an appropriate one.

In this respect, aesthetic experience is an art response, one that involves either detecting and discriminating the aesthetic properties of a work and/or contemplating the relation of the form of an artwork to its point. However, though having aesthetic experiences – or making aesthetic responses – to artworks represents one major family of art responses, it is important to stress that aesthetic experience is neither the only kind of art response, nor the only appropriate form of experiencing art.

There is a popular tendency to use the notion of aesthetic experience as a synonym for experiencing art in general. That is, "aesthetic experience" is often taken to be the umbrella concept that subsumes every appropriate art response. But that is not the view of aesthetic experience endorsed in this chapter. Here, the notion of aesthetic experience is restricted to only certain types of art responses: the detection of aesthetic properties and/or design appreciation. Undeniably, these responses are among the most important experiences to be derived from artworks in general. However, they are not the only ones, nor the only legitimate ones, nor are they even the most important ones with respect to every single artwork.

Moreover, it is crucial to emphasize explicitly and unambiguously the limited scope of the concept of aesthetic experience, because, if we do not, our understanding of art and the experience of art may become impoverished. For example, in the past, people have often used the notion of aesthetic experience ambiguously to refer both to every legitimate art response *and* to aesthetic property detection and design appreciation. As a result, they have often disenfranchised many legitimate art responses with arguments like this one:

1   x is a legitimate response to an artwork if and only if x is an aesthetic experience.
2   Responding to the representational content of an artwork and reflecting on its moral message are not aesthetic experiences.
3   Therefore, responding to the representational content of an artwork and reflecting on its moral messages are not legitimate responses to artworks.

But this kind of argument is not sound. It proceeds by equivocating on the concept of aesthetic experience. If the first premise is acceptable, then that is because "aesthetic experience" is obviously functioning as the name of *any* art response. But in the second premise, the meaning of aesthetic experience is much more narrow (perhaps referring to attention to significant form, the detection of aesthetic properties, design appreciation, or to all three). The conclusion of the argument can only be derived by trading illicitly on these different meanings of aesthetic experience. That is, this kind of argument commits the fallacy of equivocation.

Arguments like this – dismissing all sorts of legimate art responses – have been frequent in the philosophical and critical literature. The results have been to reduce our conception of art and the experience thereof. Such spurious conclusions can only be short-circuited by staying clear about the limited scope of aesthetic experience, properly so-called.

Strictly speaking, aesthetic experience is comprised of the detection and discrimination of aesthetic properties, on the one hand, and design appreciation, on the other. In this regard, standing back from a picture by Delacroix and noting its turbulence is a paradigmatic example of aesthetic experience, since it is a matter of detecting and discriminating the salient aesthetic properties of the work. As noted in the beginning of this chapter, the notion of aesthetics has been perennially associated with perception. That is why a large part of what is called aesthetic experience concerns noticing, detecting and discriminating.

Aesthetic experience also involves the constructive powers of the mind. This is especially evident in design appreciation, where the the challenge of comprehending the diverse elements of an artwork is joined by relating them to the point of the whole. Aesthetic detection and design appreciation attend very closely to the internal properties and relations of the artwork. Sometimes this centripetal attention has been misdescribed affectively as disinterestedness. But it is better to think of it as attention with a certain dedicated focus or delimited content – aesthetic properties, and forms.

Limiting the scope of aesthetic experience in this way does not disparage it. Aesthetic experience is of overwhelming importance to art. The possibility of aesthetic experience draws us to artworks in a great many cases, and it is what keeps us coming back for more. But we derive more from artworks than only aesthetic experience, including knowledge, moral insight and transformation, a sense of allegiance, an emotional workout and other things as well. Even if aesthetic experience were first among equals when it comes to our responses to art, it is not the whole story of our experience of art.

Chapter summary

"Aesthetics" has a number of diverse meanings. With respect to the philosophy of art, it most frequently occurs in connection with the audience's experience of art. Some philosophers maintain that our experiences of art are different in kind from other sorts of experiences. Reading a novel is different than reading a set of VCR instructions. Because of this, these philosophers, called aesthetic theorists of art, attempt to define artworks as objects designed to bring about, invite, or, at least, support aesthetic experiences. Such definitions are called aesthetic definitions of art. Like formalism, the representational theory of art, and the expression theory of art, the aesthetic definition of art is proposed as a comprehensive theory of all art.

The aesthetic definition of art can come in several forms, depending on its conception of aesthetic experience. Such definitions may presuppose a content-oriented account or an affect-oriented account of aesthetic experience. However, neither version provides necessary and/or sufficient conditions for art. These theories are generally too broad – including many human artifacts that are not artworks under their rubric – and too narrow – excluding anti-aesthetic art from the order of art. Thus, aesthetic theories of art are not adequate, comprehensive theories of art.

Nevertheless, the notion of aesthetic experience is still an important one. Even if it cannot be used to define all art, it is frequently used to describe certain of our commonly recurring responses to art. So it seems advisable to come up with some characterization of aesthetic experience.

The most popular characterizations of it are affect-oriented and rely on the concept of disinterested attention. But upon scrutiny, this concept appears inadmissible, since it confuses motivation with attention. This suggests that the affect-oriented account of aesthetic experience is a dead end.

Instead, a better approach to characterizing aesthetic experience is in terms of its content: aesthetic experiences are experiences *of* aesthetic properties and formal relations. The experience of formal relations is what was called design appreciation in both this chapter and the previous one. To experience aesthetic properties is to detect and discriminate them – to notice the distinctive plangency in the music, for example.

There is some question, however, about whether or not this is the correct characterization of aesthetic experience. Some skeptics argue that we do not detect aesthetic properties, but merely project them. Skeptics cite the protracted disagreements about attributions of aesthetic properties as a major piece of evidence on behalf of the projection theory. But the significance of this evidence is open to question. Disagreement may in fact give us a better reason to suppose that aesthetic properties are objective rather than subjective, and, consequently, that aesthetic experience is a matter of detection rather than projection.

The conception of aesthetic experience arrived at in this chapter is narrow. Aesthetic experience is comprised of design appreciation and the detection of aesthetic properties – a matter of attention to and contemplation of aesthetic qualities and artistic forms. In opposition to aesthetic theories of art, we have maintained that aesthetic experience does not represent the only kind of legitimate response to art available to us. Cognitive and moral experiences, among others, may be equally appropriate. Aesthetic experience is an important dimension of our experience of art, but it is not the whole shooting match. To suppose that it is, as aesthetic theorists do, reduces both our conception of art and our sense of its variety, as well as our experiences thereof.

Annotated reading

The notion of the aesthetic has a rich history. One place to find a useful, though adversarial, overview is George Dickie's *Art and the Aesthetic* (Ithaca, New York: Cornell University Press, 1974). A characterization of the relation of the philosophy of art and aesthetics is also available in Noël Carroll, "Beauty and the Genealogy of Art Theory," *Philosophical Forum*, vol. xxii, no. 4 (Summer, 1991), pp. 307–334.

Important statements of the aesthetic definition of art include: Monroe Beardsley, "An Aesthetic Definition of Art," in *What is Art?*, edited by Hugh Curtler (New York: Havens Publishers, Inc., 1983), pp. 15–29; Harold Osborne, "What is a Work of Art?," *British Journal of Aesthetics*, vol. 23 (1981), pp. 1–11; and William Tolhurst, "Toward an Aesthetic Account of the Nature of Art," *The Journal of Aesthetics and Art Criticism*, vol. 42 (1979), pp. 1–14. See also: Bohdan Dziemidok, "Controversy about the Aesthetic Nature of Art," *British Journal of Aesthetics*, vol. 28 (1988), pp. 1–17.

For discussions of aesthetic experience consult: Monroe Beardsley, *The Aesthetic Point of View: Selected Essays*, edited by Michael Wreen and Donald M. Callen (Ithaca, New York: Cornell University Press, 1983). Section I of this text and the article "Aesthetic Experience" in Section IV are especially useful. The characterization of the affect-oriented account of aesthetic experience in this chapter was derived from Jerome Stolnitz, *Aesthetics and the Philosophy of Art Criticism* (New York: Houghton Mifflin Co., 1960), pp. 32–42. For a classic refutation of the notion of aesthetic disinterestedness, see George Dickie, "The Myth of the Aesthetic Attitude," *American Philosophical Quarterly*, vol. 1 (1964), pp. 56–65. Objections can also be found in Noël Carroll, "Art and Interaction," *The Journal of Aesthetics and Art Criticism*, vol. XLV, no. 1 (Fall 1986), pp. 57–68.

For a broad introduction to the topic of aesthetic properties see Göran Hermerén, *The Nature of Aesthetic Qualities* (Lund: Lund University Press, 1988). Skepticism about the objectivity of aesthetic properties is defended by Alan H. Goldman in his "Realism about Aesthetic Properties," *The Journal of Aesthetics and Art Criticism*, vol. 51, no. 1 (Winter, 1993), pp. 31–38. Representations of the realist viewpoint are available in: Philip Pettit, "The Possibility of Aesthetic Realism," in *Pleasure, Preference and Value*, edited by Eva

Schaper (Cambridge: Cambridge University Press, 1983), pp. 17–38; and Eddy M. Zemach, *Real Beauty* (University Park, Pennsylvania: The Pennsylvania University Press, 1997).

One much-debated issue concerning aesthetic properties that is not discussed in this chapter concerns whether or not aesthetic concepts are condition-governed. For an introduction to this topic, see: Frank Sibley, "Aesthetic Concepts," *Philosophical Review*, vol. 68 (1959), pp. 421–450; and Frank Sibley, "Aesthetic and Non-Aesthetic," *Philosophical Review*, vol. 74 (1965), pp. 135–159. For a critical engagement with Sibley's views, see: Peter Kivy, *Speaking of Art* (The Hague: Martinus Nijhoff, 1973).

CHAPTER 5
Art, definition and identification

5
Art, definition and identification

Part I
Against definition

Neo-Wittgensteinianism: art
as an open concept

Throughout this book, we have examined successive attempts to define art. The representational theory of art, neorepresentationalism, the expression theory, formalism, neoformalism, and aesthetic theories of art are all attempts to provide comprehensive definitions of all art. But each of them appears inadequate in turn. Undoubtedly, this has led some readers to suspect that maybe one cannot define art at all; the diversity of objects we call art may seem too great to be encompassed by a single definition. Or, perhaps some of you thought this from the very beginning; perhaps you started reading this book with the opinion that art cannot be defined and, as a result, regarded each of the theories that we reviewed as predestined to fail. Maybe the entire project struck you as quixotic from the outset. But however you came to the conviction that art cannot be defined, you may feel reassured to learn that it is also a philosophical position, sometimes called Neo-Wittgensteinianism.

Throughout the twentieth century especially, philosophers of art have attempted to define art. Probably one reason that Western philosophers have been preoccupied with defining art for the last century or so is that it is during this period that we have found ourselves confronted with a dazzling array of different kinds of art whose sheer variety is unprecedented. On the one hand, there have been the multifarious creations of the avant-garde which, from Romanticism onwards, have consistently challenged settled ideas of art with their radical departures from conventional practice.

And, on the other hand, during the same period, Westerners grew more and more familiar with the art of other cultures, which, though deviating from the canons of Western art, nevertheless have a *prima facie* claim on art status. Whereas for centuries art developed slowly and smoothly in ways that could be accommodated tacitly within everyday understanding, by the twentieth century matters were getting confusing. There was such a diversity of stuff on offer that it became pressing to tell the art from the nonart.

It is at least plausible to suppose that if we had assembled a group of informed art lovers at some imaginary point around the middle of the eighteenth century and paraded a selection of objects before them – pictures, shovels, poems, bills of sale, cavalry regiments, pieces of music, pieces of artillery, sailing ships, racks, apple orchards, ox carts, and dances – they would have been able to agree, to a surprising extent, about which of the objects were art and which were not. They would not have needed a definition to guide them. They possessed a shared, though often unarticulated, understanding of art upon which they could rely to deliver consistent and convergent judgments about what was and was not art.

Artists, too, shared in this common understanding, and they created what audiences expected. No one had to be told explicitly what was art. Everyone just knew implicitly; the concept was more or less embedded in the language. And the practice more or less confirmed that that unarticulated common understanding was reliable. Just as today we all know what an ice cream cone is without needing a definition of one, we may hypothesize that the concept of art was likewise generally implicit and untroubled two hundred years ago.

But the appearance of revolutionary art movements, like Romanticism, and the initiation of progressively accelerating velocities of change by the various proliferating avant-gardes, in addition to the influx of non-Western art from all over the world, altered that situation forever. Telling the art from the nonart was suddenly difficult.

Identifying art became a pressing issue; one could no longer suppose that there was a tacit or implicit cultural understanding ready-to-hand, since avant-garde art was designed to problematize any such conventional, unexamined premises, and non-Western art hailed from other cultures, with potentially different prevailing assumptions, anyway. The situation was now becoming one in which, as the old saying has it, you couldn't tell the players without a scorecard.

It is important to be able to identify art – to be able to tell the art from the nonart – for many reasons. Whether or not something is art might determine whether or not it is eligible for an award from a government arts agency or whether its sale or import should be taxed. For example, a question arose over the importation of Brancusi's abstract sculpture *Bird in Flight* as to whether it was an artwork or a collection of industrial metal. If industrial tubing, a customs fee would have had to have been paid; but if art, it could enter the U.S. duty-free.

Of course, determining whether or not something is art is not merely important for the purpose of settling practical and political questions like these. Identifying whether something should be classified as art or not is crucial to ascertaining how we should respond to it. Should we attempt to interpret it? Should we explore it for aesthetic properties? Should we try to fathom its design? These sorts of questions begin to be answered when we know that something is art.

For instance, suppose we come across, as we might at a garage sale, a stuffed angora goat wearing an automobile tire around its middle and standing on a canvas. Should we chalk it up as a random assemblage of articles, imagining that the owner had no place else to put the tire, or should we try to interpret it – should we try to ask just what it means and why this accumulation of things should mean exactly that? Of course, if we identify it as an artwork – as Robert Rauschenberg's combine *Monogram* to be precise – that's exactly what we'll do; we'll try to interpret it. But otherwise it looks just like things shoved into a forgotten corner of the attic and as unworthy of attention as any other old pile of junk.

Identifying something as art, then, is indispensable to our artistic practices. That something is art signals how and even whether we are to respond to it interpretively, aesthetically, and appreciatively. If we have no way of classifying art – no means of determining whether something belongs to the category of things that warrant art responses – then our artistic practices would cave-in. Prior to the modern period, people knew tacitly how to match objects with the appropriate responses. They could tell whether things were being put forth to be interpreted – perhaps theologically – pretty much by looking (and listening). But the advent of revolutionary and avant-garde art, along with the arrival *en masse* of art from other cultures, made this a thornier affair.

The philosophy of art in the twentieth century reflects this situation. As the question of identifying art became more and more perplexing, the solution to the problem seemed obvious: come up with an explicit definition of art. If the old implicit ways of identifying art no longer work, define the concept of art explicitly so that it can cover every case. The representational theory of art, neorepresentationalism, the expression theory, formalism, neoformalism, and aesthetic theories of art can all be viewed in this light. They are all attempts to provide an explicit way of analysing the concept of an artwork by means of a definition that provides necessary and sufficient conditions for counting something as an artwork. Is Brancusi's *Bird in Flight* an artwork? Is Rauchenberg's *Monogram*? Look to the correct definition of art to tell.

This approach to identifying art – by defining it – seems pretty straightforward and commonsensical. However, by the 1950s, a significant group of philosophers grew suspicious of this approach. They noted, as many of you may have, that every attempt to define art in the past has failed. This doesn't prove that future attempts will also fail. But it does give one food for thought. Specifically, these philosophers asked whether or not there might be some deep philosophical reason why this project kept coming up with such unsatisfactory results.

Similarly, these philosophers also were impressed by how many different, and amazingly diverse kinds of art there are in the world. What does an oratorio by Handel have in common with a readymade by Duchamp? Thus, they wondered whether any definition could cover every single artwork nonvacuously – that is, in a way that was informative and noncircular. Formalism and the expression theory were, of course, informative – they excluded many candidates from the corpus of art. But, as we have seen, they were also false; they excluded too many candidates. The history of art theory seemed to be littered with successive conjectures, each refuted.

Of course, neither of these considerations – that past definitions have failed and that the data are incredibly complex – proved that art could not be defined. But such observations did encourage philosophers to review the project critically. And once reviewed critically, many came to believe that the project of defining art was inherently misguided. The continued failure of the project to define art was not the result of a lack of imagination, intelligence or ingenuity on the part of theorists of art. Rather, there was a deep philosophical reason why art theories always foundered. The reason was that art is *necessarily* indefinable.

The philosophers who believed that art cannot be defined were often influenced by Ludwig Wittgenstein's book *Philosophical Investigations*. Thus they can be called "*Neo-Wittgensteinians.*" The Neo-Wittgensteinians thought that the philosophy of art, up to their intervention, rested upon a mistake. The mistake was to attempt to define art essentially (that is, in terms of necessary conditions that are conjointly sufficient). They agreed that we need some way to identify art, but they thought the proper way to go about it is not to frame a definition of art and then to apply it to particular cases. Following Wittgenstein, they thought the procedure that we should follow is what they called the method of family resemblances.

Many of the concepts that we employ in everyday life, like the concept of chair, largely go undefined. But we are able to get along without definitions. When we are confronted with a new kind of object for sitting purposes, we decide whether or not it is a chair by comparing it to already existing chairs. Is the so-called bean-bag chair really a chair? We determine whether or not it belongs to the category chair by comparing it to things already squarely in the category. That is, we ask whether it resembles what we antecedently believe to be chairs enough to be counted as one of their number. Many of our concepts are like this. Many of our concepts lack definitions in terms of necessary and sufficient conditions, but are applied on the basis of resemblance, rather than by means of a formula. Could the concept of art be like this?

The Neo-Wittgensteinians say yes. One argument that they advance on behalf of this conclusion is simply that art cannot be defined and, since it cannot be defined, it cannot be that we classify objects as falling under the concept of art by means of a definition. We must have some other method: the method of family resemblances.

But before saying what this method involves, there is a prior question. Why were the Neo-Wittgensteinians so sure that art, on logical grounds, cannot be defined? Perhaps the best way to give you the flavor for their reasoning is to quote a passage by the most frequently cited Neo-Wittgensteinian, Morris Weitz. His argument is called the *"open concept argument"* and he states it this way:

> "Art" itself is an open concept. New conditions (cases) have constantly arisen and will undoubtedly constantly arise; new art forms, new movements will emerge, which will demand decisions on the part of those interested, usually professional critics, as to whether the concept should be extended or not. Aestheticians may lay down conditions but never necessary and sufficient ones for the correct application of the concept. With "art" its conditions of application can never be exhaustively enumerated since new cases can always be envisaged or created by artists, or even nature, which would call for a decision on someone's part to extend or to close the old or invent a new concept.
>
> What I am arguing, then, is that the very expansive, adventurous character of art, its ever-present changes and novel creations makes it logically impossible to ensure any set of defining properties.
>
> (Weitz, 1956, "The Role of Theory in Aesthetics")

What Weitz seems to be saying here is that art – the practice of art – is always, at least in principle, open to revolutionary change. This is not to say that art must always be expansive. Some artistic traditions will value stasis over change – a classical Chinese painter may be valued more for his approximation of a pre-existing paradigm than for his innovations. In fact, innovations may be discouraged in certain traditions. Art is not required to be original in order to count as art. Nevertheless, the practice of art – or our concept of the practice – is such that it must accommodate the permanent possibility of change, expansion or novelty. Our concept of art is such that there must always be room for artists to do something new.

But if this is so, Weitz argues, then the attempt to arrive at a definition of art in terms of necessary conditions that are conjointly sufficient for determining art status is incompatible with the conception of the practice of art as that which affords the permanent possibility of change, expansion and novelty, since (Weitz appears to presume) conditions would place limits on the range of artistic innovation. The concept of art cannot be closed (by necessary and sufficient conditions); it must be an open concept (not a condition-bound concept) in order to be consistent with the permanent possibility of innovative artistic creativity.

Weitz believed that the central error of preceding philosophers of art was that, by assuming that art could be defined, they treated art as a closed concept rather than as an open concept. This is the reason why all art theories that conceive of their task as defining art fail. Moreover, since, according to Weitz, this is how art theory is conceived in the philosophical tradition, all art theories are fundamentally in error.

Here it is important to notice that Weitz is not saying that, since all known definitions of art have failed, any future attempt is, *most likely*, doomed. His argument is not a simple inductive argument like this one, based on enumerating the past failures of such theories. It is an argument that any attempt to define art must fail *necessarily*, as a point of logic.

According to Weitz, art cannot be defined, as previous philosophers of art had assumed, because art is an open concept, a concept denominating a field of activity where originality and invention are permanent possibilities. If art were defined by necessary conditions that were conjointly sufficient, then, Weitz maintains, this would imply that there were limits to what art can be – limits beyond which artistic creativity cannot extend and still be counted as art. But this would be incompatible with our conception of the practice of art. That is, the presupposition that art can be defined by virtue of sets of necessary conditions that are conjointly sufficient *contradicts* our concept of art as an open concept – a concept congenial logically with the permanent possibility of radical change, expansion and novelty.

Perhaps the history of twentieth-century art will illustrate the problem that Weitz has in mind. Philosophers propound art theories at a certain point in history – theories that in the best case apply to most of the art made up to the moment in time when the theory is propounded. But once contemporary artists learn of the theory, they make artworks that confound it, as Duchamp did with *Fountain*. The theories in question deny *Fountain* art status, but art history moves on, and, as *Fountain* becomes generally regarded as a masterpiece, the theory is discarded. Art theories attempt to close the concept of art, but artists strive to exceed closure, and ultimately our concept of art is more sympathetic to the artists than to the art theorists. The reason for this is that art is an open concept, whereas philosophers mistakenly treat it as a closed concept, and that is allegedly incompatible with its profound receptivity to innovation.

Weitz's open concept argument can be stated as a *reductio ad absurdum* of the view that art can be defined:

1   Art can be expansive.
2   Therefore, art must be open to the permanent possibility of radical change, expansion and novelty.
3   If something is art, then it must be open to the permanent possibility of radical change, expansion and novelty.
4   If something is open to the permanent possibility of radical change, expansion and novelty, then it cannot be defined.
5   Suppose that art can be defined.
6   Therefore, art is not open to the permanent possibility of radical change, expansion and novelty.
7   Therefore, art is not art.

But this is an absurd conclusion. It is self-contradictory. How are we to dispel this contradiction? One of the premises must be false. Which one? Probably the one that we added – by supposing it – to the otherwise acceptable looking set of premises. And that premise, of course, is premise #5. So, let us infer that premise #5 is false in order to rid ourselves of the contradictory conclusion in step #7. But this suggests, then, that the supposition that art can be defined is incompatible with the concept of art, or, simply: art cannot be defined.

But if art cannot be defined, how do we go about identifying art? After all, we do do it. This calls for an explanation. The Neo-Wittgensteinian is not a skeptic about the possibility of identifying art, but only a skeptic about the adequacy of definition as the model for how we discriminate the art from the nonart. This is where the family resemblance method comes into play. It is the Neo-Wittgensteinian's explanation of the way in which we identify art.

What is this family resemblance method? Neo-Wittgensteinians elucidate the idea by referring to Wittgenstein's analysis of games in his *Philosophical Investigations*. Wittgenstein pointed out that there are many different kinds of games. Some involve equipment; some don't. Some involve competition; some don't. Some involve boards; some don't. And so on. For any perceptible feature of some games that you can mention, there will be some other games that lack them. So there are no perceptible features of games that represent necessary conditions that all games must possess, nor is there some set of conditions that picks out all and only games. How, then, do we determine whether some heretofore unencountered activity is a game?

We do this by taking note of whether or not it resembles in significant respects some things that we already regard as paradigmatic games. When certain computer activities arrived on the scene, we counted them as games because of their many similarities to things that we already regarded as paradigmatic games: they involved competition, scoring, turn-taking, counters, leisure time, and so on. There was no fixed number of similarities required to obtain between these new candidates and our paradigmatic examples. Rather, when the similarities mounted, the weight of reflection upon the correspondences gradually led us to decide in favor of the game status of the computer arrays. Moreover, when confronting a skeptic about the status of a recent candidate for gamehood, we would point to resemblances between our paradigms of games and new arrivals as the appropriate way of arguing on behalf of something like *Donkey Kong*.

Similarly, according to the Neo-Wittgensteinian, we do not identify art by means of a definition. That seems unlikely not only given the open concept argument, but also because, if it were true that we had such a definition at our disposal, even if only implicitly, then why would it be that no one seems able to articulate it? If ordinary folk can identify art on a daily basis by means of a definition, why can't philosophical special-ists, whose expertise is conceptual analysis, say what it is? If we use a definition of art, if only subconsciously, why is it so elusive that not even hypnosis can unearth it?

The Neo-Wittgensteinian says that that is because we do not possess a definition of art, even implicitly. Instead we identify artworks in terms of their resemblances to paradigmatic artworks. We start with some things that everyone agrees are artworks – *A Midsummer Night's Dream*, the *Pietà*, *Bleak House*, *Canterbury Tales*, *The Scream*, *The Goldberg Varia-tions*, and the ballet *The Nutcracker*. Then, when inspecting a new candi-date for art status and arguing on its behalf, we note similarities between it and various features of our paradigms.

The new work will not be an exact replica of any of our pre-existing paradigms. It shares some similarities with some of our paradigms in some respects and other similarities with other paradigms in other respects. Just as a family member's appearance may recall his mother's coloring and his grandfather's nose, so a candidate artwork may correlate with some of the expressive properties of *The Scream* and with the structural complexity of *The Goldberg Variations*. No correspondences are necessary or sufficient, yet the accumulation of family resemblances between a candidate and the standing family of art supplies the grounds for calling a new work, includ-ing an avant-garde one, an artwork.

The background metaphor here is that of a family resemblance. In our families, there are several generations – say, grandparents and their relatives, their descendants (our parents and their relatives) and our generation (us, our siblings, and our cousins). When a new baby is born to one of us, we start to note her similarities to other members in the family: her red hair is like her father's; her powerful legs are like her mother's; her taciturn temper is like her uncle's.

These similarities shoot out in every direction; there is not one dimension of resemblance that is *the one and only* family resemblance, like the Hapsburg jaw. There are many strands of family resemblances along different dimensions, and they connect up with many different preceding and current family members. Art is like a family for the Neo-Wittgensteinian, and membership in that family is decided on the basis of whether the many different strands of similarity between new candidates for inclusion and the antecedently acknowledged members of the family are impressive.

The family resemblance account seems to accord better than the definitional approach with how we actually go about defending a claim that such and such a work is art. If I say that Spalding Gray's performance piece *Gray's Anatomy* is art, but you deny it, I try to persuade you by pointing to the way it resembles things you already are prepared to call art. For example, I note that like *Midsummer Night's Dream*, it involves acting, narrative, comedy, and a certain kind of dream logic. I also remind you that, like many of the poems and songs that we already regard as art, it is a soliloquy. I do not attempt to sway you by producing a definition of art. The Neo-Wittgensteinian says that I couldn't do so, even if I wanted to. But, in any case, arguments like these about the status of a candidate for arthood rarely proceed definitionally; instead they usually proceed by trading examples and reflecting upon them. Thus, the family resemblance method accords nicely with actual practice, and that is certainly a consideration in its favor.

When applying the family resemblance approach to the question of whether or not a given candidate is an artwork, we do not simply compare the new work to one of our paradigms. A new work may resemble one of our original paradigms or a recognized descendant of one of them in terms of expressivity, be similar to yet another one in terms of form, and remind us of still another in virtue of its subject matter. We look for many different strands of similarity across various dimensions between the new works and often more than one of our paradigms. Different new works may resemble past paradigms in different respects. There is no single set of respects nor number of correlations between a new work and our paradigms (and descendants thereof) that must obtain before we categorize it as art, but as the number of connections swells, the classification of the new work becomes irresistible.

The family resemblance approach does two inter-related things for the Neo-Wittgensteinian. On the one hand, it offers an account of how we succeed in identifying art. This is something any philosophy of art should do. Insofar as philosophy is concerned with our concepts, it should offer an account of how that concept is applied in practice. It should explain how we use it successfully to classify art in contradistinction from nonart. This is something that we do do. Philosophy should explain it. The Neo-Wittgensteinian explains it by means of the family resemblance method.

But the family resemblance account also adds another argument – to the open concept argument – to consolidate its case against the definitional approach. For the definitional approach also suggests an explanation of how we go about identifying and classifying works as artworks. It is an explanation with some intuitive appeal. It alleges that we identify artworks by means of a definition that we possess, if only tacitly. So, the definitional approach and the family resemblance method can be seen as competing explanations for the same phenomena – our successful identification and classification of certain objects as artworks. This then raises the question of which explanation is superior.

The Neo-Wittgensteinian argues that hers is. Against the definitional approach, she can point out that it is astonishing to say that we identify art by means of an implicit definition if no one, after centuries, can say what it is. On the positive side, she can point out that reflecting on resemblances between paradigms and their recognized descendants, on the one hand, and new cases, on the other, fits more accurately with what we actually do when deliberating and debating about new candidates for art status, whether they be avant-garde experiments or art from other cultures. Thus, the Neo-Wittgensteinian argues that, since the family resemblance method provides a better explanation of how we identify and classify art than the definitional approach, that, along with the open concept argument, gives us good grounds to reject the supposition that art can be defined. For that supposition appears to have little plausible explanatory value.

The Neo-Wittgensteinian points out that many of our concepts are not governed by definitions replete with necessary and sufficient conditions. The concepts of game and chair reputedly are not. Indeed, there are very few concepts – save formal definitions, such as those in geometry – to which the definitional model appears applicable. In the remaining majority of cases, the relevant concepts must be applied in some other way, such as by means of reflection upon resemblances. This gives us good reason to explore the possibility that the concept of art is like this. That the family resemblance method supplies a plausible explanation of how we apply the concept whereas the definitional approach does not – since every attempt to reconstruct the relevant definition fails – gives us solid grounds for suspecting that the concept of art is more like the concept of a game than it is like the concept of an equilateral triangle.

The family resemblance approach differs sharply from the definitional approach. The definitional approach rests on tracking common properties – common properties that reputedly define essentially the phenomena in question. The family resemblance approach, in contrast, depends upon noticing strands – discontinuous but interweaving strands – of resemblances. The family resemblance approach explains how it is possible for us to sort the art from the nonart without invoking the arguably unavailable common features that essentially define art. The family resemblance approach is thus a more feasible account of how we identify art, since resemblances are something we have access to, whereas no one seems to have a glimmer of the essential defining features of art.

The family resemblance method also fits like a glove with the open concept argument. If art, as a matter of the logic of the concept, must be in principle so unpredictable that no set of conditions can ever be laid down, but, at the same time, it is also the case that we can continue to classify works as art, then what resources enable us to do this? Resemblance to artistic paradigms and their already recognized descendants, the Neo-Wittgensteinian suggests, is the only live candidate.

Neo-Wittgensteinianism is a philosophy of art. It presents an account of the concept of art – art is an open concept. And it proposes a view of how that concept is applied – in virtue of family resemblances. It is not a theory of art where the term "theory of art" means "an essential definition" (a definition in terms of necessary conditions that are conjointly sufficient). In fact, it regards all art theories, conceived of as definitions, to be foundationally flawed. And, since the Neo-Wittgensteinians believe all art theories make the fundamental error of conceiving their project in terms of essential definitions, Neo-Wittgensteinians think that all art theory is wrong.

Does this mean that the history of art theory is completely worthless? Here the Neo-Wittgensteinian still has some kind words for the past. Art theorists in the past, like the expression theorist and the formalist, were mistaken in believing that they could provide an essential definition of art. In that they were attempting to do the impossible, and their efforts were futile. But, without knowing it, they were also doing something else, and that "something else" is valuable. What was it? Art criticism.

Clive Bell thought that his theory of significant form disclosed the eternal nature of art. He was wrong about that. But his writing was not totally in vain. For what he proposed as the essence of all art – significant form – was really an insight about what was important in certain kinds of art, such as the art that he loved most, neo-impressionism. Though limited as a theorist of art, Bell was a very good critic: he told people what to look for and what to value in newly emerging art movements.

Bell imagined that he was speaking as a philosopher about art for all time. But, the Neo-Wittgensteinian claims, it is possible to re-read him as an astute critic for his own time, informing the English-speaking world about the way in which to understand modern art. He showed them how formal possibilities that were recessive or neglected in previous artistic practices, like realism, were really the thing to attend to in the new art. He taught people how to appreciate the new art. Thus, his writing, reconstrued as art criticism, has lasting value, even if his theory was fatally defective.

Similar recuperative readings, the Neo-Wittgensteinian suggests, can be offered of many other past theories of art. The expression theory of art, for example, can be reconceived as offering critical insight into the art of the Romantic period as well as certain modernist tendencies that flowed from it. Even the representational theory of art can be re-read as instructive art criticism: by stressing the importance of mimesis, Aristotle was telling his fellow Greeks what was the most important feature of dramatic poetry – he was saying what audiences should attend to in order to get the most out of tragedy.

The Neo-Wittgensteinian philosophy of art, then, has three parts. First, there is the open concept argument. This has a positive side and a negative side. The positive side is the characterization of the concept of art as an open concept. The negative or critical side is the rejection of the proposition that art can be essentially defined by means of necessary and sufficient conditions. The second part of the Neo-Wittgensteinian view is the family resemblance method. This part can be called reconstructive: it attempts to reconstruct the way in which we go about identifying and classifying objects as art. The last part of the position is rehabilitative: it proposes to recuperate what is worthwhile in existing art theories by re-reading them as unconscious contributions to art criticism.

Neo-Wittgensteinianism, therefore, is not simply a skeptical position, noteworthy only for its dismissal of the definitional approach. It is also a coherent, comprehensive philosophical view that includes a positive account of the concept of art, a conception of how we classify art, and a re-reading of the history of the philosophy of art. Were Neo-Wittgensteinianism merely a form of skepticism, it might not appear so formidable. It's easy to say no, but unless you have something to put in the place of what you're rejecting, such skepticism is rarely persuasive. That Neo-Wittgensteinianism is able to weave its "no to definitions" into an ostensibly informative philosophy of such apparently broad breadth makes it particularly attractive. For that reason, it was the dominant philosophy of art for much of the 1950s and 1960s.

Objections to Neo-Wittgensteinianism

The open concept argument and the family resemblance method work very effectively together. They are a neat package of hypotheses. The first says that art cannot be defined; the second says "But not to worry," since we can get along nicely without definitions – we can explain, by means of the family resemblance method, how we go about classifying objects and performances as artworks, without definitions. Indeed, the family resemblance approach does a much better job of capturing more accurately what we do in debates about art status than the definitional approach does.

The open concept argument, so to speak, clears the ground for the family resemblance method, since if there can be no definition of art, the pressure to come up with an alternative explanation is especially acute. Thus, the first place to start interrogating Neo-Wittgensteinianism is to review the open concept argument.

Recall that according to that argument:

1   Art can be expansive.
2   Therefore, art must be open to the permanent possibility of radical change, expansion and novelty.
3   If something is art, then it must be open to the permanent possibility of radical change, expansion and novelty.
4   If something is open to the permanent possibility of radical change, expansion and novelty, then it cannot be defined.
5   Suppose that art can be defined.
6   Therefore, art is not open to the permanent possibility of change, expansion and novelty.
7   Therefore, art is not art.

This argument seems compelling, but it trades on a very dubious ambiguity. When the Neo-Wittgensteinian maintains that art cannot be defined, he is talking about the attempt to craft necessary and sufficient conditions for what counts as an *artwork*; but to show that this is impossible, he then adverts to the *practice* of art, the very concept of which he maintains must be open to the permanent possibility of expansion. Thus, in effect, the Neo-Wittgensteinian is arguing that a closed concept of *artwork* is incompatible with an open concept of the *practice* of art. But here the levels of generality between the two concepts of art ("art" as artwork; "art" as practice), though related, are hardly the same. Why must an allegedly closed concept of art in the first (artwork) sense be incompatible with the reputedly open concept of art in the second (practice) sense? The Neo-Wittgensteinian never says why, nor is it obvious. Moreover, the failure to keep the two concepts of art separate indicates that there may be a fallacy of equivocation in the argument.

The conclusion of the argument (step #7) is that art is not art. But "art" here is not being used univocally: so there is no genuine contradiction here; no real incompatibility is being demonstrated. In premise #3, when we say that something is *art* only if it is open to the permanent possibility of radical change, expansion and novelty, we are talking about the *practice of art*. Clearly it makes no sense to say of an individual artwork that it is open to the permanent possibility of radical change, expansion and novelty; the individual artwork is what it is.

But in premise #5, when we suppose that *art* can be defined, we are talking about artworks; after all, the debate is about whether the concept *work of art* can be essentially defined – that's what the Neo-Wittgensteinian accuses his predecessors of doing. But if we apply these clarifications throughout the argument, then it is obvious that there is no real formal contradiction in step #7. For there is no inconsistency in saying that an artwork is not the practice of art – nor that the concept of art is not the concept of the practice of art. The conditions that differentiate artworks from nonartworks may differ consistently with the conditions that differentiate the practice of art from other practices (like religion and science). Moreover, there is no reason to suppose that the concept of a practice may be open, while the concept of the objects of said practice (in this case artworks) is closed.

Why does the Neo-Wittgensteinian imagine that there is any real, logical tension here? Let us grant that the practice of art is open to the permanent possibility of radical change, expansion and innovation. What does that have to do with the conditions requisite for the status of artwork? Talk of the permanent possibility of expansion only makes sense with reference to the practice of art; it sounds virtually nonsensical to say of completed artworks that they need to be literally open to the permanent possibility of change and innovation; few artworks would ever be completed, if that were the case. It is simply a category error to maintain that completed artworks must be open to radical change (save perhaps in the special case of environmental-process artworks). Therefore, the open concept argument fails, precisely because it equivocates on the relevant concepts of art involved, and it neglects to forge any logical connection between definitions of art, on the one hand, and the concept of the practice of art, on the other.

This refutation may leave some unconvinced. They may be haunted by the residual suspicion that somehow if we "lay down" necessary and sufficient conditions for artworks, we may be really stipulating limitations on the kinds of things that artists can do – on the kinds of experiments and innovations they may introduce into the practice. Neo-Wittgensteinianism, in this light, gives voice to the perennial fear that by defining art, philosophers are trying (improperly) to legislate what artists can do.

But there is no reason in principle to suppose this. That artworks might possess defining characteristics does not logically preclude the invention of new works that instantiate the relevant conditions in innovative, unexpected, and unforeseeable ways. An adequate definition of science would not preclude innovative, unexpected, and unforeseeable research. That is, if we read premise #4 as pertaining to artworks, then it is false.

Of course, if a definition of art precludes artistic experimentation, that is a problem. But it is a problem with the particular definition in question, not with the very idea of defining art itself. There is no reason to imagine that, in principle, defining art is necessarily a barrier to artistic innovation. One reason for believing that this is so is that many existing definitions of art propose no conceptual barriers to artistic experiment. For example, in the next section, we will study the Institutional Theory of Art at some length. This theory does a particularly nice job of explaining why ready-mades are art. The definition is stated in terms of necessary conditions that are conjointly sufficient. But clearly any theory that countenances ready-mades as art is compatible with artists presenting any kind of thing as an artwork, since any kind of thing can be turned into a readymade.

Readymades, like Duchamp's *Fountain* and the "found sounds" of Cage's 4' 33", are indiscernible from their real-world counterparts. If a definition of art can be framed to accommodate such indiscernibilia, then clearly it will permit anything to be transformed into an artwork in the proper circumstances and for the right reasons. But if an essential definition of art can allow that *anything* can be art (not *is* art, but *can* be art), then the mere possession of necessary and sufficient conditions by such a theory places no restraints whatsoever on the scope of artistic activity.

Since there is no kind of thing that something like the Institutional Theory of Art, an essential definition of art, forfends, it is a counter-example to the Neo-Wittgensteinian allegation (premise #4) that definitions of art are in principle incompatible with the reputed openness of the practice of art to radical change, innovation and novelty. This is not to say that the Institutional Theory of Art is true, but only that it illustrates the logical point that an essential definition of what it is to be an artwork can be framed in terms of necessary and sufficient conditions without constraining the range of artistic creativity and innovation, and without legislating what kinds of things artists may and may not produce.

Still, it might be argued in response that necessary and sufficient conditions must place *some* limits on what can be an artwork, even if no limits are placed on the *kind* of thing that can be an artwork. Otherwise, they wouldn't be necessary and sufficient conditions. Several points need to be made here. First, necessary and sufficient conditions are not incompatible with an immense latitude for expansion and innovation – as much, as we shall see shortly, as anyone should want.

Second, though the concept of art (in the practice sense) may be open, it is not wide open – not anything can be art at any time for just any reason. After all, even if we agree that the practice of art is open to change and expansion, the relevant changes and expansions must be related to what precedes them, lest they would not be changes and expansions *of the practice*. That is, the changes, expansions, and innovations we have in mind cannot be utter *non sequiturs*.

Thus, we can argue that the only expansions to the practice of art that an essential definition, like the Institutional Theory and comparable theories, block are supposed "innovations" of the utter *non sequitur* variety. But this is not a problem, since the commitment of such theories to the proposition that any kind of thing can be art for the right reason is just as liberal and open as anyone should want. This in no way compromises the legitimate creativity of artists, since it allows that artists can present any kind of thing as art, from urinals, bottleracks and Parisian air, to angora goats with tires around their bellies, blocks of lard, and sections of sharks floating in formaldehyde. How much more open might we wish the practice be? Who would want to count as an artwork just anything for the wrong reason?

Undoubtedly, the family resemblance approach gets a real boost when conjoined with the open concept argument. Were the open concept argument compelling, then that would undermine the claims of the intuitively seductive definitional approach to the problem of identifying art, thereby sending us in search of an alternative account of the way in which we classify art, such as, most eminently, the family resemblance method.

But, as we have seen, the open concept argument appears ultimately unequal to its mission. Nevertheless, that does not render the family resemblance method defenseless. For it may still be argued that it has many virtues of its own to recommend it, most notably that it does an adequate job of explaining how we discriminate between art and nonart. But does it really?

According to the family resemblance approach, the way in which we go about identifying artworks – the way that we sort the art from the nonart – is by looking for similarities between works already regarded to be artworks and new candidates. Ideally, the process begins by establishing a flexible set of paradigmatic artworks – works everyone agrees are unquestionably artworks. On the basis of these, we then decide about the art status of further works. At any given moment in time, then, we will have in our possession a set of artworks comprised of paradigms and recognized descendants of paradigms. If in the present moment, we are perplexed about the status of a new work, we are instructed to look at the body of works already adjudged to be artworks and to see whether the new work in question bears appreciable similarities to the items in our existing set of acknowledged artworks.

Perhaps the new work is similar to *Tristam Shandy* in its possession of an elliptical narrative structure, like *Oedipus Rex* in its capacity to raise pity and fear, and it resembles Beethoven's *Ninth Symphony* in its sublimity. As these correspondences accumulate, we decide to classify the new work as an artwork, though no established numerical criterion determines how many correspondences are required here. Rather, we reflect on the resemblances and make an all-things-considered-judgment.

But there is a really big problem with this story. It is that the concept of similarity upon which the family resemblance method relies is too slack. For, it is a truism of logic that everything resembles everything else in some respect. For example, artists and asteroids resemble each other, if only in respect to being physical objects. Likewise, an alien carburetor from another galaxy will resemble Rodin's *Gate of Hell*, at least in respect of its material objecthood, as well as probably in a number of other respects as well.

Thus, for any candidate, it will resemble the paradigms in some ways, and if we consider the recognized descendants of the paradigms, in addition, then the number of similarities between *anything* and the other items already acknowledged to be art will be compounded exponentially. Consequently, applying the family resemblance method today, we will be able to declare that each and every thing is art by tomorrow, if not sooner. But clearly this is too indiscriminate a "method" for classifying art.

If one doubts this conclusion, take the argument in steps. We start with a large and diversified set of paradigms cases, each of which possesses many properties. From that we can generate a second generation of descendants, which also will possess a great many properties, a large number of which correspond to the properties of the first generation, but an equally or larger number of which are different. Thus, we will have an even greater number of properties with which to analogize our third generation of descendants. And then so on with a fourth, fifth, sixth . . . nth number of generations, resulting in an indeterminately large number of properties. It is, in principle, unimaginable that there is any object in the universe that cannot finally be incorporated into this progression. But, then, everything is art according to the family resemblance method, and that seems way too inclusive for any classificatory procedure.

But, you may say, wait a minute. Throughout this book, we have taken readymades and found objects, including found sounds, to be artworks. So maybe it is not really problematic for a classificatory procedure to arrive at the conclusion that everything can be art. Isn't that a just consequence of taking readymades and found objects seriously?

Not really. To agree that readymades *can* be art accepts the principle that any *kind* of thing could be an artwork, but not that everything *is* an artwork. The family resemblance method entails that everything *is* an artwork. And that is far too ecumenical.

Second, let us agree that Duchamp's *In Advance of a Broken Arm* – an ordinary, factory-made snow shovel – is a work of art. It is a work of art because, among other things, it possesses the aesthetic property of being humorous – it alludes to what can happen (heaven forbid) when you use a snow shovel. *In Advance of a Broken Arm* is an artwork for the right reasons. But if the family resemblance method is put in motion, then, of course, not only *In Advance of a Broken Arm*, but every other snow shovel will be an artwork, since every other snow shovel will resemble *In Advance of a Broken Arm* in a million ways. But surely that is the wrong reason to count any snow shovel as an artwork. It is not the reason why we accepted *In Advance of a Broken Arm* as art; but it will supply the grounds to say that anything *is* art, on the family resemblance model. Thus, the family resemblance approach amounts to the *"too open* concept" of art.

On its own, resemblance unqualified, then, is just too broad a relationship to employ to pick out artworks, since everything is similar to everything else in some way or another. However, you might think that there is a clear-cut way to repair the family resemblance method: simply require that the similarities between candidates and the paradigms (and recognized descendants thereof) be of a certain sort. Material objecthood, for example, is ruled out of court as a relevant similarity for art status. But to talk about required sorts of similarities is, of course, to revert to the idea of necessary conditions for art status, and that is exactly what the family resemblance method eschews. The reintroduction of talk of necessary conditions is inconsistent with the point of the family resemblance approach.

But perhaps there is another way of preventing the "here-comes-everything" effect. Instead of requiring that candidates possess certain properties, let us draw up a long list of the properties of our paradigms and their recognized descendants that we think are art-relevant; and then let us propose that if a candidate resembles already existing art in some of these respects, then it will be art. Our list will be a long disjunction of art relevant properties – either x has a or b or c or d and so forth. If x has a or b or c or d etcetera, then x is art. This gets around the problem of necessary conditions, since neither a nor b nor c nor d are necessary conditions of all art.

But this strategy will not save the family resemblance method either, since a disjunctive set of properties like this will supply us with a list of sufficient conditions for art status. And the proponent of the family resemblance account is as opposed to the notion of sufficient conditions as he is to the notion of necessary conditions. Thus, drawing up a disjunctive list of art relevant properties is also inconsistent with the point of the family resemblance approach.

The family resemblance model, then, is caught on the horns of a dilemma: either it employs the concept of resemblance without qualification, which results in the conclusion that everything is art; or, to avert that conclusion, it qualifies what kind of resemblances are relevant for art status, thereby reintroducing either necessary or sufficient conditions or both, with the consequence that we are now back in the definition business. That is, the family resemblance approach either entails that everything is art, which is to give up altogether the idea of sorting art from nonart, or, if conditions are added to avoid this alternative, then the approach is no longer the family resemblance approach, but some kind of condition-governed, definitional approach. Either way, the family resemblance approach fails to make good on its promises.

When Neo-Wittgensteinianism first appeared in the 1950s, it struck many philosophers as very convincing. A virtual moratorium on attempts to define art ensued. However, as time wore on, chinks began to appear in the Neo-Wittgensteinian armor, as questions were raised about both the open concept argument and the family resemblance method. Confidence in the project of definition gradually returned and then, by the 1970s and 1980s, it was in full throttle once again. In the next section, we will discuss two of the more influential definitions of art from that period: the Institutional Theory of Art, to which we have already alluded, and the Historical Definition of Art.

Part II
Two contemporary
definitions of art

The Institutional Theory of Art

There are a number of different versions of the Institutional Theory of Art. The one that we'll spend most of our time looking at was defended by George Dickie in the early 1970s. Since then, he has developed a more complicated position, which can be called the Theory of the Art Circle. The justification for dwelling primarily on his earlier theory instead is twofold:

it is the best known and most widely discussed version of the Institutional Theory of Art, and it illustrates nicely how the current revived interest in defining art grew out of a careful consideration of the shortcomings of Neo-Wittgensteinianism.

Institutional Theorists like Dickie were impressed by a certain criticism of the family resemblance method, which, though related to the objections rehearsed above, had a slightly different inflection. Suggested by Maurice Mandelbaum, the objection scrutinizes the central metaphor of Neo-Wittgensteinians – family resemblance – and finds it wanting.

The Neo-Wittgensteinian talks about family resemblances: we compare new candidates for art status with previously acknowledged paradigms and their recognized descendants, and we look and see whether or not they bear a family resemblance to their predecessors. But upon reflection, it should be obvious that the notion of a *family* resemblance is really misplaced here. Real family resemblances – say the similarity between your hair and your grandmother's – are not *mere* resemblances, mere correlations of features. Even if my eyes are exactly the same color as Gregory Peck's, they do not bear a *family* resemblance to Gregory Peck's for the straightforward reason that, no matter how great the similarity between my eyes and Peck's, we are not members of the same family – not members of the same gene pool.

For resemblances to be genuine *family* resemblances, there must be some underlying mechanism – such as genetic inheritance. If a similarity is to count as a family resemblance, it must have been *generated* in the appropriate manner. If Bill Clinton resembles a big teddy bear in certain respects, that is not a family resemblance, since presumably Clinton and the teddy bear don't belong to the same gene pool. Though they may look alike, the resemblance is not a family resemblance.

Does it really make a difference, if the Neo-Wittgensteinians were talking improperly about family resemblances? Yes. One reason it is important is that once we realize that they are not talking about family resemblances, but only mere resemblances, then, as we saw in the preceding section, their so-called method will have the "here-comes-everything" effect. But when the resemblances are called family resemblances, this consequence is obscured for the reason that genuine family resemblances really are selective because they presuppose, in addition to similarity, an underlying mechanism that accounts for that similarity. Family resemblances are condition-governed, since in order to be a *family* resemblance, the similarity must obtain between people who meet the necessary condition that they belong to the same gene pool.

Thus, either Neo-Wittgensteinians were really talking about family resemblances, in which case they were presupposing necessary conditions for art status, or they were talking about mere resemblance, in which case their approach was not selective enough, since everything resembles everything else in some respect. So far, of course, this is just a different way of getting at some of the objections that we've already seen against Neo-Wittgensteinianism. However, this way of approaching the problem is suggestive in a way that our previous formulation was not.

For this way of stating the matter hints at a possible solution to the problem of how we go about identifying art. The Neo-Wittgensteinian advised us to *look* for family resemblances. He misspoke, because family resemblances are not something that you can determine simply by looking. Family resemblances also depend on something that you cannot see – genetic inheritance. How the resemblance came about – its *genesis* – is crucial for calling a resemblance a family resemblance. This is what the Neo-Wittgensteinian ignored, but, at the same time, it provides a clue for how we identify artworks, namely that the genesis of a candidate is crucial for its art status.

We do not classify people as members of the same family because of the way they look. Two people may exhibit or manifest the same properties, but we do not say they belong to the same family on that basis. It is only when they are genetically linked that we say they belong to the same family. We will call two people sisters, even if they do not look alike, if they are genetically linked in the right way. Nonmanifest properties – genetic properties – are what make for family membership, not perceptible resemblances that, as the Neo-Wittgensteinian says, you can detect by looking and seeing (or listening and hearing). That art status might rely as well on a candidate's possession of certain nonmanifest or unexhibited properties is the clue that Institutional Theorists of Art learnt from Mandelbaum's criticism of the Neo-Wittgensteinian's misuse of the notion of family resemblance.

Of course, artworks are not the product of genes. They originate socially, not biologically. They are generated within a social context wherein the activities of the artist and the audience are co-ordinated by certain underlying social rules. Being an artwork is a function of certain social relations. These relations are not something that the artwork wears on its face; they are not something that one can detect by simply looking. They are nonmanifest or unexhibited social relations. Thus, the Institutional Theorist suggests that if we can isolate those features of the social context of the practice in virtue of which a candidate for art status is deemed an artwork, we will have a way of sorting art from nonart.

Neo-Wittgensteinianism has an obvious problem dealing with ready-mades and found objects. If *In Advance of a Broken Arm* is an artwork, then any snow shovel that is indiscernible from it, including yours and mine, should be an artwork as well. If we simply attend to the perceptible features of the shovels in question, they should all count as artworks, since they are perceptually indiscernible. Moreover, this kind of problem could result with any kind of object, since any kind of object could be a found object. But this result is wrongheaded. *In Advance of a Broken Arm* is art, but my snow shovel is not, despite the fact that it looks exactly like Duchamp's. What is the difference? The Institutional Theorist appeals to certain nonmanifest, relational properties that *In Advance of a Broken Arm* possesses and that my snow shovel does not, namely, its position within a certain set of co-ordinated social practices – that is, its location in a certain social context.

The Institutional Theorist calls the relevant social practice "the art-world." The artworld, he claims, is a social institution, like religion, insofar as it is underwritten by rules and procedures. Candidates are artworks because they abide by the pertinent artworld rules and procedures. In other words, an artwork is generated by playing by the required rules and procedures. These social rules are the underlying factors that make art-works possible (they are analogous to the genetic mechanisms that account for *family* resemblances). The relation of the artwork to the rules is not a manifest property of the artwork – you cannot eyeball it by concentrating on the object in isolation; it is a function of the social context into which the artwork is inserted.

What are these rules and procedures? According to the Institutional Theory of Art:

> x is an artwork in the classificatory sense if and only if (1) x is an artifact (2) upon which someone acting on behalf of a certain institution (the artworld) confers the status of being a candidate for appreciation.

This theory comprises two necessary conditions that are conjointly sufficient. The Institutional Theory of Art is advanced as a comprehensive definition of all art. As indicated in the last section, it has been designed in such a way that it allows that any kind of object can be an artwork, so long as it is put forth in accordance with the right procedure. It does not impede any imaginable type of artistic experimentation, and, therefore, it is a counterexample to the central contention of the open concept argument (that an essential definition is incompatible with artistic innovation). However, though it allows that anything can be art in principle, it does not err – in the way the family resemblance method does – by proposing a procedure for identifying art that entails that everything is art now.

According to the Institutional Theory, a work of art must be an artifact. Here "artifact" should be understood liberally. To be an artifact requires that the candidate must somehow be a product of human labor, although the extent of the labor may be exceedingly minimal. Something may be an artifact because a human has worked it up out of raw materials. But it will also be an artifact, for the Institutional Theorist, if someone has merely framed or indexed the object; a readymade is an artifact if someone puts it forth for exhibition purposes, or even points to it and says that it is an art object, as Duchamp once did with the Woolworth Building in lower Manhattan. A performance can be an artifact in this sense, since it is a product of human labor; not only objects, that is, satisfy the artifactuality condition. Moreover, the artifactuality condition is also meant to indicate that the work in question must be publicly accessible.

Many theorists of art would agree that a necessary condition for art status is that the candidate be an artifact in the broad sense. It is the second condition of the theory that is most distinctive. It maintains that something is an artwork only if it has had the status of candidate for appreciation conferred on it by some person or persons acting on behalf of the institution of the artworld. The conferral of status here is a procedure. That is why Institutional Theories of art are called procedural theories. Procedural theories of art contrast with functional theories, like the aesthetic theory of art, because procedural theories adjudge a candidate to be art in virtue of its conformity with certain rules, and not in terms of its results or functions (such as the production of aesthetic experience).

But what is this strange-sounding procedure – the conferral of the status of candidate for appreciation? The model for this procedure is something like a bishop's conferring holy orders on a priest, or the queen's conferral of knighthood on some luminary, or a university's conferral of the status of bachelor of arts upon a graduating senior. Just as a couple acquires the status of "married" when the justice of the peace pronounces them man and wife, so an artifact is an artwork when someone acting on behalf of the artworld confers the status of candidate for appreciation upon it.

Nevertheless, who are the people who confer this status on artifacts? In the great majority of cases, they are artists. They confer the status of candidate for appreciation on artifacts by making the objects and then putting them out in the world for people to attend to appreciatively – that is, artists confer the status of candidate for appreciation on artifacts by creating artifacts with understanding such that audiences can size them up and assess them with understanding. Generally the understanding exercised by the artist and that exercised by the audience are roughly complementary.

This is the most standard case. However, on occasion, the person who confers the relevant status on the object may not be the creator of the object. A museum curator might display a tribal implement, like an Eskimo fishing hook, as a candidate for appreciation because of its striking aesthetic properties and thereby transform a tool into an artwork. But in the general case, the conferral of status occurs when an artist makes an artwork and puts it forward for appreciation, or when an artist selects a found object and displays it for others to size up and assess.

Here, it is important to note that the artist does not confer the status of artwork on her artifact. The status that she confers on the artifact is candidate for appreciation. Also, presenting something as a candidate for appreciation does not guarantee that it will be appreciated by anyone. The artifact is simply nominated for appreciative attention. But just as a candidate for Vice-President who has been duly nominated may lose the election, so an artifact can be nominated as a candidate for appreciation and then go unappreciated.

The basic social interaction that the Institutional Theory describes is one that is quite familiar. An artist makes something and presents it to spectators for their attention and understanding; it is up to the audience then to decide whether or not it is worth their efforts. The Institutional Theorist describes this familiar interaction in unfamiliar terms – like "conferral of status" and "candidate for appreciation" – in order to call our attention to the way in which this ordinary transaction is governed by social rules and roles. Just as there is a framework – a social context with underlying rules and roles – in place when we buy a newspaper, there is also a framework – an institutional network of relations – in place that makes the inter-related production and consumption of artworks possible.

In the standard case, it is the artist who confers the status of candidate for appreciation on the artifact, though, as mentioned, sometimes others may function in this role or capacity. A curator, a critic, or a distributor might elect an object as a candidate for appreciation and put it forward for display. A critic, for example, might recommend the water colors of a certain chimpanzee to his readers as something interesting to look at, due to their aesthetic properties, for the purpose of appreciation. In this case, it is the critic, not the chimp, who confers status on the objects. Recently, the art historian Mia Fineman has recommended the paintings of elephants for our attention. But this is an exceptional case. In the main it is the artist who confers status on the artifact on behalf of the artworld.

But what does it mean to confer status on *behalf of the artworld*? Why is it that the artist and the critic are empowered to act on behalf of the artworld, but the chimpanzee and the elephant are not? What is the nature of their authority? It is like the authority of a philosophy professor who, on the basis of her knowledge of the field, advises that a paper proposal does or does not address a philosophical problem. Similarly, a scientist in a given area judges, on the basis of her experience in the field, whether or not a research proposal is likely to be "in the game."

Analogously, the people who play the role of conferring status on behalf of the artworld do so in virtue of their knowledge, understanding, and experience of the artworld. Artists have the requisite background knowledge, understanding, and experience, acquired through study and practice, as do critics, curators and the like. Artists create and put forward candidates for appreciation with *understanding*. Thus, it is their knowledge and experience that give them the authority to confer on artifacts a certain status *on behalf of the artworld*.

The artist Duchamp, by virtue of his knowledge, understanding, and experience, had the authority to confer the status of candidate for appreciation on the urinal that he entitled *Fountain*. A plumber reading the reviews of *Fountain*, on the other hand, could not show up at the gallery the next day and present his own bathroom fixtures as artworks. Why not? Because he is not empowered to act on behalf of the artworld. Is this sheer elitism? No. For the plumber doesn't know anything about art; he does not put forward his plumbing fixtures on the basis of any understanding of art theory and art history, whereas Duchamp does. Similarly, it is the critic and not the chimpanzee who confers status on the water colors, since the critic knows about and understands artistic form and aesthetic properties, whereas the chimp does not.

It is the knowledge and understanding of art – its history, prevailing theories, and practices – that qualify someone to act on behalf of the artworld as a conferrer of candidate for appreciation. The Institutional Theory really claims no more than what we all admit about the social practice of art; that the people with the authority to put artifacts forward for our attention be people who know something about what they are doing – know something about art, about how it works, about its history, about what the current state of the practice is, and so on.

If a 2-year-old child with no knowledge of chess comes upon two adults playing the game and moves the pawn of one of the players into a position where it would hold the opponent's king in checkmate, we do not say that the child checkmated the king, not only because the child was not a player, but more importantly because the child did not know what he was doing. He has no knowledge of the rules, the strategies, or the point of chess. Likewise, and for the same reasons, a plumber who merely imitates Duchamp without understanding does not confer status on behalf of the artworld when he unveils *Fountain: The Sequel*.

The Institutional Theory of Art is often criticized for being anti-democratic. But this is really unfair. Democracy doesn't require that everyone be empowered to do just anything – not just anyone can walk into a hospital and perform brain surgery. Similarly, not just anyone can act on behalf of the artworld. On the other hand, the artworld, according to the Institutional Theory of Art, is an equal-opportunity employer, since anyone, in principle, should be able to become an agent of the artworld by acquiring the relevant sort of knowledge, understanding, and the right sort of experience.

This is why the artworld – as the Institutional Theory portrays it – is not elitist or anti-democratic. Anyone can act on its behalf, if only they acquire some knowledge and understanding. This can be done without great difficulty in modern, literate cultures. It need not be very much knowledge, and you can acquire it on your own; you need not go to art school, though obviously that makes things somewhat easier. Nor is the artworld a dictatorship, since the agents of the artworld only nominate candidates for appreciation – for example, for design appreciation. It remains a possibility that no one will find the candidate worthy of the scantest attention. Thus, the Institutional Theory of Art allows for bad art of fairly awful proportions. In this, it is a classificatory theory of art, not a commendatory theory.

Undoubtedly, it is not difficult for something to qualify as art in accordance with the Institutional Theory of Art. Many of us have enough knowledge to put an object forth with sufficient understanding as a candidate for appreciation. But this is not a shortcoming of the theory, since it is not really very difficult to create art. The trick is to create art that is actually worthy of appreciation.

Unlike Neo-Wittgensteinianism, the Institutional Theory does not locate the criteria for art status in the manifest properties of the artifact. The crucial determinant of art status is the social genesis of the artifact – has it emerged from the social network of the artworld in the right way (have the right kind of qualified people put it forward for the right reasons?). Since previous philosophies of art, including formalism, the representational theory of art, the expression theory, aesthetic theories of art, and Neo-Wittgensteinianism neglect the social genesis of artworks, this gives the Institutional Theory a wider reach than most previous approaches to identifying art.

At the same time, the Institutional Theory possesses the means to exclude candidates from the order of art. If the wrong person (a person without the requisite knowledge and understanding of art) puts forward an artifact, he will not possess the capability to confer the appropriate status upon it, and the object will not be art. This is not arbitrary; if a child with no knowledge of art history brings a snow shovel to an art gallery, we will not regard it as an artwork. Moreover, even if the person in question is properly informed – even if the relevant person is an artist – we will not count his artifacts as art, unless they are presented for the right reasons (as candidates for appreciation). That is, if an artist makes a pizza for lunch, it is not an artwork. Thus, though generously inclusive, the Institutional Theory of Art is not so liberal that it accepts everything as an artwork.

Perhaps the greatest accomplishment of the Institutional Theory of Art is that it has alerted philosophers to the importance of social context for determining art status. As we have seen, preceding theories of art paid scarcely any attention to the social dimension of art, focussing primarily on internal properties of the art object, such as significant form, expressive and aesthetic properties, representational properties, and the like. The Institutional Theory emphasizes that there is a social practice with rules and designated roles underpinning the presentation of such things and that the instantiation of these social forms and relations in the required way is crucial to art status. In this, the Institutional Theory of Art has had a lasting impact on the debate about "What is art?"

However, even if the general social thrust of the Institutional Theory is widely applauded, the precise details of the theory have been subjected to intense scrutiny and criticism. It may be the case that no theory of art has garnered as much comment and inspired so much fault-finding as the early version of the Institutional Theory we have been discussing. Some of these criticisms have been repeated so often that they have become virtually canonical.

The first line of criticisms pertains to the notion that art is an institution. Is the Institutional Theorist warranted in calling art a social institution, or is his usage forced? The Neo-Wittgensteinian misspoke in his invocation of family resemblances. Does the Institutional Theorist misdescribe art by alleging that it is an institution?

Think about unexceptionable cases of institutions, like the Catholic Church or the legal system of the United States. Those institutions have designated roles with duties, responsibilities, and powers attached to them. The Institutional Theory claims that art, too, possesses analogous roles, for example the role of conferrer of the status of candidate for appreciation. But is the role of conferrer of status anything like the roles of a bishop or a justice of the peace?

The Institutional Theorist says they are parallel, since they all confer status: the bishop confers priestly status (ordination) on a postulant, the justice of the peace confers marital status on the couple, and the artist confers the status of candidate for appreciation on her work. But in order to be a bishop or a justice of the peace, one has to meet certain specific, publicly ascertainable criteria. One cannot be a bishop unless one is a Catholic and has been appointed to that office by the proper authorities. Nor just anyone can ordain a postulant; one must be a bishop, and there are precise conditions for occupying that institutional role.

But what are the publicly ascertainable criteria for being a conferrer of the status of candidate for appreciation? Suppose one says that usually one has to be an artist. But what are the criteria for being an artist? Artists in modern societies are usually self-elected; it is not an official role, connected with publicly agreed upon criteria. And what about the cases where the conferrer of status is a critic? What are the criteria for that role? In

America, it is said, everyone is a critic. Arguably, holding a staff position on publication is neither a necessary nor a sufficient condition for being a critic; and, in any case, one can always publish oneself. Is mouthing off on the Internet enough to count one as a critic?

In short, there is a strong disanalogy between the agents who supposedly act on behalf of the artworld and the agents of established social institutions like the Catholic Church or the legal institution. In order to fulfill the roles of an established social insitution, the people in question have to meet certain well-entrenched, generally formal criteria; that, in part, is what it means to call these institutions established. To be a bishop requires that one go through certain procedures which themselves require certain credentials, which, in turn, depend upon meeting pre-established criteria. With genuine institutional roles, that is, there are established criteria that specify what it takes for someone to be acting on behalf of the relevant institution; there are requirements that an institutional agent, like a bishop, must meet before they are empowered to confer the status of, say, priest upon candidates.

But, with respect to the Institutional Theory of Art, there seems to be very little by way of established criteria that specify what it takes to be acting on behalf of the artworld. There don't appear to be any meaningful constraints on becoming an artist, a gallery owner, a distributor, a producer or a critic. People, it would seem, can and do just declare themselves to be in this line of business. On the other hand, with most authentic institutional roles – like being a lawyer – there is some process of certification *and*, where the role is connected with some form of knowledge that the person who occupies the role must exhibit at a certain level of understanding, whether someone possesses the required level of understanding is judged formally by previously certified practitioners.

However, there does not appear to be anything like this with respect to the artworld. True, many artists may undertake some kind of formal training, and nowadays most critics are probably university trained. Yet an academic degree is not a necessary condition for being an artist, a critic, a gallery owner, a movie producer, and so on. There are no known certification procedures; it is all very informal. But if it is all very informal, does it really make sense to call art an institution? Or is the Institutional Theorist just drastically misusing language?

An institution is not only a set of inter-related practices. An institution also has formalized relations of authority – that is, some person or persons, meeting a set of formalized criteria, have the authority to declare what is or is not an activity falling within the range of the institution, as well as the authority to decide upon appropriate expansions of the insitution. But there are no formal criteria for determining who acts on behalf of the artworld; there are no established procedures for appointing them. So, in fact, the artworld is not strictly analogous to a social institution in any rigorous sense, and there is, therefore, nothing approaching a genuinely institutionalized role of conferrer of the status of candidate for appreciation.

There are similar problems with the notion of a candidate for appreciation. To be a candidate for a public office – say, President of the United States – certain criteria must be met: the candidate must be over thirty-five years old and must be native born. Before someone can be nominated for this office, they must meet these criteria. Yet what are the criteria for being nominated as a candidate for appreciation? Institutions not only have strict criteria for who may occupy what roles; there are also criteria with respect to the execution of those roles. Before a justice of the peace may marry a couple, the couple must satisfy the requirement of being over a certain age – even a duly appointed justice of the peace cannot marry two infants. And one can only baptize a human being; one cannot baptize a potato. But what are the constraints on the artifacts upon which agents of the artworld may confer the status of appreciation? There seem to be none. But, then, the procedure hardly seems to be an institutionalized one.

Institutions have strictly defined rules about who can do what to what. The artworld has nothing like the relevant sorts of formalized criteria. Therefore, it is argued, art is not an institution, properly so called, and the elements of the Institutional Theory of Art that refer to "conferrers of status" and "candidates for appreciation" are nothing but strained and misleading metaphors that in the last analysis are empty.

Surely, the critic of the Institutional Theory has a point; art is not a social institution in the strict sense that the Catholic Church is a social institution. But how much really hangs on this? Suppose the Institutional Theorist agrees that art is not a social institution, strictly speaking, but goes on to say that it is nevertheless a social practice. Putting forward a work of art involves a sender and a receiver – a sender who makes and presents a work with understanding which is intended to be suitable for reciprocal understanding on the part of the potential audience. Moreover, at any given point in time, what comprises understanding on the part of the maker/presenter of the artifact and the complementary understanding on the part of the audience is determined by social practice. With these amendments, a revised Institutional Theory would claim; that x is art in the classificatory sense if and only if (1) x is an artifact (2) created and/or presented with understanding by an agent to an audience prepared to understand it in the appropriate manner.

Of course, this is not sufficient, since it would apply to many things that are not art. A yearly corporate shareholders' report meets these criteria. Clearly, the second condition of the revised Institutional Theory needs to say: that x is created and/or presented with artistic understanding by an agent to an audience prepared to understand it artistically. But there are two problems that critics have repeatedly raised with proposals like this.

The first is that it disallows the possibility that art can occur outside a network of social practices. The Institutional Theory's great claim to fame is the philosophical recognition that art occurs in a social context and that art status can be identified as a function of social relations. This is allegedly a necessary condition of both the early Institutional Theory of Art and the revised version. But can't art occur outside a network of social practices?

Suppose a Neolithic tribesman finds himself lost in a valley with pretty stones of different colors. He arranges some of them in a way that stirs visual pleasure in him. Also, suppose that no one in his tribe has ever done this before – maybe no living creature has ever done this before. Nevertheless, isn't this an artwork, indeed, an abstract artwork?

Note that in this case, the creator is not making or presenting the work with understanding born of social practice, since there is no relevant social practice. Nor is he making it for an audience – perhaps he believes that he will never see his fellow tribesmen again – and, in any case, he is not making it for an audience prepared to understand it artistically, since there is no such thing as artistic understanding available in his native culture for himself or others.

This objection cuts against the early version of the Institutional Theory, since it makes no sense to say that this Neolithic tribesman is conferring the status of candidate for appreciation on the stones on behalf of the artworld, since there is no artworld. Nor can we say that the stones are presented and intended to be received with artistic understanding, since there is no such thing as artistic understanding yet. Thus, if this Neolithic arrangement of stones is art, there can be art without an artworld, artistic understanding or any existing artistic culture whatsoever. But art does not, then, require, as a necessary condition, that there be a social practice in place. There can be examples of solitary artists creating one-off works of art outside of any institution or even outside any nexus of understandings rooted in social practices.

People may respond differently to counterexamples like this. Some may argue that the Neolithic arrangement of stones is obviously an artwork and that this shows that any sort of Institutional Theory is false, since it shows that solitary, nonsocial art is possible. Others may be less convinced. A defender of the Institutional Theory, in either its early or revised form, may say that if this is just a one-off affair, if the tribesman develops no conception of what he is doing – no conception that is at least in principle communicable to others – then we should not regard the arrangement as an artwork. That is, if our Neolithic artificer does not realize that the kind of thing he has made could be presented to others as a source of visual pleasure – that the visual pleasure in question is communicable – he has not created an artwork. It is a happy accident for him that he contrived such a pleasing configuration of stones, but it is not an artwork.

Archaeologists chancing upon his stones millennia later, it may be said, will not presume the stones constitute an artwork; archaeologists will wait for further evidence that the arrangement was intended for an audience prepared to receive it with whatever made for Neolithic artistic understanding, if there were such.

The argument, of course, will not end there. Of the archaeologists, it may be claimed that, if they behave in the manner described, that only shows that they presuppose that art is a social practice which, in this context, simply begs the question at issue. We want to know whether or not art is social. That certain social scientists assume that art is a social practice comes as no surprise; after all, they're *social* scientists. Better evidence that the arrangement of stones is art is that ordinary folk, using their ordinary understanding of our concept of art, would probably say the stones were art.

Here, the Institutional Theorist might respond that a plain speaker would say this because the plain speaker is imagining that others, such as himself, could look at the arrangement of stones and derive visual pleasure from it. But then the plain speaker would, in effect, be assuming that there is an audience capable of viewing it with the relevant sort of artistic understanding, thereby satisfying the second condition of the revised Institutional Theory. But did the Neolithic tribesman present it with artistic understanding? Surely, it might be argued, he must have realized that others might respond as he did, if only they saw it; otherwise whatever he believed he was doing when he composed his arrangement would be utterly mysterious.

In addition, the proponent of the Institutional Theory might add that there are few, if any, noncontroversial cases of solitary art. Most art occurs within the context of social practices. This is not simply a feature of high art. Clog dancing, folk music, quilt making, and so on are all part of social practices – they have histories that are taught, if only orally; they have techniques and conventions for creation and presentation that are learned, and stories about illustrious predecessors spring up about these practices, which prepare members of the subculture in the ways of artistically understanding works in the tradition. Amateur painters too learn their craft socially and, even if they do not show their work, they make work which is accessible to others because they employ techniques, conventions and knowledge of a sort that viewers are prepared to respond to with socially shared understanding. Even the mentally disturbed who produce drawings and the like have some exposure to existing social traditions of artmaking.

Institutional Theories of Art can encompass all of these cases; Institutional Theories are adequate for all known cases of art, since all known art is social. That there may be some controversial, conjectural cases, such as our imagined Neolithic tribesman, should not weigh too heavily against the theory. The theory is as powerful a theory as we've got. Every theory is liable to inspire some disputed borderline cases. One does not abandon an otherwise successful theory just because of a highly controversial, imaginary counterexample.

Whether the tale of our imagined Neolithic tribesman, and similar fabricated stories, defeats the Institutional Theory, is an unresolved question. There may be arguments on both sides of the debate. But there is still another problem with the Institutional Theory which merits our attention.

The earlier version of the theory maintains that status is conferred upon a candidate by an agent acting on behalf of a certain institution. Which institution? The *artworld*. Likewise the revised theory has it that an agent creates and/or presents the artifact with understanding for an audience that is prepared to understand it in the appropriate manner. But what kind of understanding is it that the agent and the audience possess? *Artistic* understanding. However, then both versions of the Institutional Theory are circular.

In order to ascertain whether a domain of activities is an artworld, one would have to be in a position to determine whether those activities involve artworks. And what is artistic understanding, if not understanding that pertains to artworks? Institutional Theories of Art are supposed to define the notion of artwork in the classificatory sense. But it turns out that in order to apply the theory, we must already know how to classify artworks, since, on the one hand, an artworld is a practice whose currency is artworks, while, on the other hand, artistic understanding is a matter of understanding artworks. How can we determine whether artists or audiences are creating, presenting, and responding to artifacts with the relevant understanding, unless we can satisfy ourselves that they are dealing with *artworks* in an appropriate manner? Thus, both versions of the Institutional Theory are effectively presupposing the concept of an artwork for the purpose of defining it. This seems blatantly circular and inadmissible.

Institutional Theorists have long been aware of this criticism. Their official answer to it is that definitions can be viciously circular or not. A definition is viciously circular if it is uninformative. "Art is art" is viciously circular. However, a definition may be circular and, nevertheless, still be informative; you can learn something from it. A definition may be circular but it may be a circle with a wide diameter, not a tight circle like "Art is art."

Given this distinction, the Institutional Theorist maintains that his circle is a nonvicious one; it is informative. From his definition, you learn that art is a social affair, that it involves artists and audiences engaged in co-ordinated roles, underwritten by reciprocal forms of understanding. Through the theory, you can come to appreciate that art occurs against a broader social context, the artworld, and that this forum of social activity is structured in terms of roles that presuppose symmetrically inter-related social knowledge.

Does this exonerate the Institutional Theory from the damning charge of circularity? There are those who will balk at the distinction between vicious and informative circularity. The Institutional Theorist will claim that most social concepts are circular, or "inflected," in the way that he says art is, and that, as a result, most definitions of social phenomena will finally be circular. Thus, what is important is that we try to assure that our definitions of social concepts be informative in their circularity, not vicious. Whether or not this is so is certainly open to debate, as is the question of whether any circular definition is ultimately satisfactory.

But even if it is true that some circular definitions are acceptable, a question also arises about how informative Institutional Theories really are. Supposedly, we learn from them that art is a social affair. We learn that artists present artifacts to audiences prepared to understand them. Undoubtedly, this specifies a social relationship, but how informative is it to be told that art requires such a relationship? What co-ordinated human activity does not require such a relationship? Jokes require tellers who understand humor and audiences prepared to understand them in terms of comic amusement; the custom of shaking hands as a form of greeting requires two parties who understand what they are doing and the circumstances appropriate to what they are doing. Does the Institutional Theory really teach us anything that isn't obvious: that art, like every other co-ordinated human activity, requires mutual understanding between concerned parties? Saying that the understanding is *artistic* yields no added information, since on that point, the definition remains stubbornly circular, if not viciously so.

Moreover, does the fact that the understanding in question is co-ordinated warrant the claim that art is either an institution or a social practice? The theory does cite a social relationship: the relationship of the artist and the audience, bound together by mutual understanding. But does a social relationship like this constitute a social institution, or even, to speak less rigorously, a social practice?

A man dying of thirst meets someone from another culture in the desert. They do not speak the same language. The dying man gestures to his mouth, sticks out his tongue, and rolls his eyes. He is trying to get the other person to understand that he needs water. He plans his gestures deliberately and with understanding. Suppose he is understood, which would not be unlikely, given the circumstances. There are no shared, pre-existing conventions here. There is a social relationship. But have these two strangers just initiated a social institution or a social practice? It would seem far-fetched to say so. Institutions and practices require some kind of framework, with established roles, techniques, conventions, and the like. But not every kind of social relationship is this involved. The relationship between the thirsty man and his savior is quite simple. Maybe there are social relationships between artists and audiences which likewise are neither institutional nor full-blown social practices.

Perhaps our Neolithic tribesman could gesture at his arrangement of stones to a fellow tribesperson. Even if the newcomer got the point, would that warrant saying that an institution or a practice was then in place? Granting that art involves social relationships, as thinly described as they are by Institutional Theorists, that would not seem to support the claim that there is always an artworld institution or a socially established artistic practice in place.

Indeed, one response that we offered on behalf of the Institutional Theory, to the case of the Neolithic tribesman was that his stone arrangement would not be truly solitary, if it were configured with the realization that others might also derive visual pleasure from it. We also said that the Neolithic artificer's behavior would be scarcely intelligible, unless he had some such understanding. But if we count his activity as social just because it is undertaken with the peripheral awareness that others might derive pleasure from it, then doesn't it seem as though the notion of what is *social* has become excessively attentuated? Arguably, there is not even a social relationship here, let alone a social institution or practice.

Admittedly, Institutional Theories are very comprehensive. They certainly capture all the central cases of known art. This art is social in the sense that it is made and presented by artists who have some background in the social practices of the art of their culture or subculture; and such art is received and appreciated by audiences who have learnt to understand it in the process of their acculturation. However, there are still some pressing questions about Institutional Theories. Must all art emerge from a preexisting network of social relations? Is the theory viciously circular? Is it really informative? Does it only appear to be informative? Does it depend upon stretching the notions of social institution, social practices, and social relationships beyond the breaking point? These are controversial issues best left, for the present, for readers to debate.

Defining art historically

As we have seen, a major bone of contention with regard to Institutional Theories of Art is the question of whether art can be produced by a solitary artist operating outside of any social institution, practice or relationship. The Institutional Theorist is apt to reject such a possibility on the grounds that humans are enculturated beings and that art, wherever it exists, is a function of that enculturation. People always, as a matter of fact, learn about art and artmaking as part of their socialization. This is true whether we are talking about high art, folk art or tribal art.

If Robinson Crusoe made art on his lonely island, he would have been able to do so, the Institutional Theorist argues, only because he learnt about art during his upbringing in England. He was not a solitary, acultural artist. He had already been educated in the practices of an artworld. And, furthermore, whatever he made would have been, as a result, accessible to a culturally prepared audience of fellow Europeans who themselves had been trained to understand it. Art is not made by wolf children; art is the product of social beings who are initiated into the artworld in the process of their socialization.

Artmaking, of any sort, requires knowledge. That knowledge is not innate, so it must be socially acquired. For any existing artwork, the Institutional Theorist claims, he will be able to show that it emerged from a social practice from which the artist in question derived the conceptual resources and basic artistic skills necessary to produce the relevant artwork. Given human nature – human social nature – it is a practical impossibility that anyone creates art outside a context of social practices from which the possibility of making art emerges.

These are serious considerations. However, the opponent of the Institutional Theory, though agreeing that this is how most art originates – and perhaps that this is how all historical art has originated – argues that nevertheless it is a logical possibility, even if it is a practical impossibility, that someone could create art outside of a social practice. One can imagine societies without art, like the culture of our Neolithic tribesman, where someone chances upon the idea of arranging pretty stones for the purpose of stirring visual pleasure and never shares that discovery with anyone else. If this is a logical possibility, then the Institutional Theory of Art has failed to show that all art necessarily involves social relationships – even social relationships as thin as the requirement that artists make and/or present artworks with understanding for audiences prepared to respond to them with understanding.

This criticism of the Institutional Theory of Art is the starting point for the Historical Definition of Art, a viewpoint defended by Jerrold Levinson.

Levinson accepts the possibility that someone could make an artifact in the manner of our imagined Neolithic tribesman and that we would have no conceptual difficulty regarding it as an artwork. Even if the Neolithic tribesman did not have the concept of artwork in his cognitive stock – where the possession of such a concept admittedly would require a social background – still we will count the arrangement of stones as art under *our* concept of art.

What enables us to count the stone artifact as art? What makes the Neolithic display an artwork? According to the defender of the Historical Definition of Art, it is the intention that the maker had in producing the arrangement of stones. His intention was to promote visual pleasure. Moreover, from our perspective, promoting visual pleasure is a well-precedented intention for making art. Thus, we would have no problem classifying the stones as art, since this is a widely recognized motive for creating artworks.

Of course, the promotion of visual pleasure is not the only intention with which an artist might create an artwork. Some artists do make art with the governing intention that the results have the capacity to engender visual pleasure. But other artists make artworks with the intention to thwart visual pleasure. Many German Expressionists made artworks intended to elicit disgust as a way of signaling their attitude to their times; they made works expressive of moral horror. But we count their artifacts as artworks because that intention, too, is a historically well-precedented one.

We call the Neolithic tribesman's stones art because they are intended to promote visual pleasure; we call the German Expressionist's paintings art because they are intended to promote visual disgust. The intentions couldn't appear more different. And yet there is a common thread that runs between them: in both cases, the intentions have through the course of history been acknowledged as artistically relevant intentions. That is, making artifacts with the intention that they be regarded as sources of visual pleasure or as sources of visual disgust both traffic in what the Historical Definition of Art calls well-precedented *art regards* – ways of regarding something as a work of art.

Many different art regards have emerged in the course of history, including: regarding an artifact as an expression of feeling, as a representation, as a display of form, as an articulation of cultural ideals, as a reflection upon the nature of art, and so on. According to the Historical Definition of Art, something is an artwork only if it is intended to support some well-precedented art regard.

This approach is called a *historical* definition because it connects candidates to the history of art. We know that many historical artifacts are artworks, whether or not we have a definition. We also know how those

242 PHILOSOPHY OF ART

works were intended to be regarded by audiences. We can use that knowledge to construct a definition of art. Something will be an artwork only if it was made with the intention to encourage at least one of the many well-precedented art regards that have emerged in the course of history. This principle is what gives our concept of art its coherence.

As we have seen, there is little hope of crafting a definition of art simply in terms of the internal properties of things. Nor can we hope to find a common thread between artworks on the basis of their actual effects – not simply because those effects may be so diverse and conflictive, but also because many of the effects of artworks, such as sensuous pleasure, can also be secured by other means, such as drugs. So, instead, the Historical Definition of Art draws our attention to another possible shared property of artworks: that they all be intended to support some acknowledged art regard, some way of correctly responding to art that is well-precedented historically.

This way of thinking unifies our concept of art. It makes of art a coherent body of artifacts. All artworks are related to each other historically in the sense that they all share some or another intended, well-precedented art regard. Unlike the family resemblance approach, the Historical Definition of Art does not rely upon tracking the manifest properties of candidates. It focusses on a nonmanifest property, namely the artistic intention to proffer objects for acknowledged art regards on the part of potential audiences. Moreover, this property is a genetic property of the works in question, for the genesis of the object is in the artist's intention. That the intention is to promote acknowledged *art* regards also explains why the object is art.

Furthermore, this approach is different from the Institutional Theory of Art, since there is no requirement that the intention be formed within the context of an institution or a social practice. One could come upon the intention to promote a certain art regard – such as visual pleasure – outside any social context whatsoever. Yet it will still count as an artistic intention, if, even unbeknownst to the artist in question, the intention is one that we now acknowledge is historically well precedented. Of course, we are rendering this judgment from the perspective of our artworld. But the artist need not be a member of our artworld, or of any other.

The Historical Definition of Art is an account of our concept of art, and, though our concept of art evolved historically in our society, our concept of art can be applied to artifacts outside of our society and even to artifacts produced in contexts where there is no concept of art nor even an artworld or artistic practices. We recognize the Neolithic tribesman's stones as art, even if he and his culture lacked the concept of art and an artworld, because his intention that the stones be regarded as sources of visual pleasure, if only by him, happens to correlate with a historically well-precedented artistic intention.

That an artifact be intended for a well-precedented form of art regard is a necessary condition for art, according to the Historical Definition of Art. In addition, the definition also requires that the artist have a proprietary right over the object in question. That is, the artist must own or have the right to use the materials and objects she intends an audience to art-regard in some historically well-precedented way. This condition is meant to block certain types of found objects from entering the order of art.

For example, as noted previously, Duchamp attempted to appropriate the Woolworth Building as a readymade. Many have claimed that this is one readymade that Duchamp failed to enfranchise as art. The reason, according to the Historical Definition of Art, is that Duchamp neither owned the Woolworth Building, nor did those who did endorse his attempted transfiguration of it into art. That is, Duchamp lacked the required proprietary rights with respect to the Woolworth Building.

The art-regard condition and the proprietary-right condition are both necessary conditions for art, according to the Historical Definition. Together they are conjointly sufficient. Combining the two conditions, we get:

> x is an artwork if and only if x is an object of which it is true that some person or persons (1) who have a proprietary right over x (2) nonpassingly intend (or intended) x for regard-as-a-work-of-art – i.e., for regard in any way (or ways) in which objects already in the extension of "artwork" are or were correctly or standardly regarded.

The proprietary right condition requires that I have rights to the object in question. I cannot simply declare your sofa to be an artwork – even if I intend that it be regarded in the way people regarded *Fountain* – unless I have your permission to do so. Further, the art-regard condition requires that I intend the art regard in question *nonpassingly*. This means that the intention must be fairly serious, long-lived, and deliberate. It should not be a passing whim. I do not make my model airplane an artwork, if, while gluing it together, I have a momentary thought that it might be a source of visual pleasure. My intention must be a fairly influential one throughout the process of creation; it must be a presiding intention, not a passing thought. As well, it should be at the heart of my production of the artifact, its influence radiating integrally throughout the work.

What I must intend is that the object support some acknowledged form of regard-as-a-work-of-art. This regard is explicated as any sort of regard in which objects already in the extension of "artwork" are or were correctly regarded. The reason for the locution "the extension of 'artwork'" here is to avoid charges that the Historical Definition of Art is circular. The extension of "artwork" is just a list of all artworks. Thus, we could replace "the extension of artwork" with a list of artworks. In this way, the term "artwork" in the definition is merely an abbreviation for this list and could be replaced, albeit cumbersomely, with the list itself.

Consequently, the concept of artwork is not being used to define the concept of art; all that is being invoked is a list of all artworks, and such a list need not ever mention the term art. The definition does not, then, use the concept of artwork in a circular fashion. It only uses "artwork" as a shorthand place-holder for the list of all previous artworks, or all previously known artworks.

The definition does presuppose that we know what the previous artworks are, or, at least, a substantial number of them. And it presupposes that we know the ways in which those works were correctly regarded. This amounts to a knowledge of the histories of the arts, but comparable knowledge is presumed in many other approaches to identifying art. How can we debate about whether definitions of art are adequate, unless we know something about art history – not only what works count as art, but also which ways of regarding them are appropriate? When the Institutional Theorist talks about artifacts being made and received with understanding, he has in mind understanding the ways in which it is appropriate or correct to regard artworks. And where else would this come, except from the history of the arts?

There are two ways that someone can present an object for regard-as-an-artwork. She can do it indirectly; she can expressly present the work to be regarded in some way or combination of ways that art has been regarded in the past. Here she will have to know art history, and that knowledge will make her part of an ongoing social practice.

However, she may also present the work for art regard directly. That means that she need only have the intention that the work be regarded in some way or ways that has been acknowledged to be an art regard. She need not know that the regard in question is a historically well-precedented art regard; she need not know any art history. Her work will count as art, even if it just happens coincidentally to invite a historically acknowledged art regard. And this, of course, does not require that the artist herself be a member of an ongoing social practice.

It is in this way that the Neolithic tribesman's stones can be classified as an artwork. He directly intended his work for regard-as-an-artwork, even though he knew nothing of the tradition of art, because what he intended – that the stones be regarded as sources of visual pleasure – turns out, unbeknownst to him, to be an acknowledged art regard. That is why we are disposed to accept his rudimentary sculpture as an artwork. Thus, if you are inclined to find the case of the solitary artist compelling, then the Historical Definition of Art is especially attractive in contrast to Institutional Theories of Art.

In addition, the Historical Definition is very comprehensive. It is hard to imagine any work of art that is intended to support no well-precedented art regard at all. If the regard in question were totally unprecedented, and if the work supported no other antecedently acknowledged art regard, how would we know how to respond to the object, and why would we call the response an art regard?

Avant-garde art grows out of the past, modifying pre-existing art regards. But even in modifying or defying some pre-existing regards, it still appeals to others. Duchamp's *Fountain* frustrates attempts to regard it in terms of visual pleasure, but it can still be regarded as amusing, as surely it was intended to be. An object that intentionally spurned every known art regard, including that it is intended to be regarded as a source of subverted expectations, is hardly imaginable. And, in any case, it would be unintelligible. Moreover, if a candidate strikes us as utterly unintelligible, that scarcely encourages us to classify it as an artwork.

Though the Historical Definition of Art has many virtues, it also raises a number of questions. The proprietary condition, for example, seems rather strange. It requires that the artist have a proprietary right over the artwork. But graffiti artists do not have such a right. They steal into train-yards at night and paint their figures all over parked subway cars. They do not own the subways, and the municipalities that do have forbidden graffiti artists to draw on the subways. It is against the law. Does this mean that their drawings are not artworks? And what if Picasso had been a graffiti artist? If he had painted his *Portrait of Dora Maar* on the side of a subway car, would it be art?

To say that the same configuration when painted on a canvas that Picasso happened to own is art, but when painted on the side of a subway car, it is not art, sounds completely arbitrary. And what if Bernini had stolen the stone and the chisels that resulted in his statue of St. Theresa? He might not have owned the work; but surely it would have been a work of art.

The intention behind the proprietary condition is to limit the possibilities for creating found objects and readymades. Duchamp supposedly could not turn the Woolworth Building into an artwork, and I cannot turn your car into an artwork by pointing at it and instructing bystanders to appreciate its visual beauty. Allegedly, the reason for this is that the artists in question do not own the relevant artifacts. Perhaps, then, the proprietary condition should only be taken to pertain to cases involving found objects.

But even there, the proprietary condition does not seem convincing.

Imagine a school of artists who specialize in stolen found objects, which they call outlaw readymades. The only readymades they present are ill-gotten ones. Their point, let us suppose, is to underline the complicity of traditional art with capitalism and the system of private property. They want their objects to be regarded, as among other things, social criticism, a well-precedented art regard.

Obviously, any gallery, museum, or collector who acquires such outlaw readymades is likely to become embroiled in all sorts of legal hassles. But then that is part of the point of outlaw readymades – to call attention to the complex inter-relations of art and the law. Outlaw readymades may turn out to be illegal. But is there any reason to say they cannot be art? Much social protest art in the past has been illegal, but legality and art are different, nonmutually exclusive categories. If Duchamp's appropriation of the Woolworth Building and my appropriation of your car fail, we should probably seek explanations elsewhere than in property law.

The proprietary right condition does not seem to be a necessary condition for art, even in the restricted case of found objects. The art-regard condition would appear to have to provide us with necessary and sufficient conditions for what it is to be an artwork. But clearly the art-regard condition is not sufficient.

One reason for this is that the art-regard condition makes no provision for the fact that art regards can pass out of existence. Thus, someone may make an artifact today, nonpassingly intending it either directly or indirectly for a well-precedented art regard, but one that is no longer in force. Consider home videos or polaroids. Marietta brings her camera on the family vacation. As she records the family excursion, she proceeds very deliberately. She intends to produce a reliable likeness of the event. This is not a passing intention; it preoccupies her. It is her intention that people will be able to regard her recording as an arresting specimen of verisimilitude. This, of course, is a widely acknowledged form of art regard. This is what artists in the western tradition from the Greeks into the nineteenth century aspired towards. Most probably Marietta knows this, but even if she doesn't, it is still an acknowledged art regard. So isn't it art according to the Historical Definition of Art (even if we add the proprietary right condition, since Marietta owns her camera and the film)?

But the problem here is that such an art regard – the simple appreciation of an image for its perceptual versimilitude – alone is no longer quite as decisive as it was even one hundred years ago. Thus, the many thousands, maybe millions, of amateur snapshots and videotapes intended to promote this regard are not art. But the Historical Definition must count them as such, since the intention solely to promote an appreciation of perceptual verisimilitude once was an intention to promote a living art regard. But isn't this too broad a theory of art?

Perhaps it will be said that Marietta's intention here is not only to invite appreciation in terms of verisimilitude, but to make a keepsake for her family. But even if that is so, two things must be said. First, even if in addition to intending that the pictures be regarded for their verisimilitude, Marietta has some other intentions that are not acknowledged art regards, that should not deny her recordings the status of artwork, since a great many historical works of art have mixed intentions. It should be enough to satisfy the Historical Definition that Marietta's picture be supported by at least one integral, nonpassing intention that her work afford some well-precedented regard-as-an-artwork. And like David's portrait of Napoleon, it does.

Second, Marietta may intend her pictures as keepsakes. But it is perfectly possible to imagine some other amateur who makes video recordings solely for the purpose of using his equipment to capture the visual appearances of things. He may do this simply to impress viewers with the capabilities of his equipment for producing recognizable likenesses. The Historical Definition must count these recordings as artworks. But that is far too inclusive.

These counterexamples have relied upon the fact that the Historical Definition of Art has no statute of limitations on art regards. But the problems with inclusiveness that these examples suggest are even deeper, since there are many still robust, well-precedented art regards that creators may intend nonpassingly as appropriate to their creations which nevertheless do not guarantee that the ensuing creations are artworks. Let us say that intending an object for visual pleasure is such a robust art regard. To make something nonpassingly intended to afford visual pleasure, then, according to the Historical Definition, is to make an artwork. But then consider how much art there is.

Alice plants her lawn carefully, waters it, and tends it assiduously. She has a nonpassing intention that the lawn appear visually pleasing. This is a well-precedented art regard. Are her lawn and countless other, deliberately well-cared-for lawns in suburbia world-wide artworks? By this reasoning, every lawn in my neighborhood, except mine, is an artwork.

Similarly, George paints his house with utmost deliberation, choosing paint that will capture the light nicely, and maybe adding a trim to set off or accentuate the color. He has a nonpassing intention that his house afford onlookers visual pleasure. Since this is a well-precedented art regard, according to the Historical Definition of Art, his house is an artwork. Again, the consequence is that your average-sized suburban village is likely to contain as much art as the Metropolitan Museum of Art. Moreover, it is easy to see where examples like these are headed. The Historical Definition is far too broad.

The Historical Definition does not say that candidates must be like past art objects in respect of their pertinent, manifest features, but only requires that the candidates be intended for some well-precedented regard-as-an-artwork. But art regards can be detached from what we standardly think of as art objects and they can be intended of things that we never conceive of as artworks. Perhaps Alice intends her lawn to be regarded – in terms of visual stimulation – in the same way that many people regard landscape paintings of lawns (i.e., as merely attractive). The art regard condition is just too encompassing to provide a sufficient condition for art. Nor will invoking the proprietary right condition save the day, since Alice owns her lawn, George his house, and so on.

Clearly, the art regard condition is not sufficient for art. But is it a necessary condition? It would still be a major accomplishment of the Historical Definition of Art, if it captured at least a necessary condition for art. So, must it be the case of any artifact that in order to be classified as art, it must have been intended, either directly or indirectly, to support some well-precedented art regard?

In favor of the Historical Definition is the fact that probably most things that we think of as art are, in fact, underwritten, directly or indirectly, with the intention to afford some well-precedented art regard. Even where we are not in a position to interview the creator about her intentions, the way she has made the artifact, especially if it belongs to a well-known artistic genre, provides reassuring evidence that it was non-passingly intended to support recognized and appropriate responses – well-precedented art regards.

On the other hand, the opponent of the Historical Definition will argue that there are notable exceptions. Sometimes we place artifacts on display in our museums that were not intended for any recognized art regard. In previous chapters, we have discussed statues of demons and warrior shields intended to frighten off viewers. The producers of these artifacts did not intend them – directly or indirectly – to be contemplated with any known art regard. Most probably they intended the faces on the shields to undermine the possibility of any imaginable art regard and to strike such overwhelming terror in any viewer that entertaining any thought other than flight be impossible.

Nevertheless, museums and art galleries are full of artifacts like this. People collect them, perhaps calling them tribal artworks. But if the creators of such works do not intend them to afford any appropriate, well-precedented art regard, why do we say these artifacts are artworks? Here, the opponent of the Historical Definition will maintain *because they can perform an acknowledged function of art*. The creators of these artifacts may not have intended these works to perform these functions – such as stimulating visual interest – but nevertheless these artifacts can be used by others to perform these functions. These tribal shields are artworks, then,

ART, DEFINITION AND IDENTIFICATION 249

not because of their creators' actual, historic intentions, but because they can be used successfully by us to serve a well-known function of art – to sustain visual interest, to afford expressive properties for inspection, and so on.

The Historical Definition of Art maintains that it is a necessary condition of art that it be underwritten by a certain intention on the part of its creator: the intention to proffer the artifact for some acknowledged art regard. The opponent of the Historical Definition denies that such intentions are always necessary. Sometimes the mere fact that an artifact can be used to serve an historically acknowledged, artistic function suffices to call an object art, irrespective of the original creator's intention. This debate between intention versus function is a profound one. Opinions can be arrayed on either side of the question. But unless and until the defender of the Historical Definition can supply an argument that says why artworks require the relevant intention, the central claim of the Historical Definition – that artifacts must necessarily be intended to support acknowledged art regards – remains controversial. This is not to say that no arguments for the necessity of the art regard condition are imaginable, but only that the burden of proof rests with the proponent of the Historical Definition.

Part III
Identifying art

Definition and identification

Recent attempts to define art, such as the Institutional Theory of Art and the Historical Definition of Art, have proven thus far to be inconclusive. Both supply useful clues to how we go about identifying art. But neither is a satisfactory reconstruction of the way in which we go about identifying art. And yet we *are* able to identify art – to classify candidates as artworks – with a very high degree of consensus. Thus the question of how we manage to do it remains pressing.

Moreover, this is not merely an academic question. Classifying artifacts as artworks is central to our practice of art. Classifying a candidate as an artwork – subsuming it under the category of art – is integral to determining how we should respond to it. Should a scattering of dirt and grease on the floor be interpreted or cleaned up? Should we attend to the expressive properties of a amalgam of crushed and mangled automobile chassis or

consign them to the junkyard? If art, these objects bear scrutiny and interpretation. If not, we call the Department of Sanitation.

Furthermore, the concept of art is an important one for the characterization of social reality. It supports many significant generalizations, such as:
that every known culture has artistic practices; that there is more art today
than there was in the fifteenth century; that the production of art is a
major social activity in Bali; that art is an important factor in the creation
of cultural identity; and so on. The concept of art also figures in certain
counterfactual generalizations, e.g., that any society without art would be
humanly diminished. And, as we have seen, the concept of art can also play
an explanatory role: Why are they writing so much about that urinal?
Because it is an artwork.

The concept of art is indispensable for social life as we know it. But how
do we go about applying it? How do we identify objects as artworks; how
do we classify artifacts under this concept? Throughout this book we have
encountered a number of attempts to treat this as a matter of applying an
essential definition. The representational theory of art, neorepresentationalism, the expression theory, formalism, neoformalism, aesthetic definitions, institutional theories, and the Historical Definition of Art have all,
in turn, tried to articulate necessary and sufficient conditions for art status.

In this, there is an underlying assumption that we identify candidates
by subsuming them under a definition. That definition is one that many
philosophers have supposed we possess, if only implicitly, and that we
apply to candidates tacitly. Successive theories have attempted to recover
it and to make it explicit.

Clearly, a certain view of the nature of concepts underwrites all these
attempts. Concepts are regarded as essential definitions. That is, concepts
are taken to be definitions that supply necessary and sufficient conditions
for membership in the category they designate. Art is a concept; so, the
story goes, the concept of art must have necessary and sufficient conditions for application to particular instances.

But, as the Neo-Wittgensteinians suggested, it may not be the case that
all of our concepts are to be understood on the model of definitions with
necessary and sufficient conditions. Indeed, quite a few of our concepts go
undefined, and yet we are able to apply them successfully. Might not art be
such a concept?

The Neo-Wittgensteinian claims that it is. On behalf of this conclusion,
she offers an argument that it must be, since defining art is not consistent
with the expansionary nature of art, *and* she further hypothesizes that we
apply the concept of art in virtue of the family resemblance method, not in
virtue of definitions replete with necessary and sufficient conditions.
Unfortunately, neither of these claims is ultimately successful, for reasons
that were explored in the first part of this chapter.

But despite the failure of these specific arguments, the possibility remains that neither is art the sort of concept that is structured by necessary and sufficient conditions nor that we do classify artifacts as artworks by means of definitions. Evidently, we do not identify artworks in accordance with the family resemblance method. But the defeat of that hypothesis does not entail that there is not some other nondefinitional method upon which we rely to sort artworks from other sorts of things.

We cannot presume that on the basis of the past failure of definitional theories of art that art cannot be defined. Perhaps one day someone will construct a perfectly noncontroversial, comprehensive definition of all art. But, at the same time, it should also be apparent that we do not go about determining what is art and what isn't on the basis of such a definition. If we do possess such a definition, albeit implicitly, why is it so damnably hard to excavate?

On the other hand, it is widely acknowledged that many of the concepts that we use with admirable effectiveness are not governed by essential definitions. This supplies us with at least a *prima facie* reason for exploring the possibility that we apply the concept of art, as we do so many other concepts, without relying – explicitly or implicitly – on definitions.

Undoubtedly, there is a great tradition in philosophy that presupposes that concepts must be understood in terms of necessary and suffficient conditions. But that tradition has been presented with serious challenges on many fronts, including not only Neo-Wittgensteinianism, but what is called prototype theory in psychology and the causal theory of reference in the analysis of natural kinds. It is not important, at this juncture, to examine each of these challenges. It is enough to note that the authority of the definitional approach to concepts is not unqualified. That at least warrants inquiry into alternative models of the concept of art. And once such a model is set forth, it remains to be seen whether it does a better job of explaining how we identify artifacts as artworks – how we classify candidates as art – than competing approaches do, including not only definitional approaches, but the family resemblance method as well.

Identification and historical narration

One way to approach the question of how we classify artifacts as artworks is to consider how we proceed in problem situations. That is, what do we do when the question of whether or not a candidate is art arises? How do we establish that a proposed artwork is an artwork in cases where the suspicion is abroad that it is not art – or even, perhaps, that it is a hoax? Such situations should reveal something about the way in which we identify candidates as artworks because, in circumstances like these, our thinking about what makes something art comes to the fore. A challenge to the art status of a work forces us to become explicit about the grounds upon which we generally classify something as art.

Notably, throughout the twentieth century, given the continuous activity of the avant-garde, accusations have abounded that this or that candidate is not art. Some examples include: Duchamp's readymades, Jackson Pollock's drip paintings, Merce Cunningham's choreography, Robert Mapplethorpe's photography, and, more recently, pieces by Damien Hirst and Janine Antoni. Frequently such misgivings are voiced not only by bewildered and sometimes disgruntled members of the viewing public, but also by their critical representatives in the fourth estate. Declaring that something is not art – or worse, that it is a confidence trick – is always good for an indignant, spirited newspaper editorial.

How are such challenges, when they occur, met? If we look at the course of such debates, we find that generally the proponent of the work in question responds by telling a story that links the contested work to preceding art – and to art-making practices and contexts – in such a way that the work under fire can be seen to be the intelligible outcome of recognizable modes of thinking and making of a sort already commonly adjudged to be artistic.

This mode of proceeding, like the Historical Definition of Art, of course, presupposes that we already know that some objects are art, that we understand what is important about these objects, and that there is agreement about this. Then, using this antecedent knowledge as a baseline, we attempt to show how the new work at issue evolves from work already acknowledged to be artistic, guided by concerns regarded by all as central to the practice. Thus, the figural distortion of German expressionist painters is not dismissed as an inept attempt at verisimilitude and, therefore, as defective or pseudo art, but as an intelligible and well-precedented artistic response – a revolt – against realism (a revolt undertaken for the sake of securing a widely and antecedently acknowledged artistic value, namely expressivity).

Typically, the question of whether or not x is an artwork arises in a context in which some skeptic fails to see how the object under dispute could have been produced within the network of practices with which she is familiar – that is, if those practices are to remain the same practices. There is a perceived gap, so to speak, between the anomalous, usually avant-garde, production x and an already existing body of work with an antecedently acknowledged tradition of making and thinking. In order to establish the status of x as an artwork, the prononent of x must fill in that gap. And the standard way of filling in that gap is to produce a certain type of historical narrative, one that supplies the sequence of activities of thinking and making required to, in a manner of speaking, fill in the distance between a Rembrandt and a readymade.

To counter the suspicion that x is not a work of art, the friend of x has to show how x emerged intelligibly from acknowledged practices via the same sort of thinking, acting, decision-making and so forth that is already familiar in the practice. This involves telling a certain kind of story about the work in question: namely, a historical narrative of how x came to be produced as an intelligible response to an antecedently acknowledged art-historical situation about whose art status a consensus already exists. With a contested work what we try to do is place it within a tradition where it becomes more and more intelligible. And the standard way of doing this is to produce an historical narrative.

For example, when Andy Warhol's *Brillo Box* appeared in 1963, questions about its status as art were raised. After all, it looked just like the cartons of Brillo in the grocery storeroom. Those weren't artworks. Why regard Warhol's, which looked just like them, as artworks? Wasn't the whole thing just a prank, or, worse, a scam?

In order to meet this objection, the defender of *Brillo Box* begins by pointing out something about the art-historical context in which the work appeared. For much of the twentieth century, a great deal of art had been dedicated to addressing the question of the nature of art. Much modern painting has been overtly flat precisely for the purpose of asserting the idea that, in reality, paintings are flat, two-dimensional things, not the illusions of three-dimensional objects they were often said to be. Painters in this tradition – which would include Braque, Picasso, Pollock, Klein, and so on – were thought to be involved in a philosophical venture, the project of defining the nature of their artform. This was a reflexive enterprise – a matter of artworks reflecting on their own nature as artworks.

In this historical context, Warhol's *Brillo Box* can be seen as a contribution to an ongoing dialogue or conversation in the artworld. That is, Warhol's *Brillo Box* poses the question "What is art?" in a particularly penetrating way, asking of itself what makes this object an artwork when its indiscernible counterparts – everyday Brillo Boxes – are not artworks? Warhol's *Brillo Box* thus addressed an antecedently acknowledged, ongoing artworld concern in a creative way by focussing the reflexive artworld question "What is art?" in a canny and strikingly perspicuous manner, reframing and redirecting it as the question: "What makes artworks different from real things?"

Seen in its historical context, Warhol's *Brillo Box* is an intelligible contribution to an evolving artworld project. Once one is made aware of the historical context of the work, Warhol's *Brillo Box* can be placed as a rational, if not ingenious, expansion upon antecedently acknowledged artworld modes of making and thinking. If those antecedent modes of thinking and making – from Cubism forwards – resulted in artworks, then *Brillo Box*, as an extension of acknowledged artworld practices, is art as well. That is, if one can construct an accurate historical narrative that renders intelligible the emergence of *Brillo Box*, as the result of rational decision-making from accepted artworld practices, then that establishes the art status of *Brillo Box*, or, at least, it shifts the burden of proof entirely onto the skeptics.

Of course, in some cases, skeptics may not accept the starting point of the historical narrative that we wish to recite. Perhaps some skeptics will query whether Cubism is art, and, therefore, will not – until Cubism's credentials are established – accept developments from it, like Warhol's *Brillo Box*, as artworks.

However, here, the friend of Warhol merely needs to start her historical narrative earlier, at some point in art history that the skeptic accepts as an exemplary moment. Suppose, in the case at hand, that the skeptic accepts impressionism as art. Then, our narrative defense of *Brillo Box* will begin with impressionism and its consequences, such as neo-impressionism, illuminating the way in which the relevant reflexive preoccupations were evident even in the nineteenth century. Then we shall go on to show the intelligible maturation of this concern through Cubism to Warhol. That is, our response to the skeptic will still be a historical narrative, though a historical narrative that starts a bit earlier than the first one we told.

So far the situations to which we have been alluding are ones where an artwork is put forward and is then challenged. That challenge, it seems, is generally met by telling an historical narrative, an historical narrative that *explains* why the artifact in question is an artwork. However, it is also frequently the case that such historical narratives are told *before* skeptics raise their objections. These narratives – which may be recounted in manifestos, gallery handouts, interviews, lecture-demonstrations, critical reviews, docents' talks, and so on – are not advanced simply to forestall criticism, but to enable viewers to understand where the artist is coming from, to see why her choices make sense given the logic of the artworld situation in which she finds herself.

When an artwork is challenged or likely to be challenged, our response is not a definition, but an explanation. That is, we do not produce a definition and apply it to the case at hand, since, as we've seen, it is exceedingly difficult to find any noncontroversial definition. Instead, we try to explain why the candidate is an artwork. We point to acknowledged artworld precedents, practices, and aims, including the antecedents of the work in question, the artworld problematic that the new work addresses, and the rationale for the choices the artist made given the options available to her. This explanation takes the form of a historical narrative. If the narrative is an accurate and reasonable one, this generally suffices to establish that the candidate is an artwork.

If this is how we generally establish that a candidate is art in cases where there is some dispute, it also reveals something about how we incorporate objects in the category of art in the ordinary course of affairs. Where we can weave the candidate into the ongoing history of art as we know it, we are disposed to classify an artifact as an artwork. We classify a candidate as an artwork by placing it in a tradition. We use our knowledge of the tradition – including our knowledge of its genres, its history, and its aims – to determine whether a new work belongs to the tradition.

Where a candidate can be shown to be a continuation of an antecedently acknowledged artistic tradition – where we are able to understand it as an intelligible development or outcome from standing artistic practices (and not from other well-known practices) – then we are satisfied that it is art in the classificatory sense. A historical narrative may not establish that a candidate is good of its kind; but it is typically enough to establish that it is art.

It is an important feature of art that it develops; even in relatively static traditions, there is development. As we have seen throughout this book, developments in art history have been a problem for the philosophy of art. Attempts to define art have often failed because they do not anticipate the future developments in the history of art. Representational theories of art scarcely anticipated the rise of abstract art; expression theories hardly forsaw the revolt against expression; and so forth. One advantage of the narrative approach is that it is sensitive to the tendency of art to evolve along often unpredictable pathways, since narrative itself is a tool for rendering change intelligible.

The narrative approach attempts to handle the developmental aspect of art – including its local developments – by treating it as a conversation. As in a conversation, so in artistic practice there is an expectation of artists that they be concerned to make original contributions to the tradition in which they work. These contributions can range along the creative scale from slight variations in established genres to wholesale revolutions. Art history is analogous to a conversation, in certain respects, in that each artist-discussant makes, or, at least, is expected to make a contribution.

However, as in a conversation, the contribution must have some relevance to what has gone before. Otherwise, there simply is no conversation. In relation to their predecessors, artists must be posing or answering some relevant question, amplifying what someone else has proposed, or disagreeing or even repudiating it – demonstrating that some neglected option is possible – and the like. In such ways as this, the artist's contribution should be pertinent to the already existing practices of the artworld – to its abiding concerns, procedures and interests. What the narratives we have been discussing do is to make salient the relevance of new works to the evolving conversation of art history. For, of course, if such works are completely irrelevant to art history, there is no reason to suppose that they are artworks.

The problem frequently presented by avant-garde art is that some of the artist's interlocutors – the general public and its representatives among the critical estate – often fail to catch the relevance of the artist's "remark" to the ongoing context. The audience may, so to say, discern the "originality" of the work, but not its relevance. There is, in other words, a glitch in the conversation.

But if this is the problem, there is an obvious way to repair it. Re-construct the conversation in such a way that the relevance of the artist's contribution is made evident. Bring perhaps unremarked or unnoticed presuppositions into the open. Point to overlooked features of the context. Make the intentions of the artist explicit, and show that said intentions are intelligible in terms of the conversation and its context, and so on.

Of course, reconstructing the conversation in this way amounts to a historical narrative. Where something is missing from the conversation – some connection – it is supplied by retelling the conversation in a way that historically reconstructs it, while simultaneously filling it in. Where we can produce a genuine, historical narrative of this sort, we have, generally, sufficient grounds for categorizing a candidate as an artwork. Historical narration is a reliable method for identifying art – for explaining why a candidate is an artwork – and, moreover, it has a solid claim for being the method that we generally employ.

The narrative approach to classifying artworks establishes the art status of a candidate by connecting the work in question to previously acknow-ledged artworks and practices. In this regard, it may appear to recall the family resemblance approach. However, the narrative approach is not merely an affair of similarities between past and present art. The pertinent correspondences must be shown to be part of a narrative development. Such historical narratives track processes of cause and effect, decision and action, and lines of influence.

Unlike the Neo-Wittgensteinian method for identifying artworks, the narrative approach links present art to past art not in terms of some unspecified notion of resemblance, but in terms of its descent – its genetic (or causal) linkage to earlier acknowledged artworks and artistic practices. Thus, according to the narrative approach, contemporary avant-garde works are classified as artworks in virtue of their ancestry, where that ancestry is explained by means of a narrative or genealogy. Thus, with its emphasis on genetic links between new art and past paradigms, the narrative approach not only differs from Neo-Wittgensteinianism, but avoids the problems of the family resemblance method.

Of course, many works do not require such elaborate genealogical briefs on their behalf. That is probably due to the fact that in most cases we already understand how to place them in the tradition. But where there is some question about the art status of a work *vis à vis* the tradition, as there often is with new and avant-garde art, the canonical method for negotiating the issue is historical narration. Historical narratives, whether implicitly understood or explicitly constructed, are the means we employ to identify candidates as members of the category art.

Undoubtedly, the suggestion that we sort objects into a kind (such as art) by means of a historical narrative will strike some readers as bizarre. This is because we often derive our models of kindhood from physics and chemistry, where elements are grouped in virtue of some intrinsic, microphysical property that explains its other projectible properties. But not all kinds, even in the sciences, are like this. For example, species are historical entities – they are groups of organisms that are sorted together by virtue of their common history rather than by virtue of intrinsic resemblances that they bear to each other.

The reason for this is that species, by their nature, evolve, typically showing variations not merely in some of their peripheral characteristics, but, in principle, in all of their features. No particular feature, no matter how central to our stereotype of the species – to its genotype or morphology – is essential for an organism to be a member of the species in question. What is crucial, as Darwin claimed, is descent.

Indeed, within the branch of biology called systematics, one important debate was between pheneticists – who proposed to sort species in terms of allegedly essential similarities between organisms – versus cladists – who argued that taxa are unified historically by the mechanism of common descent. In certain respects, this debate in biology repeats themes rehearsed in the philosophy of art, including not only the problem of fixing the essential properties of a kind that is essentially evolving, but also the problem of the slackness of similarity as an organizing concept.

Of course, there are also important differences between questions of art classification and speciation. We are now only speaking of selected analogies between the two. However, the fact that cladism is regarded as a respectable solution to the problem of speciation at least indicates that in certain cases history can supply the grounds for membership in a kind. And if descent is a viable condition for classifying an organism as a member of a biological species, there need be no problem, at least in principle, with supposing that candidates are also classified under the concept of art in virtue of descent as explicated by the appropriate types of historical narratives.

We have already noted that it is not the case generally that we classify objects by means of definitions. There are alternative means. For example, biologists determine species membership in terms of descent. Moreover, when we look at how problem cases go in debates about art, it seems persuasive that such debates are canonically joined by advancing historical narratives on behalf of contested works. Membership in the category of art, like species membership, also appears to be a matter of descent. Similarly, the way to identify artifacts as artworks is to explain their genealogy, where this is a matter of telling a historical narrative.

Historical narratives: their strengths and weaknesses

The claim before us is that identifying art is more plausibly understood as a matter of narration rather than definition. To weigh this claim effectively, a little more has to be said about the nature of the narratives in question. Only then can we go on to assess the strengths and weaknesses of this approach relative to competing approaches.

Though the relevant sort of narrative understanding is often merely implicit in the great many instances where we identify rather conventional candidates as art, it comes into the foreground in disputed cases, such as the more radical examples of avant-garde art. On such occasions, the way in which we defend the art status of an avant-garde candidate is to connect it to practices that are already acknowledged to be artistic. Since this kind of narrative is an *historical* narrative, it is committed to being accurate. It is by accurately narrating the descent of the new work from the tradition that we explain why the new work should be counted as art.

This way of proceeding also tells us something important about the relevant sort of identifying narratives; it tells us where they begin. They begin at some historical juncture where everyone agrees we know that artistic practices are involved. Identifying narratives must begin at such a juncture, since it is the point of this type of narrative to explain the art status of some present, disputed candidate, like *Brillo Box*, by showing that it emerged from and is connected to such an acknowledged artworld context, through a perfectly intelligible sequence of choices of a sort based on existing artistic aims that are themselves acknowledged to be alive and accepted in the artworld under discussion.

We also know where identifying narratives end; they end with the production or presentation of the artifact in question. An identifying narrative of this sort gets us from an acknowledged artworld and its practices to the prospective entry into that artworld of a new work by a sequence of intervening steps. What do those steps involve?

To simplify matters, let us consider a case where the new work is a revolutionary avant-garde production, an abstract film in which none of the images are recognizable figures. There is no story, just a disjunctive flow of shapes, as in some of the work of Stan Brakhage. Some viewers might be tempted to dismiss work like this as nothing but incoherent footage – certainly, they might say, it is not art. In its defense, however, we can offer the following narrative.

Most film-making is dominated by stories, told through moving pictures. At the same time, everyone acknowledges that film-making is a visual art. But storytelling by means of pictures designed to advance the narrative often causes viewers to forget about the visual dimension of films – to fail to attend to how films look, so wrapped up are we in following the story.

Confronted with a situation like this one, an artist like Brakhage wants to reclaim the visual attention of the audience. So, he makes films that virtually command audiences to pay attention to the look of his films. He does this by the almost willful subtraction of every other sort of source of attention – such as narrative and pictorial content – from his films. This is a coherent move for an artist like Brakhage to make – one in keeping with an acknowledged aim of film-making – given the artistic context in which he found himself.

That is, operating in an acknowledged artworld context, Brakhage assesses that context as one where insufficient attention is paid to the visual structure of films. This is an ironic state of affairs, since film is a visual art. On the grounds of such an unquestionably artistically intelligible assessment, Brakhage resolved to change the situation by making films that compelled audiences to attend to visual form, an altogether acceptable artistic aim, as all would agree, for a film-maker to have. Though the results were works that disposed some to challenge the status of Brakhage's works as films as well as their status as art, Brakhage's choices – to work without narrative, to explore radical abstraction – were eminently reasonable choices, given his options in the existing context and his resolve to change that context.

Such an account explains why Brakhage's films are art. They are art because they originate in an incontestable artistic context as the result of motivations that informed persons already agree are genuinely artistic ones – such as the reclamation of the visual. Brakhage's films can be explained in terms of the adoption of a series of actions and alternatives that are appropriate means to an end for a person like himself, who has arrived at an intelligible assessment of his artworld context in such a way that his resolve to change it is in accordance with recognizable and live purposes of the practice.

Putting this into narrative form, then, we can say: Given the artistic practices of the dominant cinema, Brakhage worried that the relentless emphasis on narrative and pictorial content repressed rather than enhanced the attentiveness of the audience to things visual – an anomalous state of affairs for an avowedly visual art. Because of his assessment, he resolved to change the situation. He searched for artistic strategies that would promote audience attention to the purely visual. He excised narrative and pictorial elements from his films so that they would not draw attention away from our concentration on the look of the film. The results are films that appear to be very different from standard filmworld fare, but which nevertheless reclaim the sheer visual potential of the medium.

If this narrative is historically accurate, and if it provides us with the best explanation of Brakhage's films, then there is little alternative but to regard his films as artworks. If there are no better explanations – no more comprehensive and accurate accounts of why they are as they are – then this explanation recommends that we classify Brakhage's films as artworks. Given the historical accuracy of this account, what other classification would make as much sense? Thus, from an explanatory point of view, a historical narrative, when accurate, provides us with a compelling argument for classifying something like a Brakhage film as an artwork. Indeed, given the details of such a narrative – supposing them to be historically accurate – it is difficult to imagine how else we might classify such an artifact.

Identifying narratives, then, are historical narratives that, like all historical narratives, are committed to accuracy. They have a beginning, a middle, and an end. The beginning of the story involves the description of some acknowledged art-historical context. The end of the story is a description of the production and/or presentation of the candidate for art status. The middle of the story connects the beginning to the end. The middle of such narratives, moreover, connects the beginning to the end by tracing the adoption of a series of actions and alternatives that supply the appropriate kinds of means for a person who has arrived at an intelligible assessment of the art-historical context, described in the beginning, such that she is resolved to change it in some way in accordance with recognizable and live purposes of the practice.

According to the historical approach, artworks are identified in virtue of their descent. Unlike the Institutional Theory of Art, tracing the ancestry of an artwork, rather than applying a definition, accounts for how we classify candidates as artworks. One strong point of the Institutional Theory is the stress it places on the importance of the reciprocal understanding shared by artists and audiences. But this insight is readily incorporated into the historical approach, because the historical approach too supposes that artists and audiences must share certain understandings, namely, an understanding of art history, its practices, and the aims and purposes that underpin those practices.

At the same time, the historical approach avoids the most frequently cited pitfall of the Institutional Theory – specifically, the charge of circularity. The reason for this is simple: circularity is a defect in definitions, not narratives. It is a requirement of definitions that they not be circular, but the identifying narratives advocated by the historical approach are not definitions. Consequently, they are not susceptible to charges of circularity. Such narratives do presuppose that we do know something about antecedent artistic practices, as does any theory of art. But since the concept of art is not being invoked to define the concept of art, the issue of circularity disappears for the historical method of identifying artworks.

The historical approach also differs from the Historical Definition of Art insofar as the former is not a definition. A major virtue of the Historical Definition of Art is that it calls attention to the importance of the artistic intention to promote acknowledged art regards. The method of historical narration is also sensitive to this constitutive element of the practice of art, since it counts the intended facilitation of accepted art regards as among the aims of art that may govern artistic choices. Brakhage intended to abet attention to the visual; Warhol intended his work to be regarded reflexively. These were both accepted art regards, and they figure importantly in the relevant identifying narratives.

However, unlike the Historical Definition, the method of historical narration does not restrict the aims that motivate genuine artistic choice to art regards. Any live purpose of acknowledged practices of artmaking – not merely the promotion of art regards – may play an enfranchising role in identifying narratives. Earlier, given the emphasis of the Historical Definition on art regards, we worried that sculptures of demons designed to send viewers running away in terror could not be art, since the intended effect of the work, if successful, appeared to preclude any acknowledged art regard. But this is not a problem for the method of historical narration, since, if causing flight is an acknowledged purpose of art in the relevant artworld, identifying narratives will track objects made under its aegis.

Moreover, that the method of historical narration stresses that the artistic aims referred to by identifying narratives be *"recognized and live"* purposes of the practice avoids another problem of the Historical Definition of Art. The proponent of the Historical Definition seemed compelled to accept home videos as art, since they are intended to support a historically, well-precedented art regard – the mere appreciation of verisimilitude. However, since the method of historical narration only endorses consideration of purposes that are alive in the prevailing practice, it does not have similar unfortunate consequences, since in today's art-world, as a matter of historical fact, the intention *simply* to promote the appreciation of perceptual verisimilitude is no longer a recognized and/or live artistic aim.

The method of historical narration avoids some of the shortcomings of its predecessors, which certainly counts in its favor. However, it is also open to some of the criticisms that beset the Institutional Theory and the Historical Definition. Like the Historical Definition, it will not count as artworks objects that we abstract from their nonartistic historical context and merely use as art, such as Eskimo fish hooks displayed by museum curators because of their beauty. But perhaps cases like this are not really so clear-cut. That we use certain things as art – like traffic signs as wall decoration – does not clearly make artworks of those things. So maybe examples like this present problems neither for Historical Definitions nor for the method of historical narration.

Like the Institutional Theory, the method of historical narration is inhospitable to the notion of the solitary artist. It regards art as a practice in which newcomers are granted entry to the artworld in virtue of their social ancestry – their relation to their precedessors, their history, customs and acknowledged purposes. Thus, artworks produced in an artworld of one are beyond the reach of identifying narratives. Is this a liability of the historical approach?

Here the proponent of the historical approach can make several replies. The first is to say that all that she claims is that an identifying narrative provides a sufficient condition for classifying artworks. Thus, there may be other grounds for identifying a candidate as an artwork, even if historical narration is the standard way. If the work of a truly solitary artist is art, then there may be some exceptional grounds for calling it such. However, that would not call into question the central claim that identifying narra-tion, with its emphasis on art as a social practice, is by far our most typical means for establishing art status.

This is a fairly conciliatory response. Of course, the proponent of the historical method might also make a stronger reply. Like the Institutional Theorist, she might argue that, given the social nature of human beings, the possibility of a truly solitary artist is at best a logical fiction. From an anthropological point of view, the prospect of utterly asocial art has the probability of zero. Thus, if we are concerned with modeling how we go about classifying art with respect to the real world, then neglecting hypo-thetical cases of so-called solitary artists is not a pressing problem. After all, if we ever encountered anything approaching the case of our imagined Neolithic tribesman, his stone edifice would probably strike us as enig-matic rather than artistic. At best, we might call it proto-art, but if we are completely unable to situate it in the context of any ongoing social practices, we will remain nervous about regarding it as an instance of art proper.

Whether either of these attempted defenses of the historical approach is creditable is a matter for readers to debate. However, there is another possible problem with the historical approach that deserves airing. We began this chapter by pointing out that the issue of identifying art has been a particularly urgent one for twentieth-century philosophy because of the cascade of new and different kinds of art – avant-garde art, on the one hand, and art from other cultures, such as tribal art, on the other hand. The method of historical narration is, we have seen, well suited to handle cases of avant-garde innovation. But what about tribal art?

At first blush, there does not appear to be a problem here. Tribal arts will have their own traditions and identifying a candidate for inclusion in that tradition will proceed, as in more familiar cases, by way of historical narration. But this answer, it might be suggested, ignores a deeper question – namely, how does someone outside the tradition in question establish that the aforesaid tradition is an artistic practice? If it is an artistic tradition, the narrative model is applicable. But how do we know with alien traditions that the narrative model is available?

In such cases, one needs to look for reasons other than narrative reasons for regarding the alien tradition as artistic. The likeliest place to look is at the earliest known stages of the alien tradition. If in its earliest stages the practices of the alien tradition (what are sometimes called protosystems) are intended to perform the same functions – such as representation, decoration, and signification – in the relevant societies that the earliest stages of our own tradition performed in our culture, then we have grounds to regard the alien tradition as an artistic practice. And once we regard the earlier stages of the alien tradition as an artistic practice, then we may go on to identify subsequent contributions to the tradition as artworks by tracing their lineage from their artistic forebears.

But this solution to the problem requires that the historical method of identifying artworks needs to be supplemented, on some occasions, by a functional analysis of the role of certain practices in alien cultures. And this entails that we have not provided a single answer to the question of how we go about identifying artworks. Is this a problem?

The proponent of the historical method is apt to say "no." The admission that sometimes, but only sometimes, we resort to functional analysis only shows that historical narration is not the only strategy we use for classifying art, but this is consistent with the claim that it is our primary means of identifying art. Historical narration does not collapse into functional analysis, since functional analysis only makes sense with respect to protosystems. We do not look for functional analogies between aboriginal art and postmodernism; we only make comparisons at the level of the earliest stages of the traditions under consideration. The fact that we employ more than one method for identifying art merely reflects the complexity of the phenomenon. It would be nice to have a single answer to the question of how we identify art, but if the data are too complex, we should not let our desire for a single answer obscure the truth.

On the other hand, the advocates of rival viewpoints, like the Institutional Theory and the Historical Definition of Art, may say that it is a notable virtue of their approaches respectively that they provide a more economical account of how we identify artworks. They will assert that, all things being equal, a single answer to the question is better than a mixed answer. But are all things equal? If the method of historical narration is not as economical as some of its competitors, does this apparent liability outweigh the advantages it offers?

Those advantages include providing an account of how we identify artworks without embracing a controversial definition of art. Arriving at a satisfactory definition of art has proven arrestingly elusive. This does not show that art cannot be defined. But inasmuch as no one has been able to do it successfully, it seems unlikely that all along we have been classifying art by means of an essential definition. We must be using some other method. The method of historical narration, sometimes supplemented the functional analysis of protosystems, seems like the most plausible one on offer. It is certainly superior to alternative nondefinitional methods, like the family resemblance approach.

Also, as already noted, the avant-garde has been a continuing problem for philosophies of art. Many of the most famous theories of art – including the representational theory of art, the expression theory, formalism, and aesthetic theories of art – have been wrecked by the appearance of avant-garde innovations. Compared to these approaches, the method of historical narration has nothing to fear from the avant-garde; as a procedure for identifying art it is well tailored to incorporating the mutations of the avant-garde into the continuous evolution of art. Of course, there are other approaches to identifying art that are also receptive to avant-garde experimentation, including the Institutional Theory, but the historical method of narration, to its comparative advantage, avoids many of the most troubling criticisms leveled at competing approaches.

This is not to say that the method of historical narration is obviously the only choice for solving the problem of identifying art. It is one view among the many that we have examined in the course of this book. Its strengths and weaknesses must be assessed against the advantages and disadvantages of a wide variety of rival approaches. It is up to the reader to ponder these alternatives critically, or to discover her own solution to the problem with a full appreciation of the complexity of the issues.

Chapter summary

The question of how we go about identifying artworks is an imperative one for philosophers of art. For without some way to identify artworks, we do not know how to respond to them appropriately. For example, we respond to *Ulysses* by interpreting it, whereas we do not interpret our toaster ovens. How do we know that *Ulysses* belongs to a category that warrants interpreting, while our toaster ovens do not? This is motivation for the question of how we go about identifying artworks.

In earlier chapters of this book, we have surveyed many attempts to answer this question, such as: the representational theory of art, neorepresentationalism, the expression theory, formalism, neoformalism, and aesthetic theories of art. Each of these approaches attempts to explain how we identify artworks by producing a comprehensive definition of all art in terms of necessary and sufficient conditions. These theories presume that we identify artworks on the basis of the sort of theory or essential definition that they reconstruct explicitly.

However, all these definitions of art appear seriously flawed in one way or another. The repeated failure of the definitional approach to the question of identifying art prompted a group of philosophers in the 1950s to contemplate the possibility that art cannot be defined and that we identify artworks without recourse to definitions. Called Neo-Wittgensteinians, these philosophers argued that art cannot be essentially defined because it is an open concept and that we identify artworks on the basis of family resemblances.

The Neo-Wittgensteinian approach was extremely influential for nearly two decades. Nevertheless, gradually philosophers came to believe that the arguments of the Neo-Wittgensteinians were not as persuasive as they first seemed. The open-concept argument claimed that art could not be defined essentially because any such definition would be incompatible with artistic innovation. However, philosophers like George Dickie were able to produce definitions of art, such as the Institutional Theory, that showed that one could propose necessary and sufficient conditions for art that were perfectly consistent with the widest conceivable latitude for artistic experimentation. Moreover, critics also demonstrated that the family resemblance method for identifying artworks was too facile – that, in short order, it would produce the unsatisfying result that everything is art.

A consequence of the defeat of Neo-Wittgensteinianism has been a return to the project of defining art essentially. At present, there is an ample variety of such theories on offer. Two of the better-known theories of this sort are the Institutional Theory of Art and the Historical Definition of Art. These are sophisticated viewpoints that call our attention to important features of our commerce with artworks. However, both theories are highly controversial and have been subjected to strong criticisms. Thus, we still appear to be in a position where no existing definition of art has been decisively proven to be adequate.

But if no one is able to articulate a satisfactory definition of art, it seems unlikely that we identify artworks by means of an essential definition. If we were possessed of such a definition, why would it be so difficult to extract? Furthermore, many of our concepts are not governed by essential definitions. So why suppose that art is?

This kind of thinking encourages the hypothesis that, as the Neo-Wittgensteinians suggested, we may not identify artworks by means of an essential definition, but that we have some other method. This method cannot be the family resemblance method, but perhaps there is another alternative.

The alternative we explored in the last part of this chapter emphasizes the importance of historical narration for identifying artworks. It proposes that narratives – called identifying narratives – rather than definitions model the way in which we identify artworks. This approach avoids several of the problems of its predecessors, including Neo-Wittgensteinianism, the Institutional Theory, and the Historical Definition of Art. But whether it has solved the problem of how we go about identifying artworks remains an open question.

Readers may discover criticisms of the method of historical narration that have not appeared as yet in the literature. And they will have to weigh its advantages against all the other approaches discussed in this book. Perhaps some will come to the conclusion that some previous theory of art, or a combination of theories, presents more promising lines of inquiry than the method of historical narration.

Or, maybe, the reader, dissatisfied with everything she has found between these covers, will feel moved to develop her own approach to the subject. That would be all to the good. This book will have served its purpose if it has equipped readers with ideas, techniques, and a sense of the complexity of the issues sufficient for them to strike out on their own. *Bon voyage!*

Annotated reading

The most comprehensive survey of recent developments regarding the topics discussed in this chapter is Stephen Davies' *Definitions of Art* (Ithaca, New York: Cornell University Press, 1991). This book also contains an extensive bibliography that is indispensable for further research on the subject.

Perhaps the most cited article with regard to Neo-Wittgensteinianism is Morris Weitz's

"The Role of Theory in Aesthetics," *Journal of Aesthetics and Art Criticism*, vol. 15 (1956), pp. 27–35. See also Weitz's *The Opening Mind* (Chicago: University of Chicago Press, 1977). Other important contributions to the anti-definitional approach include: Paul Ziff, "The Task of Defining a Work of Art," *Philosophical Review*, vol. 62 (1951), pp. 466–480; and William Kennick, "Does Traditional Aesthetics Rest on a Mistake?," *Mind*, vol. 67 (1958), pp. 317–334. A highly influential criticism of Weitz's version of Neo-Wittgensteinianism is Maurice Mandelbaum's "Family Resemblances and Generalizations concerning the Arts," *American Philosophical Quarterly*, vol. 2 (1965), pp. 219–228.

George Dickie has set forth versions of the Institutional Theory of Art in numerous articles and books. A statement of the earlier version of the theory can be found, among other places, in his *Art and the Aesthetic: An Institutional Analysis* (Ithaca, New York: Cornell University Press, 1974). A revised version of the theory is available in his *The Art Circle* (New York: Haven, 1984).

Jerrold Levinson is the leading defender of the Historical Definition of Art. He develops this approach in: "Defining Art Historically," *British Journal of Aesthetics*, vol. 19 (1979), pp. 232–250; "Refining Art Historically," *Journal of Aesthetics and Art Criticism*, vol. 47 (1989), pp. 21–33; and "Extending Art Historically," *Journal of Aesthetics and Art Criticism*, vol. 51 (1993), pp. 411–423.

The method of historical narration for identifying artworks is advanced by Noël Carroll in: "Art, Practice and Narrative," *The Monist*, vol. 71 (1988), pp. 140–156; "Historical Narratives and the Philosophy of Art," *Journal of Aesthetics and Art Criticism*, vol. 51 (1993), pp. 313–326; and "Identifying Art," in *Institutions of Art: Reconsiderations of George Dickie's Philosophy*, edited by Robert J. Yanal (University Park, Pennsylvania: The Pennsylvania State University Press, 1994), pp. 3–38. Also, Peter Kivy has used the narrative approach to explain the enfranchisement of absolute music as art in his *Philosophies of Arts* (Cambridge: Cambridge University Press, 1997), Chapter 1.

The notion of art as a conversation in the section on identifying narratives in this chapter of the present book is adapted from Jeffrey Wieand, "Putting Forward A Work of Art," *Journal of Aesthetics and Art Criticism*, vol. 41 (1983), p. 618.

There are a number of contemporary approaches to the problems discussed in this chapter that, given considerations of space, have not been reviewed in this book. Some notable ones include: Arthur Danto, *The Transfiguration of the Commonplace* (Cambridge, MA: Harvard University Press, 1981); and Robert Stecker, *Artworks: Definition, Meaning, Value* (University Park, Pennsylvania: The Pennsylvania State University Press, 1997). For a recent anthology of new work on defining and identifying art, see *Theories of Art*, edited by Noël Carroll (Madison, Wisconsin: University of Wisconsin Press, 1999).

Index